• Earthquakes in Human History

Earthquakes in Human History

The Far-Reaching Effects of Seismic Disruptions

Jelle Zeilinga de Boer

and

Donald Theodore Sanders

PRINCETON UNIVERSITY PRESS

Princeton and Oxford

NEW AGE

First Indian Sub-Continent Edition : 2006
by New Age International (P) Ltd., Publishers

This special low-priced edition is for sale in India, Bangladesh, Bhutan, Myanmar (Burma), Sri Lanka, Nepal and Pakistan only.
Originally Published by *Princeton University Press, U.S.A.*

ISBN 81 224 1961-5

es, Delhi.

9 788122 419610

PUBLISHING FOR ONE WORLD
NEW AGE INTERNATIONAL (P) LIMITED, PUBLISHERS
4835/24, Ansari Road, Daryaganj, New Delhi - 110002
Visit us at **www.newagepublishers.com**

To my wife, Felicité,
for her unwavering enthusiasm and patience

Jelle Zeilinga de Boer

In loving memory:
To my sister, Barbara Sanders Bradshaw,
and to our parents,
Hazel Broach Sanders and Theodore Peter Sanders,
for so very much, right from the beginning

Donald Theodore Sanders

• Contents

• Preface

THERE IS A WIDESPREAD PERCEPTION that the sciences and the humanities are incompatible, that they have little or nothing in common. What do history, the arts, great literature have to do with physics, chemistry, biology—or earth science? In 1959 the British scholar C. P. Snow analyzed that question in his widely read book *The Two Cultures.*[1] Snow attributed the problem to misinterpretation and lack of understanding, and in his book he attempts to reconcile the "two cultures."

The notion that Snow's two cultures are at odds is trenchantly expressed in a novel published in 1983 by the American author Trevanian in a scene where one of the characters warns another:

> Beware the attraction of the *pure* sciences. They are pure only in the way an ancient nun is—bloodless, without passion. No, no. Stick to the humanistic studies where, though the truth is more difficult to establish and the proofs are more fragile, yet there is the breath of living man in them.[2]

One of the present authors (Zeilinga de Boer) has attempted to bring the two cultures together at Wesleyan University in his course *Geological Catastrophes,* in which he demonstrates to liberal-arts students that the sciences are not "bloodless"—that, in the earth sciences in particular, something akin to the "breath of living man" can be seen in such phenomena as volcanic eruptions and earthquakes. In his lectures de Boer discusses selected geological events, describing their origins while placing emphasis on the many ways in which they have affected people, societies, cultures, even history itself.

This book grew out of de Boer's lectures. The theme of the present volume is the human dimension of earthquakes. Ways in which the humanities and volcanism are intertwined are discussed in a companion volume, *Volcanoes in Human History: The Far-Reaching Effects of Major Eruptions* (Princeton University Press, 2002).

Earthquakes are treated only descriptively in most books, the descriptions concerned mainly with the resulting destruction and the number of casualties. Many of these short-lived events, however, have had long-lasting aftereffects. Some of the events can be described as catalytic, their aftereffects giving rise to later events, whether environmental, economic, or cultural, that may at first appear unrelated.

In this book we explore nine earthquakes or quake-prone regions. In each case we briefly discuss the geological setting in terms of plate tectonics—the theory that segments of the earth's crust, virtually rigid, move about over a less rigid layer and collide, giving rise to volcanic activity and earthquakes. Then we discuss the aftereffects of the events—their consequences—in human terms.

By describing not only the immediate physical effects of earthquakes but also their long-term aftereffects, we demonstrate the inherent connections that exist between the earth sciences and the humanities. Some earthquakes have had philosophical repercussions, some have influenced religions, and some have affected entire societies and cultures, and yes, even history.

Earthquakes are manifestations of a living earth. If we think of an earthquake as the plucking of a long, tight-stretched string representing time, the string will vibrate. During the quake itself, at the point of origin where a great deal of seismic energy is being released, the vibrations will have high amplitudes and short wavelengths. They will be powerful, but each will last only a moment. Farther along on the string, with

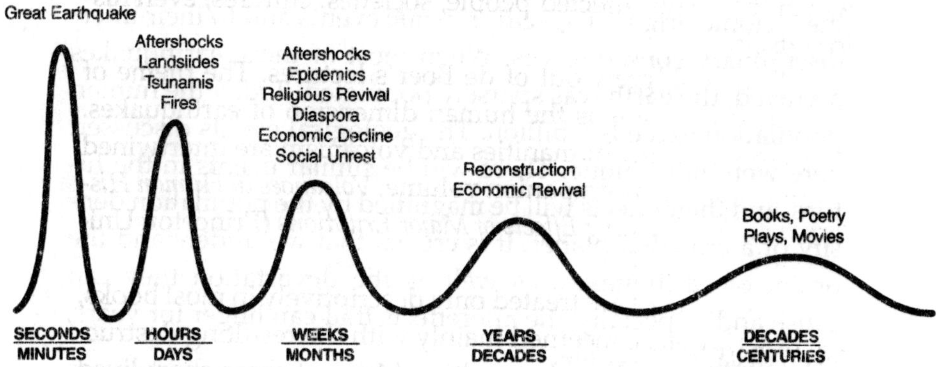

the passage of time, the amplitudes will decrease and the wavelengths increase. That is to say, the aftereffects will become less intense and they will last longer, as shown in the "vibrating string" diagram above.

For example, in 1755 a catastrophic earthquake destroyed Lisbon, the capital of Portugal. Most of the city's buildings, constructed of unreinforced masonry, collapsed, and a series of enormous quake-induced ocean waves, or tsunamis, devastated the harbor area. As many as sixty thousand people died. The damage to Portugal's economy was incalculable. In the ensuing chaos, government and church leaders vied for control. The Marquês de Pombal rose to power and became a virtual dictator; as a result, the Roman Catholic Jesuit Order lost much of its influence in Portugal. Voltaire, in his *Poème sur le désastre de Lisbonne* and his satirical work *Candide,* contradicted the then-current philosophy of optimism, that God had created a perfect world. And in both Europe and America the disaster sparked the search for a scientific understanding of natural phenomena, a search that has been unceasing. Recent geological research has focused on the offshore origin of the earthquake, and on what might happen to Lisbon if there should be a similar quake in the future. Lisbon's string vibrates to this day.

By discussing the Lisbon earthquake's "vibrating string" and eight others, we hope in this book to draw interest both to the tectonic origin of specific seismic events and to their interdisciplinary consequences. When most of those earthquakes occurred, the earth was sparsely populated. Today the human population exceeds 6 billion. The geological events discussed here were not unique. There will be similar events in the future, and their effects will be magnified by the population density of a crowded planet. It is crucial that we understand the origin of earthquakes, as well as the devastation they can cause and, especially, the aftereffects that can linger for years, even decades, to come.

Acknowledgments

THE AUTHORS GRATEFULLY ACKNOWLEDGE the guidance and keen editorial assistance of Joe Wisnovsky of Princeton University Press. For invaluable advice on specific chapters, we thank César Andrade (Lisbon), John Hale and Elena Partida (Sparta), Kenneth and Molleen Matsumura (Japan and San Francisco), Rafael Rojas (Managua), Nancy Smith (England), and David Titus (Japan). We especially thank Barbara Bode for her generous permission for us to adapt material from her book *No Bells to Toll* in writing our Peru chapter, and for her careful reviews of the manuscript.

We thank Alison Hart, Gerrit Lekkerkerker, and Mary Watson for their constant encouragement and for their thoughtful reviews of each chapter, and John Ebel, Emanuela Guidoboni, Susan Hough, and Stephen McNutt for their help with technical aspects of the book. And thanks to Melvin Marcus for suggesting that we check out Oliver Wendell Holmes's "Wonderful 'One-Hoss-Shay.'"

Joy Devorsetz, Cheryl Hagner, Jeffrey Makala, and Suzy Taraba have our gratitude for locating publications in the Special Collections and Archives Department of Wesleyan University's Olin Library. Reference librarians in Olin Library, Wesleyan's Science Library, and the town libraries of Fairfield and Madison, Connecticut, helped us locate information that was important to our work.

Special thanks go to Michael Ross, whose telephone call in 1994 led, more or less directly, to the authors' collaboration.

We also thank Edward Knappman of New England Publishing Associates, who on our behalf contacted Princeton University Press.

More personally, we thank Joan Boutelle, Barbara Bradshaw, Katherine Sanders, and Felicité de Boer for their support and help in so many ways.

• Table of Conversions

1 centimeter = 0.39 inch
1 meter = 3.28 feet
1 kilometer = 0.62 mile
1 square meter = 10.76 square feet
1 square kilometer = 0.39 square mile
1 hectare = 2.47 acres
1 cubic meter = 35.31 cubic feet

- Earthquakes in Human History

1 • Earthquakes: Origins and Consequences

A bad earthquake at once destroys our oldest associations: the earth, the very emblem of solidity, has moved beneath our feet like a thin crust over a fluid.

Charles Darwin, *The Voyage of the Beagle*

EARTHQUAKES ARE AMONG the most terrifying of natural phenomena. Striking without warning, and seemingly coming out of nowhere, they challenge our inherent assumptions about the stability of the very planet we live upon. Any shaking of the earth, whether lasting for minutes or only for seconds, seems eternal to those who experience it. A mild quake may inspire no more than passing interest, but a powerful quake can wreak awesome devastation. Figure 1-1 is an artist's interpretation of a quake that shook Naples, Italy, in 1805. A century later (in 1904) an American geologist, Clarence E. Dutton, published a seminal book about seismology (the study of earthquakes) in which he graphically described a strong temblor:

> When the great earthquake comes, it comes quickly. . . . The first sensation is a confused murmuring sound of a strange and even weird character. Almost simultaneously loose objects begin to tremble and chatter. Sometimes, almost in an instant, sometimes more gradually, but always quickly, the sound becomes a roar, the chattering becomes a crashing. . . . The shaking increases in violence. . . . Through its din are heard loud,

FIGURE 1-1. Copper engraving of devastation in Naples, Italy, during an earthquake in 1805. (Private collection.)

deep, solemn booms that seem like the voice of the Eternal One, speaking out of the depths of the universe.[1]

Dutton's figurative reference to an "Eternal One" alludes to an age-old belief that earthquakes are visited upon sinful mortals by divine wrath, either as punishment for sins committed or as a warning to those who might yield to temptation. In ancient Greece it was the god Poseidon "the earthshaker" (also the god of the sea) whose wrath was to be feared. The Bible contains many verses in both Old and New Testaments that equate earthquakes with God's anger. In contrast, many ancient myths attributed earthquakes to the stirring of giant creatures that supported the earth. In Japan it was a catfish, in China a frog. In the Philippine Islands it was thought to be a snake, and Native Americans believed the earth rested upon the back of a turtle.

The Greek philosopher Aristotle (384–322 BCE) developed a somewhat more rational, if still fanciful, explanation for earthquakes. He believed that strong winds blew through caves and clefts inside the earth, creating "effects similar to those of the wind in our bodies whose force when it is pent up inside us can cause tremors and throbbings."[2]

Among the early attempts at a scientific explanation of earthquakes was a book titled *Conjectures concerning the Cause, and Observations upon the Phaenomena of Earthquakes,* written in 1760 by John Michell (1724?–1793), a professor of geology at Cambridge University. From a study of the great Lisbon earthquake of 1755, Michell concluded that quakes were caused by shifting masses of rock many kilometers below the earth's surface.

In 1793 Benjamin Franklin, among the leading scientists of his day, suggested a mechanism for Michell's shifting masses:

> I . . . imagined that the internal part [of the earth] might be a fluid more dense, and of greater specific gravity than any of the solids we are acquainted with; which therefore might swim in or upon that fluid. Thus the surface of the globe would be a shell, capable of being broken and disordered by any violent movements of the fluid on which it rested.[3]

Scientists had to wait more than a century before they could definitely establish a relationship between shifting masses of rock (Franklin's broken "shell") and earthquakes. Then in 1891 a powerful temblor shook the island of Honshu, in Japan. Known as the Mino-Owari earthquake, it left a zone of destruction marked by a fracture, or fault, that extended across the island from the Sea of Japan to the Pacific Ocean. In some places, vertical movement had created fault scarps several meters high (see figure 1-2). From that convincing evidence a Japanese scientist, Bunjiro Koto, concluded that the quake had been triggered by the fracturing of the earth's crust, thus for the first time demonstrating a causal relationship between earthquakes and faulting.

Early in the twentieth century, by studying earthquake

FIGURE 1-2. Drawing showing the 6-meter-high scarp created by rupturing along a fault across the island of Honshu, in Japan, in 1891, causing the Mino-Owari earthquake. In the photo, notice the offset of the road, indicating simultaneous horizontal and vertical movement. (From Montessus de Ballore, *Science Séismologique*, 414.)

waves and the time it takes for them to pass through the earth, scientists deduced that our planet has a dense, at least partly molten core at its center, and that the core is surrounded by a thick layer of less dense material, which they named the mantle. Above the mantle lies the thin, rocky crust (or "shell") upon which we live. The crust can be several tens of kilometers thick where it comprises the continents, but it is only a few kilometers thick beneath the oceans. In some respects we might say that the earth resembles an apple. If an apple is sliced in two, the cross section reveals a small "core" (where the seeds are), a thick "mantle" (the edible flesh), and a "crust" (the skin). The relative proportions of those parts of an apple are not unlike the proportions of the main parts of the earth.

In the 1960s geologists began to understand that the outer part of the earth is made up of individual rigid plates, some very large, others small, as shown in figure 1-3 (and not entirely different from Benjamin Franklin's speculation in 1793). The plates move very slowly over a ductile, or plastic, layer within the mantle. The movement of these tectonic (structural) plates, typically a few centimeters a year, is responsible for most earthquakes, as well as for volcanic activity. This is the theory of plate tectonics, which revolutionized the science of geology by providing a single, unifying concept that helps explain most geological processes and features. The block diagrams in figure 1-4 illustrate the kinds of faults that develop in the earth's crust when plates collide, when they separate, and when they move past one another laterally.

The rigid tectonic plates are made up of rocky crustal material and a thin layer of the uppermost part of the mantle. Together they form what geologists call the *lithosphere* (from the Greek *lithos*, meaning "stone"). The ductile layer of mantle material over which the plates move is called the *asthenosphere* (from *asthenos*, meaning "weak").

Tectonic plates are in motion presumably because of convection currents within the mantle. The currents are thought to be driven by heat from the earth's core, much as convection

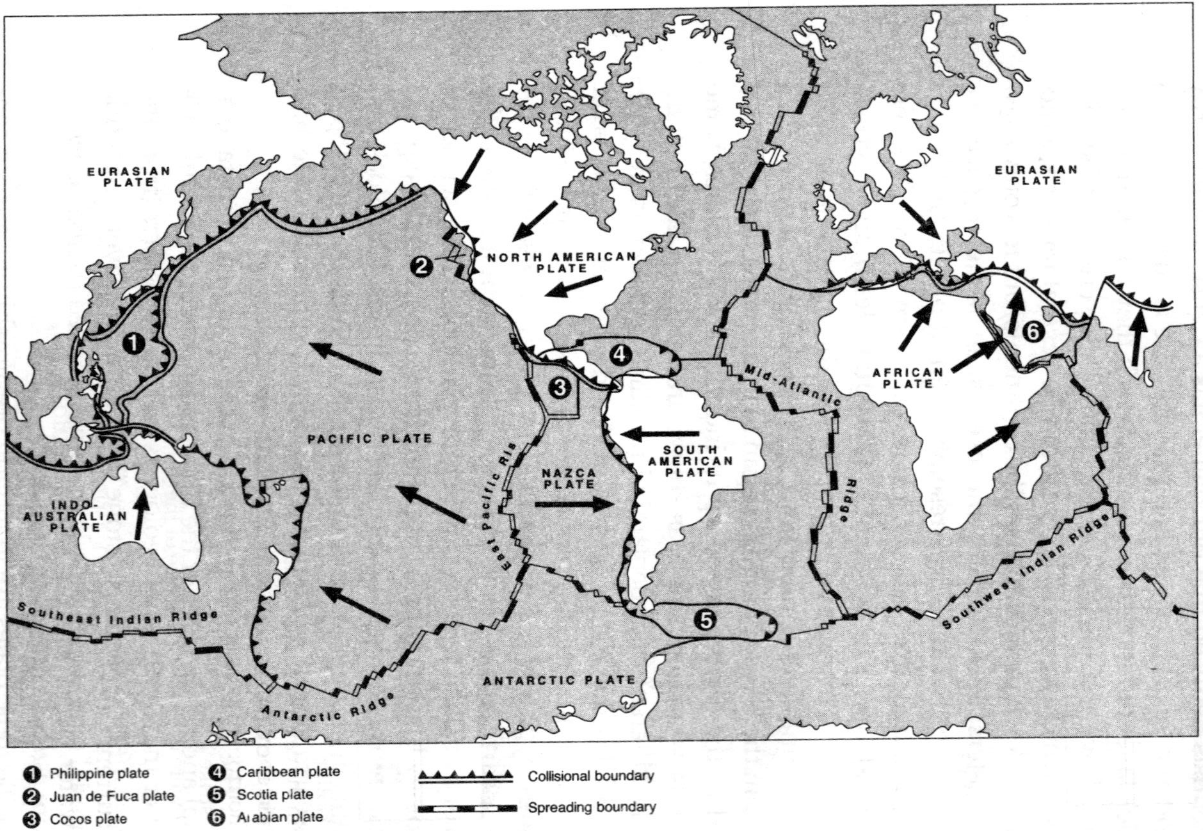

FIGURE 1-3. Configuration of the earth's tectonic plates, showing boundaries between colliding plates and between plates that are spreading apart. Arrows show the present directions of plate motion. Small black triangles at collisional boundaries indicate subduction zones.

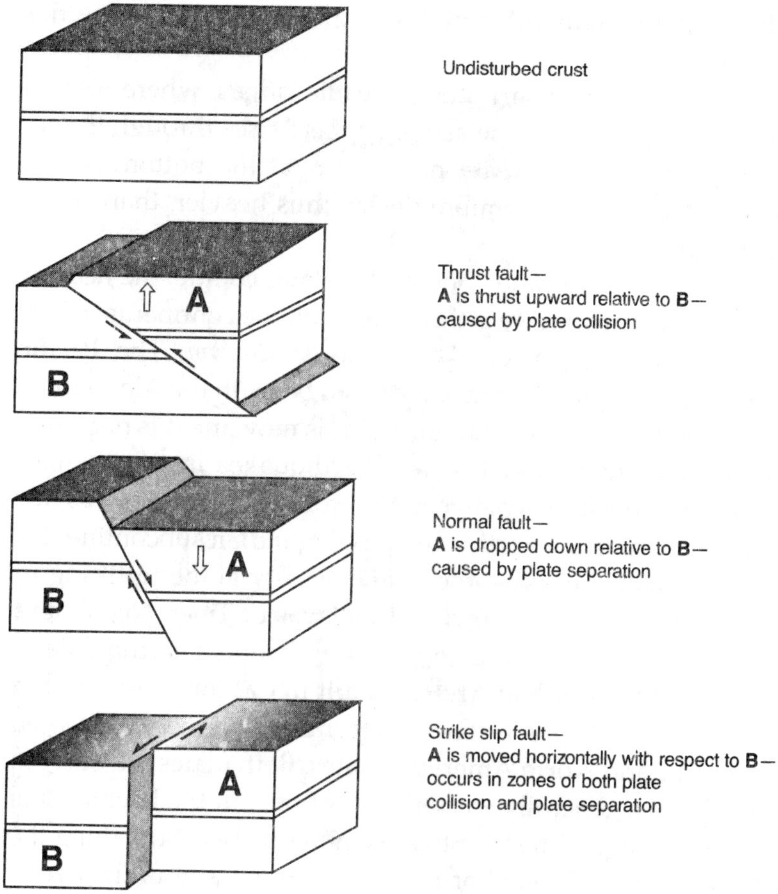

FIGURE 1-4. Block diagrams illustrating, from top, undisturbed rock layers in the earth's crust and the kinds of faults that develop in crustal rocks when plates collide, when they pull apart, and when they move past one another horizontally. Open arrows indicate crustal uplift and subsidence. The "strike" of a fault is the direction that would be taken by a horizontal line if it were drawn on a surface of the fault.

currents are created in a pot of water heated on a stove. Hot water, being less dense than cold water, rises to the surface, where it cools and becomes more dense. Therefore it returns to the bottom of the pot. A similar process is believed to be at work, albeit far more slowly, within the earth. Along their boundaries, tectonic plates may be separating from one another, colliding with other plates, or grinding past one another laterally.

Plates spread apart along oceanic ridges, where molten rock, or magma, from the asthenosphere rises through the resulting fractures to create new crust on the bottom of the ocean. Oceanic crust is more dense, thus heavier, than continental crust.

Where oceanic and continental plates collide, the heavier oceanic plate ordinarily is thrust beneath the continental plate, an earthshaking process known as *subduction*. The Pacific plate, for example, is being subducted beneath the Aleutian Islands and the islands of Japan, and this movement is responsible for volcanism and frequent earthquakes in those areas. Where the collision is between two continental plates—as, for example, where the northward-moving Indian subcontinent is colliding with Eurasia—the result usually is the uplifting of mountain ranges such as the Himalayas of Tibet, Nepal, and northern India, again accompanied by frequent earthquakes.

The infamous San Andreas fault in California lies within a highly active tectonic zone that forms the boundary between the Pacific and North American plates. Both plates are moving laterally in a generally westerly direction, but the Pacific plate is moving slightly faster. Stresses therefore build up along the San Andreas and neighboring faults within the boundary zone until, from time to time, friction is overcome in one area or another and the sudden release of accumulated stress creates an earthquake.

The boundaries of tectonic plates are by far the most common sites of earthquakes, but plate interiors are not invulnerable. The same forces that created the plates can tear them apart, as today the Arabian platelet is being separated from the African plate along the axis of the Red Sea. Branching southward from the mouth of the Red Sea is the East African rift system, a zone of crustal weakness that includes the famous African rift valleys. That region is the site of volcanic activity and frequent earthquakes. Similarly (but without volca-

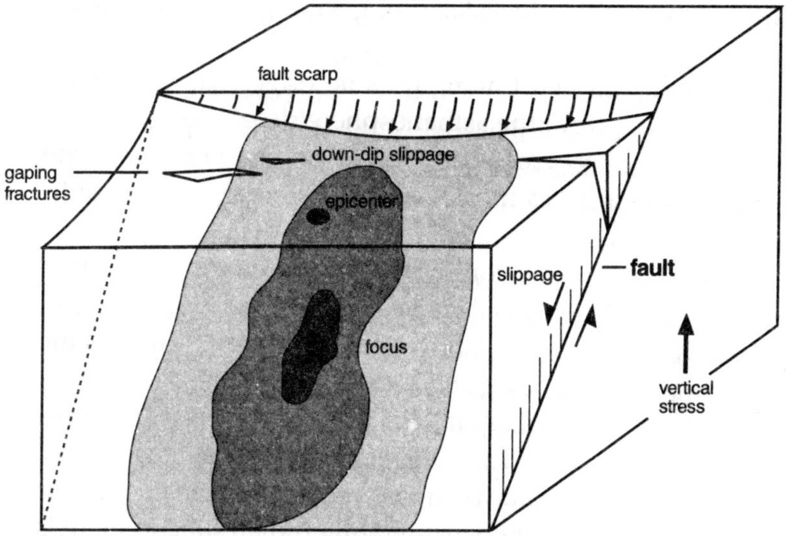

FIGURE 1-5. Block diagram showing the focus and epicenter of an earthquake caused by abrupt down-dip slippage along a fault produced by a vertical stress in the earth's crust. Such slippage often creates gaping fractures in the earth's surface, as depicted in figure 1-1. The *focus* is the place on the fault plane where rupturing originated. The *epicenter* is the location on the earth's surface directly above the focus. Rupturing expands outward along the fault in all directions from the focus, as shown by gradations in shading.

noes), the lower Mississippi Valley is underlain by an ancient rift. Presumably reactivated by the movement of the North American plate, old faults related to the rift gave way in 1811 and 1812, and the region was shaken by some of the most powerful earthquakes in American history.

• • •

Earthquakes are caused by the sudden release of energy when slippage occurs where stresses created by tectonic movement have strained the earth's crust to the breaking point. The place on a fault where an earthquake originates is called the *focus*, or *hypocenter*. The place on the earth's surface directly above the focus is the *epicenter* (see figure 1-5). The waves of seismic energy released by the rupture—called body waves—are propagated through the crust either as push-pull (P) waves or as shear (S) waves. P waves move by successively compressing and dilating crustal material in the direction of propagation, while S waves shake particles of material in directions perpendicular to that direction. In typical midcrustal rocks, S waves travel at about 3 kilometers per second, whereas P waves move at about 5 kilometers per second. The faster P waves arrive at seismographs ahead of S waves, so P waves are also referred to as primary waves, and S waves as secondary waves.

When seismic waves reach the earth's surface they move along the surface in either of two forms, known as Rayleigh waves and Love waves. Rayleigh waves, named after the British physicist Baron Rayleigh (John William Strutt), cause particles in their path to move about in an elliptical fashion. Love waves, named for a British mathematician, A. H. Love, are surface shear waves. Particles in their path move in a horizontal plane at right angles to the direction of wave propagation. Both kinds of surface waves oscillate with lower frequencies, hence with larger amplitudes, than body waves and are largely responsible for earthquake damage.

Before the seismograph was invented in the late nineteenth century, the intensity of ground shaking during earthquakes was estimated by how and where the quakes were felt and by the amount of damage they caused. In 1902 an Italian seismologist, Giuseppe Mercalli, developed a scale with ten degrees of intensity, later modified to twelve as shown in table 1-1. Because the Mercalli scale is qualitative, its accuracy depends on subjective observation or, for past quakes, the accuracy of historical accounts.

In 1935 Charles Richter, a seismologist at the California Institute of Technology, developed a quantitative scale for measuring the *magnitude*, rather than the qualitative *intensity*, of earthquakes.* Magnitudes originally were calculated from

* A Japanese seismologist, Kiyoo Wadati, had developed a quantitative scale in 1931, but it was Richter's scale that became widely accepted for many years.

TABLE 1-1 The Modified Mercalli Scale of Earthquake Intensities

I	Rarely felt.
II	Felt by few people.
III	Felt mostly on upper floors of buildings.
IV	Felt indoors by many, outdoors by few.
V	Felt by most people. Some dishes and windows broken, plaster cracked.
VI	Felt by all. People run outdoors. Some furniture moved, chimneys damaged.
VII	Everyone runs outdoors. Much damage to poorly constructed buildings, slight damage to well-built structures. Chimneys broken.
VIII	Damage great to poorly constructed buildings, considerable to well-built structures. Chimneys, monuments, walls collapse. Sand and mud ejected from ground.
IX	Buildings moved from foundations, ground cracked, underground pipes broken.
X	Most masonry buildings and some wooden buildings destroyed. Ground badly cracked, rails bent, landslides on steep slopes, water splashed over riverbanks.
XI	Few masonry buildings remain standing. Bridges destroyed, broad cracks in ground, all underground pipelines out of service.
XII	Damage total. Waves in ground surface; objects thrown upward.

the deflection measured by a particular kind of seismograph corrected for the distance of the instrument from the epicenter of the quake. In time it became apparent that such calculations did not work well for the strongest earthquakes, and seismologists have developed other, more sophisticated magnitude scales, which are used today.

Table 1-2 indicates the relative amounts of seismic energy that are released by earthquakes of various Richter magnitudes. In the table, one "energy unit" represents an arbitrary value equal to the amount of energy that would be released by

TABLE 1-2 Relative Amounts of Energy Released by Earthquakes of Various Richter Magnitudes

Magnitude (M)	Duration, in seconds	Energy released, in arbitrary units*
1–2.9	short	less than M4
3–3.9	short	less than M4
4–4.9	1–5	1 × M4
5–5.9	2–15	30 × M4
6–6.9	10–30	1,000 × M4
7–7.9	20–50	30,000 × M4
8–8.9	30–90	1,000,000 × M4

*For the purposes of this table, one "energy unit" is given an arbitrary value equal to the amount of energy that would be released by a magnitude 4 (M4) earthquake that lasted 1 to 5 seconds.

a magnitude 4 earthquake that lasted from one to five seconds. A magnitude of 4 generally is considered the threshold for causing significant damage. The amount of energy released by earthquakes increases greatly from one magnitude value to the next, as graphically illustrated in figure 1-6.

Some earthquakes are preceded by foreshocks if slippage along the responsible faults begins gradually. And many quakes are followed by aftershocks caused by continued, intermittent slippage along the responsible faults. Aftershocks have been known to continue for years.

Movement along some faults is more or less continuous, so that seismic energy is released gradually and there is no abrupt rupturing to cause any but minor earthquakes. Such faults are said to "creep." Typically, however, because of friction, faults remain "locked" for a time, in effect storing energy just as a compressed spring does—until enough stress has accumulated to overcome the friction, and the slippage occurs. In figure 1-7, erosion has exposed the surface of a fault that was polished smooth by the grinding of one block against the other.

On rare occasions, notably in California and Japan, emissions of bright white light have been reported along faults that have broken through to the earth's surface. Most likely the

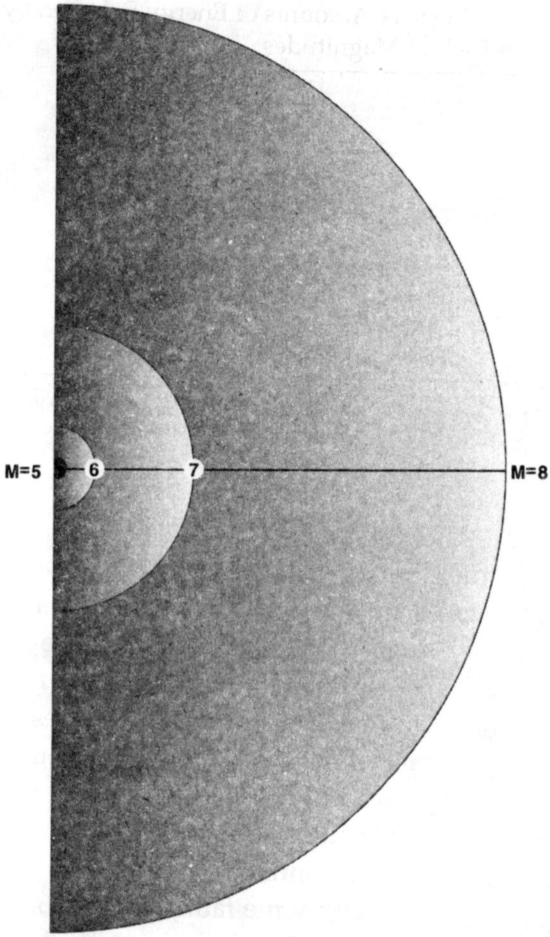

FIGURE 1-6. Schematic representation of relative amounts of energy (shown as cross sections of half spheres) released by earthquakes with magnitudes ranging from 5 to 8. Imagine each magnitude value as a three-dimensional spherical *volume*: the amount of energy released is 30 to 40 times greater from one magnitude to the next.

light is generated when electrons from the freshly ruptured rock collide with atoms in the air above the fault.

Because the earth's crust absorbs and scatters seismic waves, the intensity of ground shaking usually decreases rapidly with increasing distance from a quake's epicenter. The severity of an earthquake is also affected by local geological

FIGURE 1-7. A geologist slides down the polished surface of a fault, demonstrating the relative direction of movement of the block of crustal material that once lay above the fault. This type of fault is similar to that shown in figure 1-5.

conditions. Seismic waves in hard bedrock, for example, vibrate with higher frequencies and lower amplitudes than do waves in unconsolidated sediments. Conversely, seismic waves in unconsolidated material, such as marshes and filled land, tend to be amplified because ordinarily they vibrate with lower frequencies and higher amplitudes. For that reason buildings constructed on bedrock tend to survive earthquakes that would destroy structures built on less firm material such as reclaimed swamplands.

Major earthquakes usually are followed, in cities, by fires that result from broken gas mains, sparking electrical wires, and overturned stoves used for cooking or heating. Quake-related conflagrations often cause much more damage, and many more deaths, than the quakes themselves. Lisbon in 1755, San Francisco in 1906, and Tokyo and Yokohama in 1923 all suffered powerful earthquakes, but it was fire, not the quakes, that completed the destruction of the cities.

Faulting and displacement of the seafloor during earthquakes can produce the destructive ocean waves called *tsunamis*, a Japanese word meaning "harbor waves." Tsunamis (often mislabeled "tidal waves," though they are unrelated to tides) are fast-moving waves that can traverse entire oceans in hours. Approaching land, a tsunami can build to a great height in shoaling water and crash ashore with devastating results, especially in bays and harbors where its energy may be focused by a narrowing configuration of the shoreline.

In mountainous regions, earthquakes can produce ruinous landslides and mudflows. Damage can range from blocked roads, washed-out bridges, and disrupted irrigation systems to the destruction of entire towns and cities.

Other possible aftereffects of catastrophic earthquakes include famine, disease, economic disruption, and even political repercussions, as discussed in the following chapters.

• • •

About 75 percent of the earth's seismic energy is released along the boundaries of the Pacific plate. Another 23 percent comes from a zone of seismic activity that extends eastward from the Mediterranean area to Indonesia. The rest of the world accounts for only about 2 percent. Thus it is not difficult to predict, in general, where earthquakes are likely to happen. But any attempt to predict specifically where or when a quake may strike is fraught with difficulty.

Essential for the successful prediction of earthquakes is recognition of precursors such as geodetic changes (tilting of areas near faults) or the sudden lowering of water levels in wells. Changes in local magnetic, electric, or gravimetric fields, or unexplained changes in the velocity of seismic waves from quake activity elsewhere, all indicate local tectonic changes in the earth's crust. But none of these precursors, by themselves, are reliable predictors of seismic activity.

If part of a fault has remained inactive, or locked, for a considerable period while there has been seismic activity elsewhere along the fault, the locked segment is called a *seismic gap*. It seems obvious that such gaps are likely locations for future earthquakes—and the longer the period of quiescence, the greater the probability of recurring seismicity.

For the reasons outlined above, seismologists are loath to make specific earthquake predictions. An inaccurate prediction would not only discredit the scientists who made the prediction; it could have far-reaching social and economic consequences if towns or cities were needlessly evacuated, schools closed, and businesses shut down.

Efforts to find ways of predicting seismic activity will continue, of course, but in the meantime the most pragmatic approach to minimizing the danger of earthquakes is to assess known hazards. In her recent book *Earthshaking Science*, U.S. Geological Survey seismologist Susan Elizabeth Hough writes: "Faced with a growing awareness of the intractability of earthquake prediction and a stronger imperative to apply hard-won knowledge to matters of social concern, the seismological community has turned away from short-term earthquake prediction and toward long-term seismic hazard assessment." Hough defines a hazard as involving not any one quake but "an evaluation of the average long-term hazard faced by a region as a result of all faults whose earthquakes stand to affect that region." She goes on to point out:

> Earth scientists are careful to differentiate "hazard," which depends on the earthquake rate, from "risk," which reflects the exposure of structures, lifelines, and populations to existing hazard. Risk is generally the purview of insurance companies; the evaluation of hazard is a matter of science.[4]

Once the earthquake hazard is understood for an area, much can be done to ameliorate the risk of damage in future quakes. Building codes can be made more rigorous, and existing structures can be strengthened. Certainly the cost will be great, and we might be willing to gamble that no devastating temblor will strike any time soon. But in an area of known hazard, such a gamble would be risky indeed.

In the following chapters we describe nine historic earthquakes or quake-prone regions, in each case emphasizing the long-lasting consequences—cultural, socioeconomic, and political—of only a few moments of seismic cataclysm.

INDUCED EARTHQUAKES

Not all earthquakes are natural events. Quakes have been caused by the weight of impounded water where large dams have been built, and they have occurred where large quantities of waste fluids have been pumped into deep wells.

In the early 1930s, after Hoover Dam was built on the Colorado River, tremors began to shake the area as Lake Mead filled. In 1940, five years after the dam was completed, a stronger earthquake shook nearby Las Vegas. With a magnitude of about 5, it caused minor damage.

There were similar earthquakes after the Aswan Dam was built in Egypt in 1970. More than 100 meters high and 3 kilometers wide, the dam impounded the Nile River to form Lake Nasser, which extends almost 350 kilometers upstream. Not unexpectedly, occasional tremors accompanied the rising water. Then on November 14, 1981, a more powerful earthquake, with a magnitude of 5.6, struck the region.

None of those quakes claimed any victims—but in 1967 an induced quake with a magnitude 6.4 killed several hundred people and injured some two thousand after the Koyna Dam was built near Bombay (now Mumbai), India.

Until the 1960s such activity puzzled seismologists. They considered it unlikely that the load created by filling a reservoir could strain the earth's crust enough to cause movement along faults. Some other mechanism had to be present. The answer to the puzzle came in 1965 near Denver, Colorado. On the grounds of the U.S. Army's Rocky Mountain Arsenal, engineers had drilled a hole more than 3 kilometers deep to dispose of liquefied nerve gas. They started pumping in March 1962. A month later tremors shook the Denver area, which had been free of seismicity for many years. The frequency of the quakes initially decreased from about thirty a month to only five in December. But starting in January 1963, the numbers increased rapidly. There were as many as forty temblors in late April alone, the strongest with a magnitude of 4.3. By that time, residents of the area had become alarmed.

David Evans, a consulting geologist in Denver, suggested that the quakes might be related to the pumping.[1] Government officials denied any connection, but in September 1963 the army agreed to stop pumping for a few months. Seismic activity continued, but the quakes were less frequent. The officials concluded that no connection existed, and pumping was resumed in September 1964. The number of quakes rose sharply, to more than eighty during July 1965. Seismographs installed by the U.S. Geological

Survey showed that virtually all the shocks had originated beneath the arsenal and were clustered around the drill hole. Pumping was discontinued, and seismic activity ceased. The connection was clear.

In a press conference, with the aid of a simple model, Evans explained what he believed was happening. He had drilled tiny holes in the bottom of an empty beer can. He placed the can on a board and tilted the board, but friction held the can in place. He then poured water into the can, which immediately slid downward. A similar phenomenon, he proposed, had taken place beneath the arsenal. The fluids pumped into the earth, under high pressure, had penetrated old fracture zones, reduced friction along inactive fault planes, and led to reactivation of the faults.

Subsequently some scientists suggested that active faults might be controlled by lubricating them so they would cause many low-magnitude tremors rather than stronger earthquakes at longer intervals. The problem, however, is in knowing just where to inject fluids into faults that might be hundreds of kilometers long and many kilometers deep. Even if optimal sites could be identified, it is unlikely that anyone would want to take legal responsibility for initiating an earthquake.

In the early 1990s some Russian nuclear scientists suggested researching the possibility of developing "tectonic bombs" that could be detonated in tunnels dug into fault zones to generate earthquakes, but fortunately nothing came of the idea. Indeed, the energy released by underground nuclear tests in the United States is known to have caused movement along faults. The notion of targeting specific faults with such devices, however, is best left to the realm of horror fiction.

MARK TWAIN'S EARTHQUAKE ALMANAC

Mark Twain happened to be in San Francisco on October 8, 1865, when the city was shaken (but not too seriously) by an earthquake. He thereupon took it upon himself to compile an "almanac" for the benefit of "several friends who feel a boding anxiety to know beforehand what sort of phenomena we may expect the elements to exhibit during the next month or two, and who have lost all confidence in the various patent medicine almanacs, because of the unaccountable reticence of those works concerning the extraordinary event of the 8th inst." Following are excerpts from Twain's "Earthquake Almanac":

Oct. 17.—Weather hazy; atmosphere murky and dense. An expression of profound melancholy will be observable upon most countenances.

Oct. 18.—Slight earthquake. Countenances grow more melancholy.

Oct. 19.—Look out for rain. It will be absurd to look in for it. The general depression of spirits increased.

Oct. 20.—More weather.

Oct. 21.—Same.

Oct. 22.—Light winds, perhaps. . . . Winds are uncertain—more especially when they blow from whence they cometh and whither they listeth. N. B.—Such is the nature of winds.

Oct. 23.—Mild, balmy earthquakes.

Oct. 24.—Shaky.

Oct. 25.—Occasional shakes, followed by light showers of bricks and plastering. N. B.—Stand from under.

Oct. 26.—Considerable phenomenal atmospheric foolishness. About this time expect more earthquakes, but do not look out for them, on account of the bricks.

Oct. 27.—Universal despondency, indicative of approaching disaster. Abstain from smiling, or indulgence in humorous conversation, or exasperating jokes.

Oct. 28.—Misery, dismal forebodings and despair. Beware of all discourse—a joke uttered at this time would produce a popular outbreak.

Oct. 29.—Beware!

Oct. 30.—Keep dark!

Oct. 31.—Go slow!

Nov. 1.—Terrific earthquake. This is the great earthquake month. More stars fall and more worlds are slathered around carelessly and destroyed in November than in any other month of the twelve.*

Nov. 2.—Spasmodic but exhilarating earthquakes, accompanied by occasional showers of rain, and churches and things.

Nov. 3.—Make your will.

Nov. 4.—Sell out.

Nov. 5.—Select your "last words." . . .

Nov. 6.—Prepare to shed this mortal coil.

Nov. 7.—Shed.

Nov. 8.—The sun will rise as usual, perhaps; but if he does he will doubtless be staggered some to find nothing but a large round hole . . . where he saw this world serenely spinning the day before.[1]

* On November 1, 1755, the city of Lisbon, Portugal, was destroyed by one of the most infamous earthquakes in history.

2 • In the Holy Land: Earthquakes and the Hand of God

The Lord also shall roar out of Zion, and
utter his voice from Jerusalem;
and the heavens and the earth shall shake.

Joel 3:16

TODAY, SCIENCE PROVIDES geological explanations for many events depicted in the Bible. Two or three thousand years ago, however, in biblical times, geological events such as earthquakes raised unanswerable questions about the natural order of things, and supernatural powers were invoked to explain them. Biblical interpretations of earthquakes in Palestine, the Holy Land, are well represented in the Old Testament. Often the writers invoked the wrath of God, as in the following passages:*

- 2 Samuel 22:8—"Then the earth shook and trembled; the foundations of heaven moved and shook, because he was wroth."
- Psalms 104:32—"He looketh on the earth, and it trembleth; he toucheth the hills, and they smoke."
- Isaiah 24:18–20—"the foundations of the earth do shake. The earth is utterly broken down, . . . the earth is moved exceedingly. The earth shall reel to and fro like a drunkard."
- Jeremiah 10:10—"the Lord is the true God . . . : at his wrath the earth shall tremble."

* All quotations from the Bible are from the Authorized King James Version.

- Nahum 1:5—"The mountains quake at him, and the hills melt, and the earth is burned at his presence."
- Habakkuk 3:6—"He stood, and measured the earth: he beheld, and drove asunder the nations; and the everlasting mountains were scattered, the perpetual hills did bow: his ways are everlasting."*

The quotation from Habakkuk seems to anticipate modern concepts of plate tectonics in that land masses ("nations") were separated ("driven asunder"), with the result that parts of the earth's crust ("everlasting mountains" and "perpetual hills") were moved.

Among the most chilling references to God's wrath can be found in Numbers 16:20–33, in which, after the Exodus from Egypt, Korah, Dathan, and Abiram and their followers rebelled against Moses and Aaron. "And the Lord spake unto Moses and unto Aaron, saying, Separate yourselves from among this congregation, that I may consume them." Then "the ground clave asunder . . . And the earth opened her mouth, and swallowed them up. . . . They, and all that appertained to them, went down alive into the pit"—as graphically depicted in figure 2-1.

Palestine lies between the eastern Mediterranean Sea and the Jordan River, roughly comprising modern-day Israel and the part of Jordan known as the West Bank. It is a tectonically unstable region of frequent earthquakes, many of them catastrophic. During the last 2,500 years Palestine has experienced more than forty devastating quakes with magnitudes estimated to have been between 6.7 and 8.3. All were felt throughout the Middle East.

Most earthquakes in the Middle East have originated along a north-trending belt of tectonic deformation known as the Dead Sea rift, or fault zone, which forms the northwestern

* There are many other references to earthquakes in the Bible. Examples are found in Psalms 77:18 and 114:7 and in Isaiah 13:13, 24:18–20, and 29:6.

FIGURE 2-1. "The ground clave asunder" as Korah, Dathan, Abiram, and their followers were consigned to "the fiery pit" as punishment for rebelling against Moses and Aaron after the Exodus. (From Doré, *Sainte Bible*, 308, courtesy of Special Collections and Archives, Olin Library, Wesleyan University.)

boundary of the Arabian platelet as shown in figure 2-2. Earthquakes within the zone result mainly from movements of the Arabian platelet, which separated from the African plate some 34 million years ago and opened the Red Sea, which is still widening as the Arabian platelet continues to drift northward. Today the Dead Sea rift, up to 20 kilometers wide and more than 1,000 kilometers long, extends from the Red Sea and the Gulf of Aqaba through the Dead Sea and the Sea of Galilee to the Taurus Mountains in southeastern Anatolia, the Asian part of Turkey. The rift ends in a zone of crustal convergence where the Arabian platelet, in its northward movement, is colliding with the Anatolian platelet.

Until about 18 million years ago there was no Dead Sea rift. Palestine and the Dead Sea region moved northward together as part of the Arabian platelet. But then the Palestinian platelet (see figure 2-3) separated from the Arabian platelet, and as its northward movement slowed, the Dead Sea rift began to develop. Thus, today, the Palestine side of the rift appears to be moving southward relative to the faster-moving Arabian platelet.

Rock units east of the rift have moved more than 100 kilometers farther north than those west of the rift. The relative rate of movement has averaged 1.7 centimeters a year. The rate has varied over time and appears to have slowed during the last few millennia, possibly because of increasing resistance by the Anatolian platelet. Slower movement implies less deformation within the rift, hence fewer earthquakes—but strong quakes still shake the region about once every hundred years and continue to threaten the inhabitants of Israel, Jordan, Lebanon, and Syria.

Rupturing of faults in the densely populated area near the Dead Sea has caused eight earthquakes with magnitudes estimated to have been as high as 7 during historical time. The recurrence intervals between those quakes range from fifty to more than five hundred years. In southern Turkey, the city of

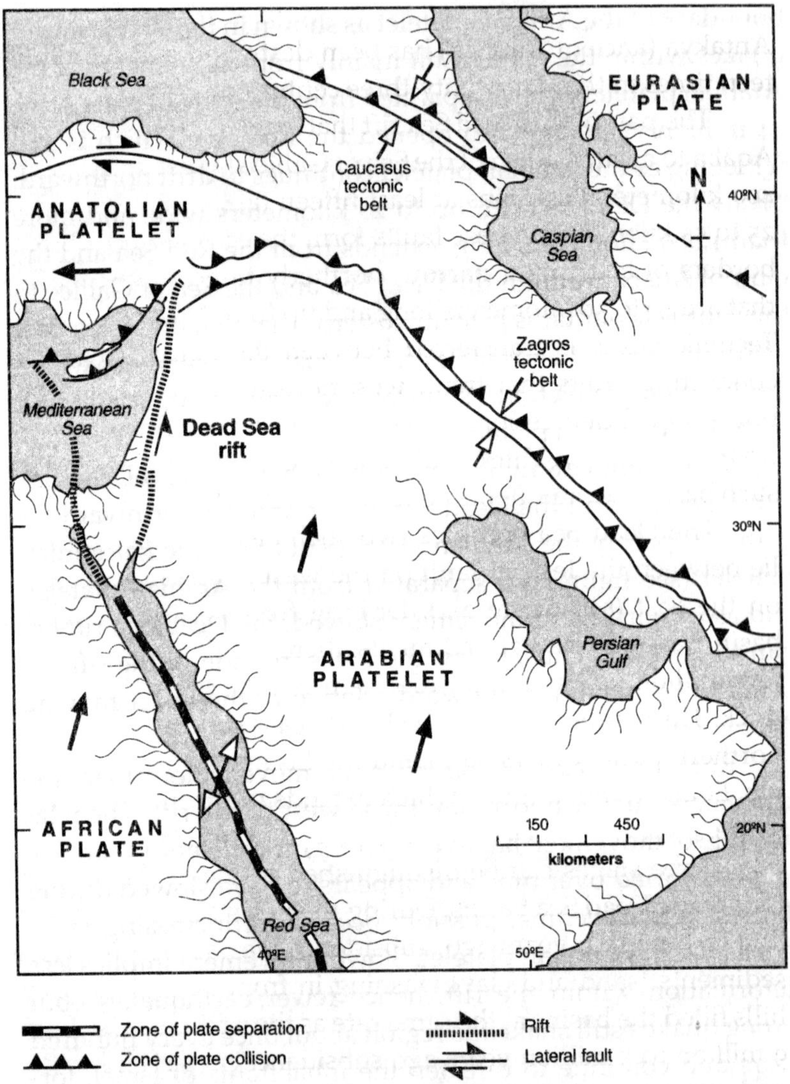

FIGURE 2-2. Plate-tectonic setting of the Dead Sea rift, or fault zone, just east of the Mediterranean Sea. The Palestinian platelet (not labeled; see figure 2-3) lies immediately west of the rift, where it underlies the eastern Mediterranean and the Sinai Peninsula. Black arrows indicate directions of plate movement. Open arrows indicate a zone of plate separation in the Red Sea, as well as zones of plate collision in the Zagros Mountains of Iran and in the Caucasus Mountains of Georgia and Azerbaijan.

Antakya (ancient Antioch) has been destroyed and rebuilt fifteen times in the last twenty-three centuries.

The part of the Dead Sea rift that extends from the Gulf of Aqaba to an area north of the Sea of Galilee (a distance of some 400 kilometers) contains at least fifteen faults with lengths of 25 to 55 kilometers. Those faults form the eastern and western borders of a string of narrow, northerly trending rift valleys that are 20 to 30 kilometers long and up to 20 kilometers wide. Tectonic stress is transferred between the border faults via connecting faults that trend west-northwest, forming rhomboid-shaped depressions called pull-apart basins as shown in figure 2-3 (inset). Thick sedimentary deposits accumulate in such basins as their floors continue to subside.

The Dead Sea occupies two such basins, both of which lie between the Jericho fault on the west and the Arava fault on the east (see figure 2-4). Drilling for oil in the southern basin has shown that sediments there, representing only a few million years of deposition, are as much as 8 kilometers thick. The southern part of the Dead Sea is separated from the northern part by marshland and the Lisan peninsula (in Arabic, *El Lisan*, the tongue), which extends out from the eastern shore.

Three stages can be distinguished in the geological history of the Dead Sea basins. During the first stage, from 18 million to 9 million years ago, subsidence was slow, and clastic sediments (sand and clay) washing in from the surrounding hills filled the basins at the same rate as the rift subsided. From 9 million to 5 million years ago subsidence increased rapidly, and water from the Mediterranean Sea invaded the Dead Sea rift through a narrow fault valley near where the city of Haifa is today (see figure 2-3). Evaporation of the seawater left a thick deposit of salt called the Sedom formation, named for Mount Sedom near the south end of the present Dead Sea. About 5 million years ago that seaway closed, and the old basins, now merged, became an isolated, hypersaline lake. New salt formations were deposited in the lake as subsidence

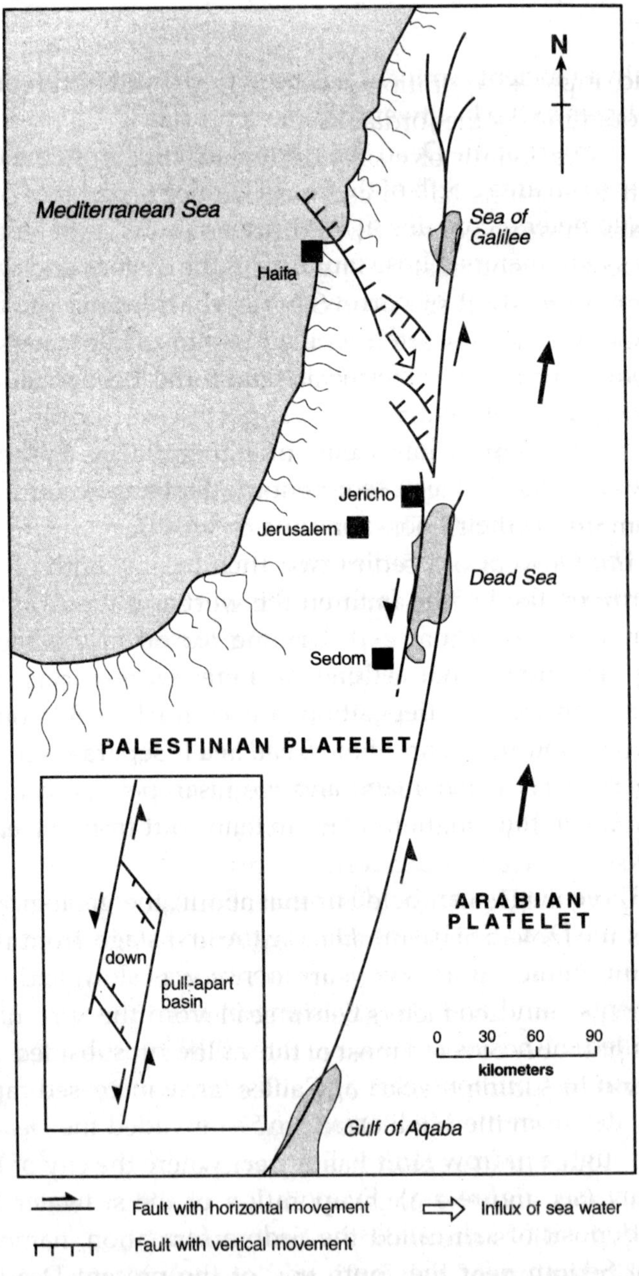

FIGURE 2-3. Schematic view of principal faults that form the Dead Sea rift. Black arrows illustrate northward movement of the Arabian platelet relative to the Palestinian platelet. The open arrow southeast of Haifa indicates the tectonic corridor along which water from the Mediterranean Sea infiltrated into the rift from about 9 million to 5 million years ago.

and rapid evaporation continued, and silts and clays were brought in by the Jordan River.

The weight of clastic sediments that overlie the ductile salt formations has forced massive volumes of rock salt upward through zones of weakness, as along faults—not unlike squeezing toothpaste from a tube. Such intrusive masses, common in the southern Dead Sea basin, are known as *salt domes*. Three salt domes are identified in figure 2-4. The southernmost extends above the surface and forms Mount Sedom, as illustrated in figure 2-5.

A third pull-apart basin lies beneath a lowland called the Arava Valley, which extends some 65 kilometers southward from the Dead Sea. The Arava basin is filled mainly with 10- to 25-million-year-old sediments; thus it is older than the two northern basins. It is apparent, therefore, that areas of deposition in the Dead Sea have migrated northward.

The surface of the Dead Sea today is about 390 meters below sea level—the lowest body of water on earth. The deepest part is some 730 meters below sea level. Climatic changes during the last 20,000 years have resulted in large variations in rainfall and fluctuations of more than 200 meters in the level of the sea. Ancient beach terraces, arranged in tiers on the hills flanking the Dead Sea, tell us that about 4,000 years ago the sea was 100 meters higher than today. And in earlier periods (from about 14,000 to 11,000 years BCE, for example) it was still higher—only 200 meters below sea level. In those days its waters probably covered most of the valley of the Jordan River up to and including the Sea of Galilee, as well as most of the Arava Valley south of the Dead Sea.

Today that region has an arid climate. High evaporation rates and the constant influx of salts, leached out of rocks in the surrounding countryside, have led to a high concentration of salt and the precipitation of evaporites (rock salt, gypsum, and rocks such as limestone, which is composed of calcium carbonate). Water in the Dead Sea is almost ten times saltier than ocean water. Evaporation under

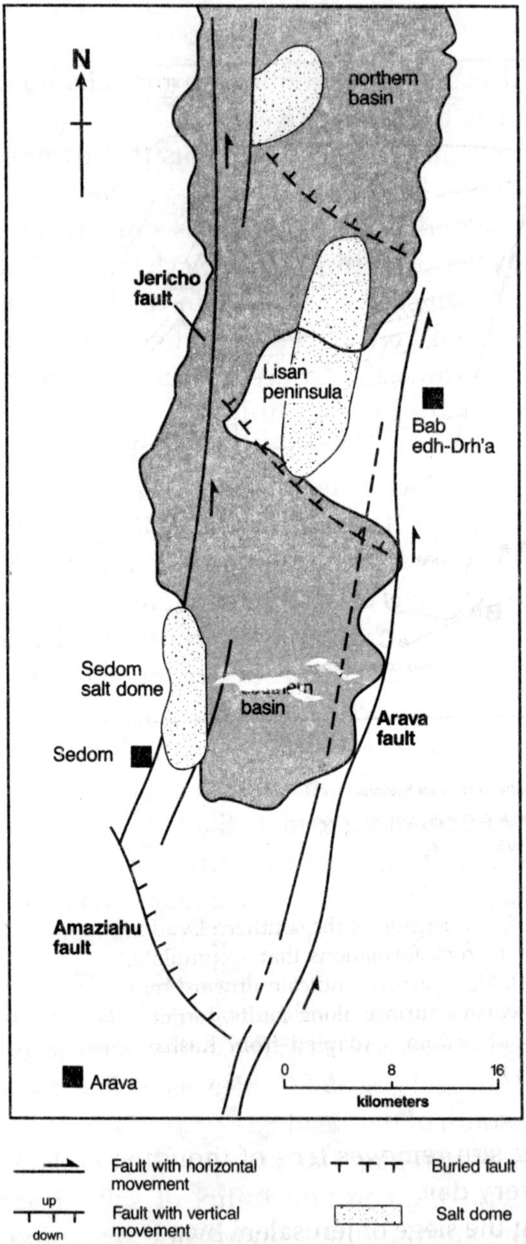

FIGURE 2-4. Southern part of the Dead Sea. The northern and southern basins have subsided to a much greater depth than the area between, where the Lisan peninsula almost bisects the sea. (Adapted from Shmuel and Amotz, "Prehistoric Earthquake Deformations," 695.) Also shown are three areas (stippled) where salt domes are located.

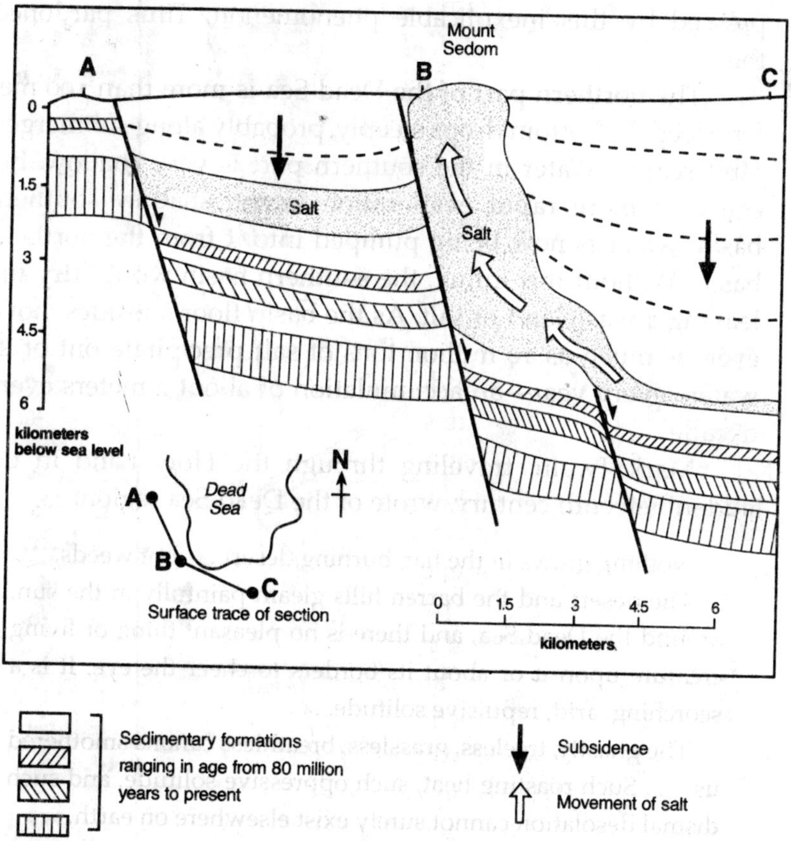

FIGURE 2-5. Cross section of the southern Dead Sea basin, showing faults and sedimentary rock formations that accumulated as the basin subsided (black arrows). Open arrows indicate upward movement of salt as it was forced to the earth's surface along faults, forming the salt dome now exposed at Mount Sedom. (Adapted from Kashai and Croker, "Structural Geometry," 34.)

the broiling sun removes tens of thousands of cubic meters of water every day.

During the siege of Jerusalem by a Roman army in 70 CE, the Dead Sea's high salt content confounded the Roman commander, Titus. Having sentenced some slaves to death, Titus had them chained together and thrown into the sea. But instead of drowning, they floated and drifted back to shore. Impressed by this inexplicable phenomenon, Titus pardoned them.

The northern part of the Dead Sea is more than 100 meters deep. Its bottom drops steeply, probably along submerged fault scarps. Water in the southern part is very shallow. Because of more rapid evaporation in the shallow southern basin, water is now being pumped into it from the northern basin. Without this influx, the southern basin would dry up, leaving a wasteland of salt. As the basin floor subsides, however, as much as 10 million tons of salt precipitate out of its waters every year—an accumulation of about 2 meters every decade.

Mark Twain, traveling through the Holy Land in the mid-nineteenth century, wrote of the Dead Sea region:

> Nothing grows in the flat, burning desert . . . but weeds. . . . The desert and the barren hills gleam painfully in the sun, around the Dead Sea, and there is no pleasant thing or living creature upon it or about its borders to cheer the eye. It is a scorching, arid, repulsive solitude. . . .
>
> The ghastly, treeless, grassless, breathless cañons smothered us. . . . Such roasting heat, such oppressive solitude, and such dismal desolation cannot surely exist elsewhere on earth. . . .
>
> It is a hopeless, dreary, heartbroken land.[1]

Yet this "hopeless land" nurtured the world's three great monotheistic religions—Christianity, Islam, and Judaism.

Ancient rock units that underlie younger sediments within the Dead Sea rift contain organic matter and sulfur (the biblical brimstone). To the east, in Saudi Arabia, Kuwait, Iraq, and Iran, and to the north in Syria, similar deposits have produced rich oil fields. Oil also has also been found, though in much smaller volumes, in sediments near the south end of the Dead Sea.

Where the faults bordering the Dead Sea rift penetrate these oil-bearing deposits, oil tends to seep to the surface and create tar pits, also known as asphalt pits or slime pits. In the

Bible the Dead Sea area is referred to as the vale of Siddim. According to Genesis 14:10, "the vale of Siddim was full of slimepits." Because the surface of the sea is about 40 meters higher now than in biblical times, many of those pits are submerged today. However, floating blobs of asphalt regularly wash up on the shores, having been detached from the submerged tar pits during earthquakes. The area's Roman conquerors were astounded by these floating "rocks," which could be made to burn.

The Greek geographer Strabo (63? BCE–24? CE) referred to the Dead Sea when he wrote, in his *Geography*:

> It is full of asphalt. The asphalt is blown to the surface at irregular intervals from the midst of the deep, and with it rise bubbles, as though the water were boiling. . . . With the asphalt there arises also much soot, which . . . is imperceptible to the eye; and it tarnishes copper and silver and anything that glistens, even gold; and when their vessels are becoming tarnished the people who live round the lake know that asphalt is beginning to rise; and they prepare to collect it by means of rafts made of reed.[2]

Strabo's invisible "soot" was in all likelihood hydrogen sulfide gas, which is known to tarnish metals. The asphalt itself was used widely as mortar in building construction, for caulking boats, and even as a medication, and considerable quantities of it were exported to Egypt for use in preparing mummies.

It was not until 1848 that scientists first visited the Dead Sea. In that year the United States government sponsored a surveying expedition to the area led by a geologist named W. F. Lynch. Lynch and his colleagues first made their way to the freshwater Sea of Galilee, which, to their astonishment, they found to be more than 200 meters below the level of the Mediterranean. In two boats they followed the Jordan River down to the Dead Sea and were surprised again. Not only did they find the Dead Sea much lower than the Sea of Galilee (390 meters below sea level): they found it so salty that it supported no life.

Mark Twain visited the Holy Land only a few years after the Lynch expedition. After going for a swim in the Dead Sea, he wrote: "It was a funny bath. We could not sink. . . . Some of us bathed for more than an hour, and then came out coated with salt till we shone like icicles." And of the sea itself he wrote, "Its waters are very clear, and it has a pebbly bottom and is shallow some distance out from the shores. It yields quantities of asphaltum; fragments of it lie all about its banks; this stuff gives the place something of an unpleasant smell."[3]

The book of Genesis (chapter 19) describes a catastrophe that befell four cities—Sodom, Gomorrah, Admah, and Zeboim—located within the vale of Siddim. Abraham's nephew Lot had settled in this fertile area when he "lifted up his eyes and beheld all the plain of the Jordan, that was well watered everywhere" (Genesis 13:10). To desert dwellers the valley must indeed have looked like the Garden of Eden. Its inhabitants benefited greatly from its natural resources. They grew rich, complacent, and morally lax—and "the men of Sodom were wicked and sinners before the Lord exceedingly" (Genesis 13:13). Retribution followed! In Genesis 19:24–28 we read:

> Then the Lord rained upon Sodom and upon Gomorrah brimstone and fire from the Lord out of heaven; And he overthrew those cities, and all the plain, and all the inhabitants of the cities, and that which grew upon the ground. . . . And Abraham gat up early in the morning to the place where he stood before the Lord: And he looked toward Sodom and Gomorrah, and toward all the land of the plain, and beheld, and lo, the smoke of the country went up as the smoke of a furnace.

The earthquake that "overthrew those cities" is thought to have occurred about 2100 BCE and to have had a magnitude of at least 6.8.[4] Fires follow many earthquakes of that magnitude. In those days a conflagration could easily have started from quake-scattered hearth coals. Moreover, when faults rupture, energy is released both as elastic shock waves and as heat. The heat generated where segments of the earth's crust slip past each other is sufficiently high to melt thin layers of rock, which, as a result, form thin layers of glass on the fault plane. Such temperatures could ignite the hydrocarbon gases and oil that tend to accumulate in fault zones. Thus the earthquake might well have been followed by the expulsion of burning hydrocarbons from the faults. As early as 1896 the geologist B. K. Emerson of Amherst College wrote:

> Earthquakes . . . overthrew the cities of the plain and caused the outpour of petroleum from the many fault fissures and the escape of great volumes of sulphurous and gaseous emanations, which, ignited either spontaneously, by lightning or by chance, furnished the brimstone and fire from heaven, and the smoke of the land going up as the smoke of a furnace which Abraham saw.[5]

Emerson's suggestion that movement along faults in petroleum-rich areas could cause spontaneous combustion was supported by nineteenth-century earthquake accounts in California. On January 9, 1857, a petroleum seep on the south flank of the San Gabriel Mountains, north of Los Angeles, was ignited during the Fort Tejon earthquake, which had a magnitude of 7.8. At night the fires could be seen from the San Fernando Valley. Fires were started during seismic activity in the Owens Valley in 1872; and after the Sonora earthquake of 1897, trees overhanging the fault were found to have been scorched.

In the book of Deuteronomy (29:20-23), Moses, addressing the Israelites for the last time before his death, recapitulated the covenant they had made with God. Moses invoked the fate of Sodom and Gomorrah in warning of the fate of any man who should break the sacred covenant:

> The Lord will not spare him . . . according to all the curses of the covenant that are written in this book of the law: . . . and the stranger that shall come from a far land, shall say . . . that the

> whole land thereof is brimstone, and salt, and burning, that it is not sown, nor beareth, nor any grass groweth therein, like the overthrow of Sodom, and Gomorrah, Admah, and Zeboim, which the Lord overthrew in his anger, and in his wrath.

Another reference to the disaster that befell Sodom and Gomorrah can be found in Strabo's *Geography*:

> Near Moasada are to be seen rugged rocks that have been scorched, as also, in many places, fissures and ashy soil, and drops of pitch dripping from smooth cliffs, and boiling rivers that emit foul odours to a great distance, and ruined settlements here and there; and therefore people believe the oft-repeated assertions of the local inhabitants, that there were once thirteen inhabited cities in that region of which Sodom was the metropolis, . . . and that by reason of earthquakes and of eruptions of fire and of hot waters containing asphalt and sulphur, the lake burst its bounds, and rocks were enveloped with fire; and, as for the cities, some were swallowed up and others were abandoned by such as were able to escape.[6]

So far no ruins have been found that can be correlated with Sodom and Gomorrah. Some authorities believe the cities were at the north end of the Dead Sea; others believe they were at the north end of the Arava Valley, along the south shore of the Dead Sea. Possibly they were located on the eastern shore, at the foot of a scarp formed by the Arava fault where it borders the Lisan peninsula. Excavations on the peninsula, at Bab edh-Dhr'a (figure 2-4), have revealed remnants of a large Bronze Age settlement, with massive defensive walls and a huge cemetery, from the period 2350 to 2100 BCE. This part of the Arava fault has been and continues to be highly active.

Some authorities believe Sodom was located not on the east side of the Dead Sea but on the west side near Mount Sedom,[7] which was formed by a salt dome. If they are correct—and certainly the names are similar—Sodom probably obtained much of its wealth by exporting rock salt dug from the mountain. The second-century Greek physician Galen is said to have mentioned "Sodom salt" and related it to the "Sodom mountains."

The presence of salt domes in the Dead Sea region probably gave rise to the biblical story of Lot's wife, who, as Lot and his family were fleeing Sodom, had been warned not to look back—but she did, "and she became a pillar of salt" (Genesis 19:26). Locally the salt domes have pushed upward for several thousand meters through overlying strata. Fracturing and erosion created elongated blocks of salt capped by erosion-resistant layers of marl impregnated with sulfur as well as conglomerate locally cemented with tar. Rain and sandstorms further eroded the salt beneath the caps, creating shapes that can be imagined to resemble human beings. A column of rock salt on the eastern flank of Mount Sedom is indeed known locally as "Lot's wife." Such columns are so numerous on that flank of the mountain that one group is called "Lot's harem."

About 8 kilometers north of the Dead Sea lies the ancient city of Jericho, also known today as Ariha. The ruins of the biblical city are marked by a hill called Tell es Sultan, about 2 kilometers northwest of modern Jericho. Archaeological work has revealed late Stone Age to Bronze Age ruins in layers some 25 meters thick. The bottom layer dates back to the seventh millennium BCE and shows that Jericho is among the oldest cities on earth. Artifacts found in the ruins suggest that the city may have housed as many as two thousand people, sustained by primitive but rapidly evolving agriculture.

Jericho owes its long life both to its strategic location and to a dependable source of water. A spring emerges from the Jericho fault nearby and has provided the city with freshwater for thousands of years. The spring is called Ein es Sultan or, alternatively, Elisha's spring, because the prophet Elisha is said to have purified its waters (2 Kings 2:21).

At least seventeen successive layers of ruins have been identified in Jericho, indicating repeated periods of destruction and reconstruction. Warfare may have caused some of the destruction, but much of it undoubtedly resulted from earthquakes.

The tectonic history of Jericho since biblical times is similar to that of the older city. Jericho was severely damaged by earthquakes three times in the seventh century CE, once each in the eighth and ninth centuries, and four times in the eleventh century. Some of those seismic events may have produced aftershocks that lasted for years. An earthquake that damaged Jericho in 1927 was followed by three years of seismic activity.

Earthquakes may have helped Joshua, who succeeded Moses as leader of the tribes of Israel, in his campaign to conquer Canaan (Palestine). The Egyptians had established a hegemony over Canaan sometime during the third millennium BCE. Joshua is believed to have entered Canaan and occupied Jericho sometime around 1300 BCE. By then Egypt's political power in Canaan had declined. Local rulers fought bloody internecine wars, and the region had slipped into anarchy. In this climate of political instability, according to the Bible, the Lord spoke to Joshua, who was east of the Jordan River with the Israelites, and said, "go over this Jordan, thou, and all this people, unto the land which I do give to them, even to the children of Israel" (Joshua 1:2).

When Joshua and his followers reached the river, they found it in full flow and were unable to cross, but after three days "the waters . . . stood and rose up upon an heap . . . and all the Israelites passed over on dry ground, until all the people were passed clean over Jordan" (Joshua 3:13–17). Quite possibly a landslide that originated in the hills on the upthrown western side of the Jericho fault interrupted the river's flow. Six such landslides, caused by earthquakes, have been recorded since 1000 BCE. Typically they have blocked the river for at least one or two days.

The fortress-city of Jericho guarded the principal route from the Jordan valley into the highlands and fertile valleys of Canaan, so Joshua had little choice but to lay siege. The Lord ordered Joshua and his people to march around the city once each day for six days, blowing "trumpets of rams' horns" (Joshua 6:3–20). On the seventh day they "compassed the city seven times," and

> at the seventh time, when the priests blew with the trumpets, Joshua said unto the people, Shout; for the Lord hath given you the city. . . . So the people shouted when the priests blew with the trumpets: and it came to pass, when the people heard the sound of the trumpet, and the people shouted with a great shout, that the wall fell down flat, so that the people went up into the city, . . . and they took the city.

The coincidence of the easy passage across the Jordan and the easy conquest of Jericho suggests the aftermath of a major earthquake. Ancient Jericho's fortifications were impressive for its time. Its Bronze Age walls were over 4 meters high and were protected by a ditch some 7 meters wide and 2 meters deep. The city's watchtower had walls about 7 meters high and equally thick. Such fortifications could not have been taken by nomadic tribesmen unless the walls had been breached, and the most likely agent for breaching such stout walls would have been an earthquake. A single severe earthquake would have had a much greater effect on city dwellers than on nomadic herdsmen. Mud-brick houses might well have collapsed, irrigation systems crumbled, and springs ceased to flow. Moreover, such an earthquake would almost certainly have breached city walls, enabling determined bands of nomads to enter and conquer.

It has been suggested that the city was destroyed by an earthquake that is believed to have shaken the Jordan valley in 1546 BCE, more than three centuries before Joshua's conquest.[8] If so, that event may have been combined with the story of Joshua as written by scribes for Judean kings in the seventh century BCE. Recent radiocarbon dating of cereal grains found in the ruins suggests a destructive event around 1315 BCE—a more likely date for Joshua's invasion.[9]

The books of Joshua and Judges provide accounts of the destruction of sixteen cities in Canaan. At least ten have been identified with reasonable confidence, but evidence for their destruction at the time when the Israelites are thought to have invaded has been found at only three—Jericho, already discussed, and Lachish and Hazor. Excavations have uncovered the ruins of Lachish at Tell ed Duweir, about 40 kilometers southwest of Jerusalem. As dryly noted in Joshua 10:32: "And the Lord delivered Lachish into the hand of Israel."

At Hazor, about 16 kilometers north of the Sea of Galilee, archaeologists have found twenty-one successive periods of development. Destruction by fire, war, or the forces of nature mark the end of each period. One layer of burnt rubble dates from the thirteenth century BCE and may be related to the biblical story of Joshua's conquest. According to Joshua 11:10–11: "And Joshua at that time . . . took Hazor, . . . and he burnt Hazor with fires." It is likely, however, that Hazor, like Jericho, had suffered from a seismic catastrophe that preceded Joshua's invasion.*

In 759 BCE Hazor was destroyed again, this time by an earthquake with a magnitude estimated to have been as great as 7.3. Hazor is only about 140 kilometers from Jerusalem—close enough for Jerusalem to have suffered serious damage as well.

Effects of the quake in Jerusalem are mentioned by the Jewish historian Flavius Josephus (37–100? CE) in describing how Uzziah, king of southern Israel in the eighth century BCE, was said to have been stricken with leprosy as punishment for "impiety toward God" in the temple:

> A great earthquake shook the ground, and a rent was made in the temple, and the bright rays of the sun shone through it, and fell upon the king's face; insomuch that the leprosy seized

* It is unlikely that the Israelites invaded Canaan as a single body, or army. More likely they trickled into the region tribe by tribe, settling among the Canaanites and only later expanding their territories and creating a unified culture.

> upon him immediately. And before the city, at a place called *Eroge*, half the mountain broke off . . . and rolled itself four furlongs . . . till the roads, as well as the king's gardens, were spoiled. . . . Now, as soon as the priest saw that the king's face was infected with the leprosy, they told him of the calamity he was under, and commanded that he should go out of the city as a polluted person. Hereupon he was so confounded at the sad distemper . . . that he did as he was commanded.[10]

In 31 BCE a strong earthquake caused widespread destruction in the lower Jordan valley and in Judea, the southern part of Palestine. Jerusalem's temple was damaged, as were King Herod's palace in Jericho and the fortifications at Masada, about 50 kilometers south of Jerusalem. Evidence from archaeological data suggests reactivation of the Jericho fault north of that city. The quake's magnitude has been estimated at 6.7.[11]

At that time Rome was governed by the triumvirate of Mark Antony, Octavian, and Lepidus. Mark Antony, in charge of Rome's eastern provinces, had abandoned his wife (Octavian's sister) and was living with Cleopatra, Queen of Egypt and daughter of Ptolemy XI. Antony gave certain provinces to Cleopatra, thus alienating the Romans. In 32 BCE, a year before the earthquake, the Roman Senate stripped Antony of his powers and declared war against Cleopatra.

Antony and Cleopatra made plans to invade Rome and sent a fleet of war galleys to the Gulf of Ambracia, an inlet of the Ionian Sea on the west coast of Greece. Octavian then sent a fleet, commanded by Marcus Agrippa, to blockade the gulf. On September 2, 31 BCE, the day of the earthquake in Judea, the opposing sides fought a great naval battle near a promontory known as Actium, and Agrippa won a famous victory.

Antony and Cleopatra, with remnants of their fleet, scurried back to Egypt. Octavian followed and captured Alexandria, Egypt's capital city. Subsequently Antony and Cleopatra both committed suicide, Antony by sword and Cleopatra, according to legend, by clasping an asp to her bosom. Octavian returned to Rome in triumph, was given the title Augustus, and became the first emperor of Rome. Thus ended the Ptolemaic dynasty in Egypt, which became a Roman province.

In Judea King Herod, an ally of Antony, had planned to join Antony's forces at Actium. Cleopatra, however, had schemed with Antony to put Herod in charge of a war against the Arabs. Her hope was that if Herod won, she would be given control over Arabia, and if Herod lost, she would gain control of Judea. Herod won one battle and was defeated in a second, but he continued to raid Arabian territory. Then, as the historian Josephus wrote, "as he was avenging himself on his enemies, there fell upon him another providential calamity; for . . . when the war about Actium was at the height, . . . the earth was shaken . . . ; but the army received no harm, because it lay in the open."[12] Destruction in towns and cities, however, was severe. At Qumran near the north end of the Dead Sea, for instance, houses and fortifications collapsed, and the central cistern was destroyed. Many sites in Judea were abandoned after the earthquake, probably because cisterns and irrigation systems were destroyed, aquifers were damaged, and springs dried up.

The Arabs, also in the open and unharmed, saw the earthquake as a good omen and took heart. Wrote Josephus, "pretending that all Judea was overthrown . . . they . . . marched into Judea immediately. Now the Jewish nation were affrighted at this invasion, and quite dispirited at the greatness of their calamities one after another. . . . Herod . . . endeavoured to persuade them to defend themselves by the following speech . . . :

> You might justly be dismayed at that providential chastisement which hath befallen you; but to suffer yourselves to be equally terrified at the invasion of men, is unmanly. As for myself, I am so far from being affrighted at our enemies after this earthquake, that I imagine that God hath thereby laid a bait for the

> Arabians, that we may be avenged on them. . . . And do you not disturb yourselves at the quaking of inanimate creatures, nor do you imagine that this earthquake is another sign of another calamity; . . . these calamities themselves have their force limited by themselves. . . . And indeed what greater mischief can the war, though it should be a violent one, do to us, than the earthquake has done?

"When Herod had encouraged them by this speech" Josephus continued, "he passed over the river Jordan with his army, and pitched his camp . . . near the enemy, and about a fortification that lay between them." Herod laid siege to the fort, eventually enticed the Arabs out to do battle, and defeated them decisively. "He punished Arabia so severely," concluded Josephus, "that he was chosen by the nation for their ruler."[13] Moreover, after the defeat of Antony at Actium, Octavian confirmed Herod as king of Judea and the lands he had conquered.

It was in Herod's time that Jesus was crucified, and the Bible states that there was an earthquake at the moment of his death. In the New Testament, according to Matthew 27:50–54:

> Jesus, when he had cried again with a loud voice, yielded up the ghost. And behold, the veil of the temple was rent in twain from the top to the bottom; and the earth did quake, and the rocks rent. . . . Now when . . . they that were with him, watching Jesus, saw the earthquake, . . . they feared greatly, saying, Truly this was the Son of God.

This account may well have been inspired by the earthquake of 31 BCE,[14] which damaged the temple in Jerusalem and led to Herod's victory.

Earthquakes are mentioned elsewhere in the New Testament as well. In Acts 16:25–31 the apostle Paul and Silas, a Hebrew leader, had been imprisoned by the Romans at Philippi, in northwestern Greece. They had been accused of disturbing the peace with their preaching:

> And at midnight Paul and Silas prayed, and sang praises unto God: and the prisoners heard them. And suddenly there was a great earthquake, so that the foundations of the prison were shaken: and immediately all the doors were opened, and every one's bands were loosed. And the keeper of the prison awakening out of his sleep, and seeing the prison doors open, he drew out his sword, and would have killed himself, supposing that the prisoners had been fled. But Paul called with a loud voice, saying, Do thyself no harm: for we are all here. Then he . . . fell down before Paul and Silas, . . . and said, Sirs, what must I do to be saved? And they said, Believe on the Lord Jesus Christ.

In Hebrews 12:26 we read, "[Whose] voice then shook the earth: but now he hath promised, saying, Yet once more I shake not the earth only, but also heaven."

Revelation 16:16–20 describes the titanic battle of Armageddon, between the powers of good and evil:

> And he gathered them together into a place called in the Hebrew Ar-ma-ged-don. . . . And there were voices, and thunders, and lightnings; and there was a great earthquake, such as was not since men were upon the earth, so mighty an earthquake, and so great. And . . . the cities of the nations fell. . . . And every island fled away, and the mountains were not found.

So we see that references to earthquakes, many of them catastrophic, are far from uncommon in the Bible. They involved powerful forces that have been at work within and upon our planet since it was created. Whether we interpret them scientifically or religiously, they are phenomena of the earth, and they can be explained in geological terms.

3 • The Decline of Ancient Sparta: A Tale of Hoplites, Helots, and a Quaking Earth

Earth! render back from out thy breast
A remnant of our Spartan dead!
Of the three hundred grant but three
To make a new Thermopylae!

Lord Byron, *Don Juan*

THE CITY-STATE OF SPARTA has been renowned through the ages as the strongest military power in classical Greece. From the nineth to the fourth century BCE its armies were almost invincible. Their heroism in battle is perhaps best exemplified, however, by a rare defeat, when, in 480 BCE at Thermopylae, Leonidas and his 300 Spartans fought valiantly to the death, holding the pass against invading hordes of the Persian king Xerxes.

The seat of Spartan power was the valley of the Eurotas River in the southern Peloponnesus, the large, irregularly shaped peninsula of southern Greece (see figure 3-1). The other Greek city-states both feared Sparta's power and admired it, looking to it for aid when they themselves were threatened, as by the Persian invasion.

Sometime around 464 BCE a powerful earthquake devastated the city of Sparta, with many fatalities. This event, while not immediately affecting Sparta's prominence, had a catalytic role in its eventual decline. The fatalities included not

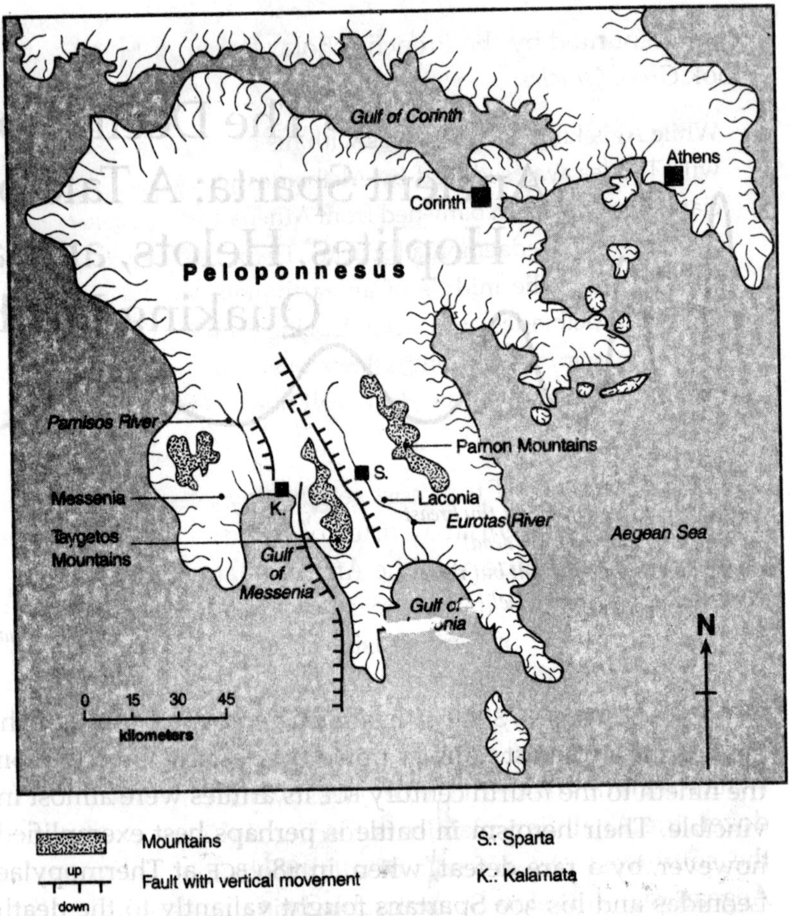

FIGURE 3-1. The Peloponnesus Peninsula of Greece, showing active faults on either flank of the Taygetos Mountains in Laconia and Messenia. Note locations of Sparta and Kalamata near faults.

only Spartan soldiers but a great many women and children as well. Thus in the following years there were many fewer births among the Spartan soldier caste, leading to the weakening of Sparta's army. This earthquake foreshadowed Sparta's gradual deterioration and disappearance from the world stage.

Seismic activity continued in the region after 464 BCE. Another quake shook Sparta about fifty years later according to a story recounted by the French scholar Robert Flaceliere in his book *Greek Oracles*:

> While Agis king of Sparta was with his army . . . in Attica, his wife Timaea was seduced by Alcibiades [an Athenian politician], who had been banished from Athens and was temporarily living in Lacedaemonia [Sparta]. Their liaison was discovered when, in the middle of an earthquake in the winter of 413–412, Alcibiades was seen leaving Timaea's room. The child she bore nine months later was named Leotychidas, though in secret Timaea used to call him Alcibiades, after his real father.[1]*

Greece is one of the most seismically active countries in the world. It is caught in a vortex of colliding tectonic plates, as illustrated in figure 3-2. The African plate is rotating counterclockwise, so that its northeastern corner is colliding with the southern edge of the Eurasian plate and forcing its way beneath it. Thus the African plate is being subducted beneath Greece. Concurrently the Arabian platelet is separating from Africa and moving northward, forcing the Anatolian platelet (which includes modern Turkey) westward. Like a titanic bulldozer, the Anatolian platelet is forcing the Aegean region to the southwest. As a result of all this tectonic activity, the Aegean region is slowly, inexorably being uplifted, hence the region's frequent earthquakes.

Geologically Greece is composed essentially of slivers of the floor of an ancient body of water called the Tethys Sea, the ancestor of the present Mediterranean Sea. Collision of the African and Eurasian plates has fractured the ancient seafloor, parts of which have been uplifted and thrust toward the west by Anatolia's westward drift. They are stacked in thick, overlapping slabs composed of highly distorted limestone and marble that overlie masses of metamorphosed clay and basalt, a volcanic rock that formed on the old seafloor. Being

* However, the Greek biographer Plutarch says it was Agis, not Alcibiades, who was frightened by the earthquake (Plutarch, *Lives*, 249).

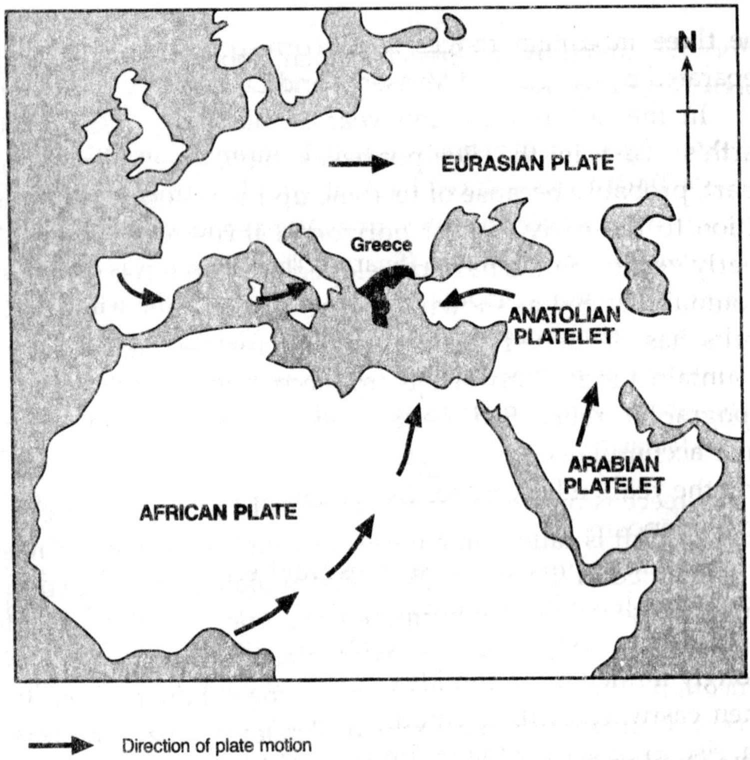

FIGURE 3-2. The convergence of tectonic plates, as shown by arrows, is responsible for the many earthquakes that plague Greece and neighboring countries.

more resistant to erosion, the limestone and marble complexes today form mountain ranges that trend north-northwest, separated by valleys where the ancient thrust faults reach the surface.

In the southern Peloponnesus, several of those overlapping slabs can be seen in the form of three more or less parallel mountain ranges named, from west to east, Pylos, Taygetos, and Parnon. The Pylos Mountains, bordering the Mediterranean in the southwestern corner of the Peloponnesus, rise only about 1,000 meters above sea level, but the Taygetos range is almost 2,500 meters high, and the Parnon range reaches almost 2,000 meters. The southern extensions of the three mountain ranges form corresponding peninsulas separated by the gulfs of Messenia and Laconia.

In the last few million years, small segments of the earth's crust in the Peloponnesus have been spreading apart, probably because of tectonic uplift. As a result, in addition to the early, almost horizontal thrust faults, sets of nearly vertical faults have developed along the flanks of the mountain ranges, as shown in figure 3-1. Motion along these faults has deepened the valleys and further elevated the mountain ranges between them, accentuating the region's topographic relief. Sediments eroded from the mountains have accumulated in the valleys between the ranges, and over the years relatively fertile soils have developed in these valley deposits.

Since antiquity the areas west and east of the Taygetos Mountains have been known, respectively, as Messenia and Laconia. Because of their height, the Taygetos Mountains strongly influence the climate of those regions. Rain develops when eastward-drifting clouds, generated above the Ionian Sea, rise to pass over the mountains. Most of the rain falls in Messenia, making it more fertile than Laconia. Moreover, the Messenian countryside is more level than Laconia's Eurotas Valley. Messenia, therefore, is better suited to agriculture.

It is in Laconia, near the Eurotas, that Sparta was founded in prehistoric times, long before the Trojan War, which traditionally has been dated about 1200 BCE. The Achaeans of Homer's *Iliad* had migrated into the Peloponnesus from the north and settled in both Messenia and Laconia. In Laconia they established a town, later to become Sparta, on a low mound of clay and marl originally deposited in a shallow lake. The sides of the mound form bluffs up to 10 meters high, capped by an indurated layer of river pebbles. providing natural lines of defense. The site commanded the only practical land routes into the valley. The Achaeans originally named the town Lacedaemon, after a son of the god Zeus. In 1830 a traveling scholar named W. M. Leake wrote of Laconia:

> One cannot help reflecting how much the former destiny of this province of Greece . . . depends upon its geographical structure and position. Those natural barriers which marked the limits of the several states of ancient Greece, and which were the real origin of the division of that country into many small independent states, . . . are nowhere more remarkable than in [Laconia]. The rugged seacoast, which forms three-fourths of its outline, combined with the steepness, height and continuity of the mountains on the land side, give it security from invasion. . . . It is to the strength of the frontiers and the comparatively large extent of country inclosed within them, that we must trace the primary cause of the Lacedaemonian power. . . . It is remarkable that all the principal passes into Laconia lead to one point. This point is Sparta, a fact which shows at once how well the position of that city was chosen for the defense of the province.[2]

Homer wrote that a Lacedaemonian king named Menelaus reigned in Laconia at the time of the Trojan War. Legend has it that the war was fought because Menelaus's wife, the beautiful Helen, was kidnapped by Paris, a son of Priam, the king of Troy. Also known as Ilium, Troy was located near the Aegean coast of what is now Turkey. The city commanded the Hellespont (now called the Dardanelles), the waterway that provides a passage from the Mediterranean to the Black Sea. Menelaus and his older brother Agamemnon, king of Mycenae, northeast of Sparta, raised an army and laid siege to Troy. As describe in Homer's *Iliad*, the siege lasted ten years. Although the legendary purpose of the Trojan War was to avenge Helen's abduction, the real purpose almost certainly was to destroy an economic rival and establish Greek influence in that strategic area.

The victorious Menelaus returned to Lacedaemon after the destruction of Troy, but the Trojan adventure had sapped his kingdom of men and wealth. His successors faced Dorian tribes, which, like the Achaeans before them, invaded Greece from the north. About 1100 BCE a Dorian army conquered

Lacedaemon. Supposedly the Dorians were led by two kings, twin descendants of the mythical hero Heracles (Hercules). Lacedaemon later united politically with four oth. Laconian towns to become the city-state of Sparta.

The Dorian conquest created turmoil throughout ancient Greece. Cities and towns fought among themselves. War and poverty led to a political and cultural dark age in Greece that lasted for two centuries or more. Some of the pre-Dorian institutions survived, however, and in Sparta they led to a brief cultural awakening, especially in art and poetry.

It was not long before the Spartans incorporated all of Laconia into their city-state. The conquered population comprised two groups, known as *perioikoi* and *helots*. The perioikoi ("dwellers about") were tradesmen and farmers who lived in largely autonomous communities. The helots were serfs, supposedly named after the residents of a conquered town named Helos who had been reduced to a servile status. In about 740 BCE the Spartans set out to annex Messenia as well. They succeeded, but only after many years of brutal warfare. The rich valley of Messenia was then divided into estates, which were assigned to Spartan soldiers. The Messenians were reduced to serfdom, forced to work the land for their absentee Spartan landlords.

The Greek poet Tyrtaeus, in the seventh century BCE, wrote that the Messenian serfs were "galled with great burdens like asses, bringing to their lords under grievous necessity a half of all the fruit of the soil."[3] Certainly the Messenians did not bear their burdens happily, and helot uprisings were not uncommon. In 640 BCE the Spartan army was able to put down a revolt only with difficulty and great loss of life.

Now weakened and in tenuous control of a subject population that vastly outnumbered its army, the city of Sparta reorganized itself into a highly regimented military state. Defective children were mercilessly put to death—thrown off a cliff in the Taygetos Mountains, some say—and boys were taken from their mothers at age seven to be sequestered in groups for training in discipline, obedience, and physical prowess. They lived in barracks and were taught to endure pain and hardship. When they were twenty years old they entered military service.

The Greek biographer Plutarch (46?–120 CE) wrote that from time to time the magistrates of Sparta would send young men into the country to kill helots, attacking them at night on the roads or by day as they worked in the fields.[4] These murderous acts were considered rites of passage, showing that the Spartan youths had attained manhood. Spartan soldiers were considered a privileged caste, membership in which was limited to native Spartans. They were encouraged to marry and have children, but they could not live with their families until age thirty, when they attained the full rights of citizenship. They served in the army until they were sixty. The ideology of Sparta compelled its citizens to live, and if necessary die, for the state.

This demanding code of citizenship produced the feared Spartan hoplites, the formidable infantrymen clad in bronze armor and crested helmets, carrying short swords and long spears, who fought ferociously in close-order phalanxes behind stout bronze shields. The laws of Sparta compelled them to win in battle or fight to the death. To survive defeat was to be disgraced. As Will Durant put it in *The Life of Greece,* the Spartan mother's farewell to her soldier son was, "Return *with* your shield or *on* it."[5] Wrote Durant:

> The Spartan code produced good soldiers and nothing more; . . . it killed nearly all capacity for the things of the mind. With the triumph of the code the arts . . . died a sudden death; we hear of no more poets, sculptors, or builders in Sparta after 550.[6]

It was about that time, the sixth century BCE, that Sparta, with a population probably approaching seventy thousand citizens and helots, attained the height of its power. The Spartans formed an alliance of city-states known as the Peloponnesian League. It was then, too, that the Persians, first under king Darius I and later his son Xerxes, began to extend the Asian empire of Cyrus the Great westward into Greece. Darius was foiled in 490 when the Athenians defeated his army at Marathon, but ten years later Xerxes, having succeeded to the throne, assembled the largest army ever seen to that time and set forth once again. He built a floating bridge across the Hellespont, and his army crossed it in 480 BCE. The Persian army easily subdued the northern Greek provinces of Thrace, Macedonia, and Thessaly, while a Persian fleet sailed south along the coast to keep the army supplied for the ultimate attack upon Athens. The Athenians met the Persian fleet in the naval battle of Artimesium, off the coast of Euboea in eastern Greece. They hoped for a victory that would destroy Xerxes' supply lines, but the engagement was indecisive.

Meanwhile some seven thousand Greek soldiers, led by Sparta's king Leonidas with three hundred Spartan hoplites, assembled at the strategic pass of Thermopylae. The name *Thermopylae,* meaning "hot gates," alludes to hot springs located along a fault at the base of Mount Kallidromos, which rises abruptly from the western shore of Maliakos Bay, a northern extension of the Gulf of Euboea. In 480 BCE there was but a narrow strip of land (the "pass") between the mountain and the bay. Since that time sediments carried down from the mountains by the Sperchios River have filled in part of the bay and moved the shoreline about 5 kilometers to the northeast.

Leonidas planned to delay the advance of the Persian hordes while the Athenian navy won a victory, which would compel the Persians to retreat for lack of provisions. When Leonidas learned that a detachment of Persians had found a way over the mountain west of the pass and were approaching his rear, he decided to release most of his army so they could retreat to make a stand elsewhere while he fought a delaying action with his three hundred Spartan hoplites. In a furious battle, in the unflinching tradition of the Spartans, the three hundred achieved immortality by fighting to the death against overwhelming odds.*

The Spartans at Thermopylae might have been inspired by the words of the poet Tyrtaeus, who wrote:

> Ye are of the lineage of the invincible Heracles; so be ye of good cheer; not yet is the head of Zeus turned away. Fear ye not a multitude of men, nor flinch, but let every man hold his shield straight towards the van, making Life his enemy and the black Spirits of Death as dear as the rays of the sun.[7]

The "black Spirits of Death" did indeed descend upon Leonidas and his men, but not until they had delayed the Persian advance for several crucial days. In a sense the Spartan king stops people at Thermopylae even today, almost 2,500 years later. Tourists pause to gaze at a heroic statue of Leonidas and read the noble epitaph on a nearby tablet: "Stranger, tell the Lacedaemonians that we lie here in obedience to their laws."

The defeat at Thermopylae forced the Greeks to abandon Athens to Xerxes' army, which pillaged the city. The Athenian fleet, however, had retreated intact to the Bay of Salamis, near Piraeus, the port of Athens. There they awaited the much larger Persian fleet and, in one of the great naval battles of history, roundly defeated the invaders by virtue of having better ships and superior tactics. What was left of Xerxes' navy fled back to the Hellespont.

Without naval support, Xerxes was forced to return to Persia with part of his army. He left perhaps 150,000 men in central Greece under a commander named Mardonius. In 479 BCE at Plataea, about 50 kilometers northwest of Athens, the Spartan commander Pausanias led some 11,000 hoplites in a downhill charge into the Persian ranks and, with Spartan discipline and superior weaponry, overwhelmed them. Mardo-

* It is thought that Leonidas's Spartans were accompanied by soldiers from one or two other city-states, some of whom are said to have surrendered to the Persians. But there is no doubt that the three hundred Spartans, true to their code, fought to the last man.

nius was killed, and the Persians retreated to a stockade camp where, later, they were routed by a Greek force comprising Pausanias's Spartans and 8,000 Athenians.

Thus Greece was saved from Asian domination. In *The Life of Greece*, Will Durant wrote:

> The Greco-Persian war was the most momentous conflict in European history, for it made Europe possible. It won for Western civilization the opportunity to develop its own economic life . . . and its own political institutions. . . . It won for Greece a clear road for the first great experiment in liberty. . . . The Athenian fleet that remained after Salamis now opened every port in the Mediterranean to Greek trade. . . . After centuries of preparation and sacrifice Greece entered upon its Golden Age.[8]

By "Greece" Durant meant Athens. Sparta did not fare so well. The Spartans, having lost a large proportion of their best hoplites in the Persian wars, were finding it increasingly difficult to suppress their helots, especially in outlying areas such as Messenia. Then, about 464 BCE,* an earthquake struck the city, virtually destroying it. Many years later Plutarch wrote:

> In the fourth year of the reign of Archidamus, . . . King of Sparta, . . . there happened in the country of Lacedaemon the greatest earthquake that was known in the memory of man; the earth opened into chasms, and the mountain Taygetus was so shaken, that some of the rocky points of it fell down, and except five houses, all the town of Sparta was shattered to pieces.[9]

The boundary between the Eurotas Valley and the Taygetos Mountains is a steeply dipping north-northwest-trending fault along which the valley floor has subsided and the mountains have risen. The fault can be traced southward for almost 100 kilometers from the central Peloponnesus to the Gulf of Laconia, where it continues beneath the sea. West of Sparta, on the eastern flank of the Taygetos Mountains, the fault forms a

* The exact year remains in question. Classical writers have mentioned dates ranging from 468 to 463 BCE.

scarp as much as 12 meters high that locally reveals an exposed fault plane. The scarp is traceable over a distance of about 20 kilometers. It represents several phases of stress release and nearly vertical slippage. During a single phase of rupturing along a fault of this length, the maximum slip usually ranges from 1 to 2 meters. This scarp, then, may represent as many as five or six tectonic events. Strong quakes associated with such ruptures are believed to occur along the Spartan fault about once every three thousand years.

Ancient Sparta was directly above the shallow part of the fault where slippage occurred in 464 BCE. The focus, or point of origin, of the resulting earthquake probably was less than 5 kilometers beneath the city. Hence Sparta received the brunt of the seismic waves. The principal shock is thought to have had a magnitude of about 7.2. It was followed by aftershocks that recurred for at least several months and possibly for as long as a year.

Fissures (Plutarch's "chasms") opened up in geologically young sediments throughout the Eurotas Valley and cut through fields, destroying farms and irrigation systems. Large masses of limestone (Plutarch's "rocky points") were shaken loose from the mountainsides, causing rockfalls and landslides that covered alluvial fans and blocked streams, forcing them to find new courses. Some wells dried up, others overflowed.

In the first century BCE the Greek historian Diodorus Siculus wrote:

> A great and incredible catastrophe befell the Lacedaemonians; for great earthquakes occurred in Sparta, and as a result the houses collapsed . . . and more than twenty thousand Lacedaemonians perished. And since the tumbling down of the city and the falling of the houses continued uninterruptedly over a long period, many persons were caught and crushed in the collapse of the walls.[10]

The Spartans suffered this disaster, wrote Diodorus, "because some god . . . was wreaking his anger upon them." That god was Poseidon. Today usually thought of as the god of the sea, whom the Romans identified with Neptune, Poseidon was originally known as "the earthshaker." It was he, in Greek mythology, who produced the tremors that so often shook the land. Poseidon sometimes caused the sea to recede during earthquakes and then roar back in the great waves we now call tsunamis. Thus he became associated with the sea. The Spartans believed that Poseidon's anger was aroused in 464 when some helots, exercising their right of sanctuary in Poseidon's shrine at Taenarum, were lured out and slaughtered by Spartan soldiers.

It is unlikely that the quake killed as many as twenty thousand in Sparta, as Diodorus wrote. Because the city was so close to the epicenter, however, thousands of Spartans must have died in collapsing houses, which were constructed of stone. Many of the victims were soldiers. Many more were boys who would never grow up to *become* soldiers. And many were women—so during the following years the quake must have led to a calamitous decline in births of native Spartan males, hence in the number of boys who were eligible, under the Spartan code, for training to serve in the army.*

In the chaotic aftermath of the earthquake, the helots in Laconia and Messenia rose in rebellion. As Diodorus described it:

> The Helots and Messenians, although enemies of the Lacedaemonians, had remained quiet up to this time, since they stood in fear of the eminent position and power of Sparta; but when

* The strength of the Sparta earthquake can perhaps be put into perspective by comparing it with one that struck Messenia's Pamisos River valley in 1986 (see figure 3-1). Part of the valley, which lies between two faults, dropped as much as half a meter. The main shock, like the quake that destroyed Sparta, originated at a depth of only about 5 kilometers. Its magnitude was 5.8. The epicenter was near the city of Kalamata, a large part of which was destroyed. The earthquake of 464 is thought to have generated fifty times more energy.

> they observed that the larger part of them had perished because of the earthquake, they held in contempt the survivors, who were few. Consequently they . . . joined together in . . . war against the Lacedaemonians.[11]

The Spartan king Archidamos organized the surviving soldiers and repelled a helot force that threatened the city. The helots then retired to the fastness of Mount Ithome in central Messenia. There, though besieged by the Spartans, they were able to conduct a war of attrition that gradually depleted Sparta's manpower. Unable to subdue the helots, Archidamos called on other city-states, including Athens, for help. The helots finally were defeated, but only after several years of warfare and great loss of life on both sides.

Before the final victory Archidamos had dismissed the Athenians who had come to Sparta's aid, apparently because he thought they might make common cause with the helots. Thus ended the alliance between Sparta and Athens, which had led only about two decades earlier to Greece's victory in the long struggle against Persia.

During the years following the Persian wars Athens had become a dominant power. Historians attribute the rise of Athens to its domination of the Delian League, created in 478 BCE as an alliance of Greek city-states bordering the Aegean Sea. The Athenians controlled the league treasury and used it, along with their navy, to support imperialistic ambitions throughout the Mediterranean region. There was continual strife between Athens and Sparta, which had formed the Peloponnesian League in 560. Historians traditionally have attributed Sparta's decline largely to the loss of manpower during the Persian wars. However, it was the lives lost in the earthquake of 464, and Sparta's preoccupation with the ensuing rebellion of helots in Messenia, that temporarily freed the Athenians from contention with Sparta and enabled them to enter into their "golden age."

The imperialism of Athens, and increasing friction with

the cities of Sparta's Peloponnesian League, culminated in the Peloponnesian War of 431 to 404 BCE. The war continued for more than a quarter of a century—a period that also saw the flowering of the great "Age of Pericles" in Athens. It was the time of Euripides and Aristophanes, of Socrates and Plato. Ultimately, however, the Peloponnesian War terminated that golden age. It involved Athenian cities throughout the Greek world, and in the end it dragged them all down. The naval power of Athens was overextended and, in the end, destroyed. Finally, in 404 BCE, Athens surrendered.

Sparta enjoyed a brief period of hegemony in Greece, but the helot uprisings and continual warfare had decimated the ranks of its hoplites. And the earthquake of 464 had ensured that there would be few replacements. Sparta was reduced to recruiting helots to serve as hoplites—without the training and ethos of the Spartan soldier caste.

Spartan hegemony meant the end of democracy in Greece as the Athenians had practiced it. There was increasing opposition to Sparta's militaristic rule, just as there had been to Athens's arrogance. In 394 BCE a Persian fleet defeated the Spartan navy in a battle off the coast of Asia Minor, some distance north of the island of Rhodes, severely limiting Sparta's sea power. Twenty years later an earthquake along the southern shore of the Gulf of Corinth delivered the coup de grâce by generating a tsunami that destroyed ten Spartan war galleys in that strategic waterway.

The city-state of Thebes, some 50 kilometers northwest of Athens, had never willingly accepted Sparta's rule. In 371 the Thebans refused to sign a peace settlement with Sparta, and in the ensuing battle of Leuctra, near Plataea, they crushed the Spartan army. Subsequently the Thebans invaded the Peloponnesus and liberated Messenia. Deprived of the labor of Messenian helots, Sparta could no longer maintain its military establishment.

And so Sparta faded into obscurity. The earthquake of 464 BCE was the catalyst for a century-long decline in which it might be said that Sparta literally bled to death as its soldiers fell in battle and could not be replaced. Plutarch believed that by 250 BCE only about seven hundred Spartan hoplites were available for the defense of their city.

Modern Sparta occupies about a third of the site of ancient Sparta. It is a bustling town, the capital of Laconia, with a population of more than eleven thousand—but except for a modest museum there are few reminders of past glories. The Sparta of Leonidas and Pausanias, with no artistic or literary legacy like that of Athens, is represented today only by undistinguished ruins, mostly just a few stone foundations, a short distance north of town.

EURIPIDES, HOMER, AND ARISTOTLE

In Greek mythology Poseidon, the earthshaker and god of the sea, had a son, Theseus, who slew the Minotaur in the Cretan Labyrinth, freed Athenian youths imprisoned there, and became the hero of Athens. Theseus married and had a son named Hippolytus. In the tragic play *Hippolytus* by Euripides, Theseus wrongly believes that his son has ravished Phaedra, whom Theseus took as his second wife after the death of Hippolytus's mother. Enraged, Theseus banishes Hippolytus and calls down a curse, demanding that Poseidon kill him. The god promptly creates a violent earthquake, followed by a great sea wave (which today we would call a tsunami). The wave crashes ashore where Hippolytus, grief-stricken because of his father's false accusation, is fleeing in a four-horse chariot. According to Euripides, the wave carries a monstrous bull, which panics the horses. They bolt, the chariot is destroyed, and Hippolytus is mortally injured. He dies later, with Theseus, realizing now what he has done, grieving at his side.

In 1962 the English writer Mary Renault published a novel, *The Bull from the Sea,* loosely based on the play by Euripides. Renault has Theseus describe the earthquake and the accompanying tsunami in the following words:

> I heard . . . a wicked beating upon the earth. . . . I stood on the prickling earth. . . . The fear of the earthquake was working in me, cold and sinking, as I had known it since a child. . . . I felt my neck-hairs rise when I faced the sea. . . . I saw the bay below. And it had moved away. Even as I watched, the waters crept out farther, showing the sea-floor no living man had seen, all weed and rotting boat-hulls. . . . All the cattle in the byres were lowing and bawling. A he-goat with wicked eyes opened his mouth in a wild cry. And with that came the earthquake. The ground jolted and jarred; there was a rumble of stones. . . .
>
> The bay was filling again; not slyly, as it had emptied, but in a great rushing wave, climbing the shores. It washed right over the . . . mole, lifting the fishing-boats upon it like toys on a child's string. Right over the chariot-road below me ran the salt sea, and climbed the plowland; spent itself, and paused, and went sucking back from the scoured land. There was a hush like death; and in this quiet . . . I heard . . . the great bellowing of a bull . . . a black bull of Poseidon, a bull from the sea.[1]

• • •

The Iliad, Homer's epic story of the Trojan War, describes Poseidon's role in turning the tide of battle when the Trojans attacked the Achaeans in an effort to capture their ships:

> The mighty Earth-shaker . . . high on the loftiest peak of . . . Samothrace . . . pitied the Achaeans as they were worsted by the Trojans. . . . At once he went down from

> the rugged mountain with quick strides, and the long ridges . . . trembled . . . beneath the immortal feet of Poseidon. . . . Three strides he made, and with the fourth he reached . . . in the depths of the sea his glorious house. . . . The Trojans . . . hoped to take the ships of the Achaeans. . . . But Poseidon who surrounds and shakes the earth, came from the deep sea. . . . So rousing them, he . . . stirred the Achaeans, and . . . those picked for bravery stood to face the Trojans. Shield pressed on shield, . . . man on man. . . . The spears bent as they brandished them in their mighty hands and their minds looked forward in their eagerness for battle.[2]

• • •

Beginning in the sixth century BCE, Athenian philosophers began to view the natural world in a more realistic way—a process of thinking that ultimately gave rise to the Western tradition of theoretical science. In their view there were four elements—earth, air, fire, and water—which provided the material foundation for nature. They considered earthquakes to be caused by interactions of those elements.

The Greek philosopher Aristotle (384–322 BCE) wrote, in his epochal work *Meteorologica*, "When an earthquake is severe the shocks do not cease immediately or at once, but frequently go on for forty days or so . . . and symptoms appear subsequently for or one or two years." He pointed out that "sound precedes the shock because sound is of finer texture and so more penetrating than the wind itself."[3]

Aristotle discussed hypotheses proposed by the philosopher Anaximenes of Miletus in the sixth century BCE and, in the fifth century, by Anaxagoras of Clazomenae and Democritus of Abdera. "Anaximenes," he wrote, "says that when the earth is in process of becoming wet or dry it breaks, and is shaken by the high ground breaking and falling." Aristotle disagreed, pointing out that "if this is so the earth ought to be sinking obviously in many places." Further, he asked, "why do earthquakes occur often in some places which . . . are by no means conspicuous for any such excess of drought or rain, as on this theory they should be?"

Anaxagoras, who thought the earth was flat, believed that "the air, whose natural motion is upwards, causes earthquakes when it is trapped in hollows beneath the earth, which happens when the upper parts of the earth get clogged by rain, all earth being naturally porous." Aristotle pointed out that "the horizon always changes as we move, which indicates that we live on the convex surface of a sphere." Therefore, he wrote, "It is silly . . . to think that the earth rests on the air. . . . Besides, [Anaxagoras] fails to account for any of the peculiar features of earthquakes, which do not occur in any district or at any time indiscriminately."

Democritus proposed that the earth is full of water and that earthquakes result when large amounts of rainwater are added, "for when there is too much for the existing cavities in the earth to contain, [the excess water] causes an earthquake by forcing its way out." Aristotle countered that "water has sometimes burst out of the earth when there has been an earthquake. But this does not mean that the water was the cause of the shock. It is the wind which is the cause, whether it exerts its force on the surface or from beneath—just as the winds are the cause of waves and not the waves of winds."

Aristotle wrote, "the earth is in itself dry but contains much moisture because of the rain that falls on it; with the result that when it is heated by the sun and its own internal fire, a considerable amount of wind is generated both outside it and inside, and this sometimes all flows out, sometimes all flows in." And "we must suppose that the wind in the earth has effects similar to those of the wind in our bodies whose force when it is pent up inside us can cause tremors and throbbings, some earthquakes being like a tremor, some like a throbbing. We must suppose, again, that the earth is affected as we often are after making water, when a sort of tremor runs through the body as a body of wind turns inwards again from without."

Aristotle's ideas were widely accepted well into the eighteenth century, more than two thousand years after his death.

4 • Earthquakes in England: Echoes in Religion and Literature

Oft the teeming earth
Is with a kind of colic pinched and vexed.

Shakespeare, Henry IV, Part 1

FEW PEOPLE ASSOCIATE ENGLAND with earthquakes. No cities in England, or in all of Great Britain, have been destroyed by quakes, and hardly any deaths there can be attributed to them. Nevertheless, at least five hundred temblors have been strong enough to have been recorded in England since the tenth century, when monastic scribes first began chronicling them. Earthquakes have influenced religion in that country ever since, and often they have been reflected in English literature.

Most earthquakes originate where moving segments, or plates, of the earth's crust are colliding and one is being forced beneath another. The British Isles, however, are securely situated on the huge Eurasian plate far from any zone of collision. The nearest such zone, where the Alps of Switzerland and northern Italy are being uplifted, is about 1,000 kilometers to the southeast. Britain's earthquakes are caused by movement along faults, or fractures in the crust, well within the bounds of the Eurasian plate. As shown in figure 4-1, most British quakes have occurred in Scotland and in northern and western England.

But it has been earthquakes in southeastern England that have had the greatest influence on British religion and litera-

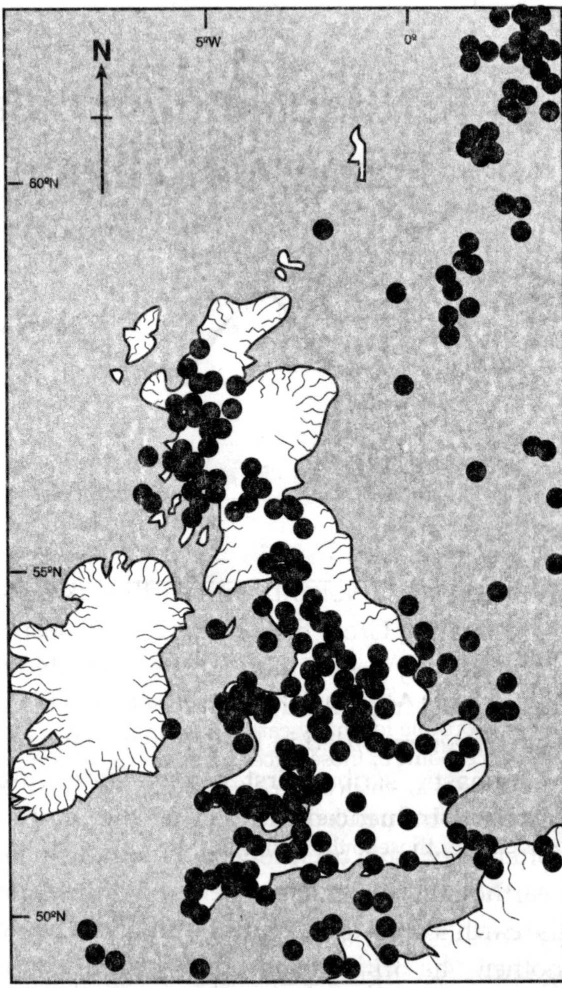

FIGURE 4-1. Epicenters of earthquakes with known or estimated magnitudes of 2 to 6 that have shaken the British Isles. (Adapted from Musson, *British Earthquakes*, 7.)

ture. Southeastern England lies above part of a broad, roughly east-west-trending belt of complex faulting that extends beneath the English Channel into northern France and southern Belgium, which share southern England's seismicity. All along that ancient trend, called the Artois fault zone after a town in France, tectonic forces within the crust generate earthquakes

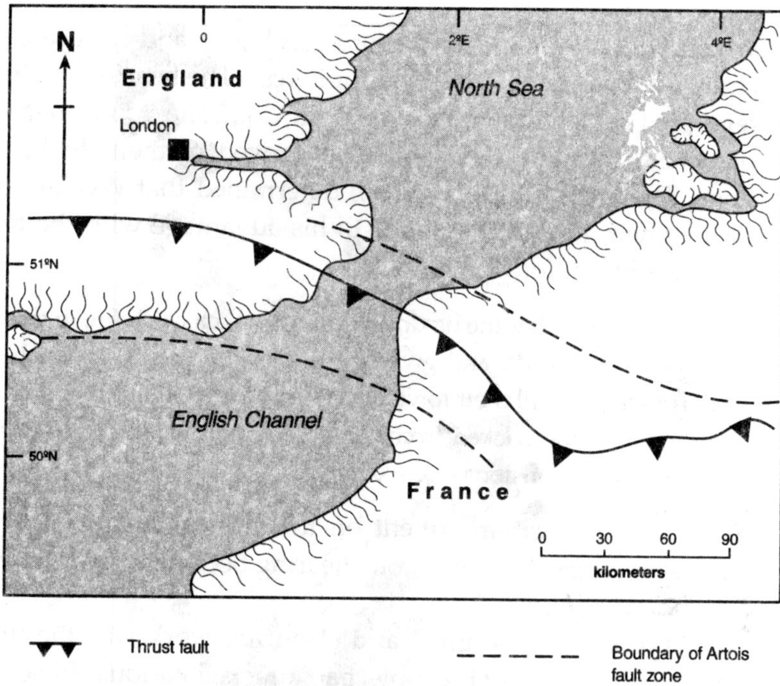

FIGURE 4-2. Within the Artois fault zone, tectonic forces generate stresses that have been responsible for many earthquakes in southern England and northwestern France. Some of those forces act horizontally, compressing the crust and causing faults in which one crustal segment is thrust over another. Along the thrust fault shown in the figure, rock formations to the southwest have been pushed over those to the northeast.

by creating stresses that are released intermittently by slippage along faults (see figure 4-2).

There was no realistic understanding of the causes of earthquakes until late in the nineteenth century, when scientists were able to correlate quakes with fractures in the earth's crust. In the Christian Bible earthquakes are cited as manifestations of God's wrath—warnings for sinners to repent, or punishment for not having already done so. In England, a quake in 1382 seemed to exemplify that biblical doctrine. The archbishop of Canterbury had convened a council of church leaders at the Blackfriars monastery in London to decide whether John Wycliffe, an Oxford theologian and advocate of church reform, should be tried for heresy. The hearing was interrupted by a temblor—a sign from God! The good prelates panicked, thinking that God disapproved of their deliberations. The archbishop, however, determined that Wycliffe be condemned, turned the quake to his advantage with the following admonition:

> Know you not that the noxious vapours which catch fire in the bosom of the earth and give rise to these phenomena which alarm you, lose all their force when burst forth? In like manner, by rejecting the wicked from our community we shall put an end to the convulsions of the Church.[1]

Reassured, the tribunal went on to condemn many of Wycliffe's writings. That infamous hearing became known as the "earthquake council."

Wycliffe, whose great and enduring work was the first English translation of the Bible, had attacked various abuses of the Roman Catholic Church. He had argued that the Holy Scriptures, not the church, were the supreme authority in ecclesiastical matters; and he had denied the doctrine of transubstantiation, which states that the Eucharistic bread and wine are literally transformed into the body and blood of Christ. Many of his followers, known as Lollards, were executed, but Wycliffe himself suffered a stroke and was allowed to live in retirement until his death in 1384.

The epicenter of the 1382 earthquake is thought to have been in the English Channel between Dover and Calais. The quake, with a magnitude now estimated by the British Geological Survey to have been 5.7, was felt throughout southern England as well as in northernmost France and the area that today comprises Belgium and Holland. In England it was strongest in Kent, in the southeastern part of the country, where it was said to have lasted as long as it takes to say the Lord's Prayer, perhaps 30 seconds. Many churches were destroyed. The bell tower of Canterbury Cathedral crumbled, and the nave was severely damaged. In London the quake damaged St. Paul's Cathedral and Westminster Abbey, and elsewhere it rocked church spires and castle towers. The quake inspired an anonymous British poet:

> Chaumbres, chymeneys, al to-barst,
> Chirches and castelles foule gon fare;
> Pinacles, steples, to ground hit cast;
> And al was for warnying to be ware.[2]

In 1580, on April 6, another earthquake shook virtually all of England as well as continental Europe from the coast of France to the vicinity of Cologne in Germany. Like the 1382 event it was strongest in Kent, where it was said to have lasted about half a minute. Near Dover a section of the famed white chalk cliff fell into the sea, along with part of Dover Castle. Church towers and castles were damaged throughout Kent, and many chimneys fell. In London, falling masonry killed two people, the first earthquake fatalities ever recorded in England. The quake rang church bells and toppled chimneys. Buildings on London Bridge were badly shaken. In England the 1580 shock is often referred to as the "London earthquake."

In the town of Saffron Walden near Cambridge in Essex, the earthquake interrupted a friendly card game, shaking the card table and indeed the whole house. The card-playing women were "dramatically transformed into kneeling penitents" according to the writer Gabriel Harvey, who lived in the town and was a fellow at Cambridge University's Trinity Hall.[3]

The strongest effects of the 1580 earthquake were felt not in England but on the Continent. In Calais, on the French coast, a number of houses collapsed and several people were killed. In Belgium, where the quake was said to have lasted long enough for two or three "paternosters" (recitations of the Lord's Prayer), more people died, many buildings were damaged, and church bells rang. As in 1382, the quake's epicenter seems to have been in the Strait of Dover. Judging from reports of ground shaking, its intensity in southern England was as high as VIII on the Mercalli scale (see figure 4-3). Aftershocks were felt most keenly in southeastern England, suggesting westward propagation of faulting that began beneath the English Channel.

The rupturing of the channel floor on April 6 generated at least two great sea waves, or tsunamis. The first is reported to have sunk twenty or thirty boats in English and French harbors. A few hours later a second wave sank well over a hundred vessels off the coasts of England and France. The tsunamis flooded coastal areas on both sides of the channel.

The 1580 earthquake is among the first events in the Western world for which the writings of monastic scribes are augmented by government archives and other secular records. Johannes Gutenberg had invented the printing press a century earlier. The introduction of printing led to the growth of literacy and vast improvements in communication and record keeping. As a result, many more documents are available about the 1580 earthquake than about earlier events. Those sources include not only government records and private journals but also religious pamphlets, sermons, and published prayers.

The wardens of various churches paid for the printing of special "earthquake" prayer books, one of which was titled *The order of Prayer . . . to avert and turn God's Wrath from us, threatned by the late terrible Earthquake.*[4] Many pamphlets warned against the danger of ascribing earthquakes to natural causes. One pamphleteer, felicitously named Thomas Churchyard, wrote:

> But perhaps, some fine headed fellowes will wrest (by naturall argumentes) God['s] doing and works, to a worldly or earthly operation, proceeding from a hidden cause in the body and bowels of [the] earth. . . . Yet those that feare God . . . will take the Earthquake to be of a nother kinde of Nature: And beholding [the] myraculous manner of the same, with open armes, and humble heart, will embrace God[']s visitation, & worthily welcome the messanger he sendeth.[5]

In an essay titled "Short and Pithie Discourse, concerning the Engendering, tokens, and effects of all Earthquakes in

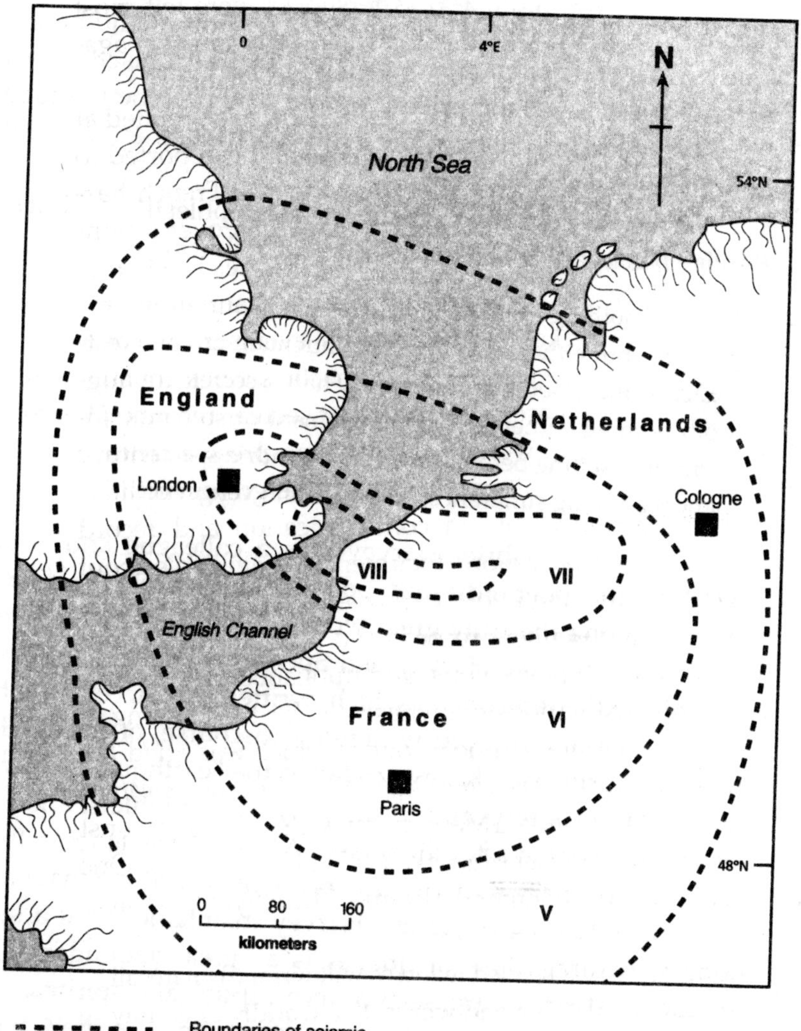

FIGURE 4-3. Zones of equal intensity of the 1580 earthquake. Roman numerals indicate values on the Mercalli intensity scale ranging from V (felt by most people) to VIII (great damage to buildings). (Adapted from Neilson, Musson, and Burton, "'London' Earthquake," 128.)

Generall," a cleric named Thomas Twyne wrote: "And herein I pray you let no man flatter or falsely persuade himself with a natural cause. . . . The Lorde is comming in maiestie to iudge the Earth, and to auenge himselfe vpon his enemies, and doubtlesse hee is not far of[f]."[6]

Further, one Abraham Fleming, in a pamphlet titled *A Bright Burning Beacon* published in 1580, had the following to say:

> There is nothing done either in Heauen aboue, or in the earth beneath, but either at the commaundement of God, or by his sufferance: . . . God I say, euery way hath a secrete counsell, and doth nothing, either by commandement or sufferance, but to some end: setting before our eies, by sundrie spectacles, . . . his patience & long sufferance, his anger and vengeance.[7]

The writer Gabriel Harvey was a colleague and close friend of the poet Edmund Spenser, author of *The Faerie Queene*, among the truly great works of English letters. After the 1580 earthquake Harvey and Spenser exchanged a series of published letters, one of which, written by Harvey, was titled "A Pleasant and pitthy familiar discourse, of the Earthquake in Aprill last." Known today as the "earthquake letter," it was Harvey's response to the prayers, pamphlets, and essays that appeared after the quake. While acknowledging that God is the primary, supernatural cause of everything that happens, including earthquakes, Harvey maintained that a secondary, natural cause of quakes is a "great aboundance of wynde, or stoare of grosse and drye vapors, and spirites, fast shut up, & as a man would saye, emprysoned in the Caves, and Dungeons of the Earth."[8] In this statement Harvey followed the conventional lay wisdom of his time, which echoed Aristotle's *Meteorologica*, written almost two thousand years earlier in Greece. Harvey felt that it was impossible to know which cause was foremost at any given time, and in a later letter to Spenser he wrote, "In earnest, I could wishe some learned, and well aduized Uniuersity man, would vndertake the matter, and bestow some paynes in deede vppon so famous and materiall an argument."[9]

Edmund Spenser, from *Calendarium pastorale*, 1732. (Courtesy of Special Collections and Archives, Olin Library, Wesleyan University.)

It was about the time of the 1580 earthquake that Spenser began writing his epic poem *The Faerie Queene*, an allegorical work in which he explores the human experience in all its complexity of virtues and vices. Three books were published in 1590, and three more in 1596.

In the poem, the "Queene," or Gloriana, represents both glory, an abstract notion, and Elizabeth I (1533–1603), the living "Virgin Queen." In the allegory twelve knights, each representing a different virtue, undertake specific quests. Prince Arthur, an angel of God who symbolizes magnanimity and seeks to find glory (the Faerie Queene), becomes involved in the knights' adventures and helps them defeat their adversaries.

The poem's first book details the adventures and misadventures of Redcrosse, the knight of holiness (the Anglican Church). He is beset by temptation in the person of Duessa, who represents deceit and shame (the Roman Church). Duessa seduces Redcrosse, who, while succumbing to her wiles and therefore committing sins of the flesh, remains confident of his virtue and thus also commits the sin of pride.

Redcrosse is set upon by a frightful giant, Orgoglio, who, personifying God's wrath, is associated with earthquakes. One day Redcrosse has removed his armor and is resting in a forest glade when,

> Till at last he heard a dreadfull sownd,
> Which through the wood loud bellowing, did rebownd,
> That all the earth for terrour seemed to shake,
> And trees did tremble. . . .
>
> But ere he could his armour on him dight,
> Or get his shield, his monstrous enimy
> With sturdie steps came stalking in his sight,
> An hideous Geant horrible and hye,
> That with his talnesse seemed to threat the skye,
> The ground eke groned under him for dreed. . . .[10]

Orgoglio subdues Redcrosse and imprisons him in a dungeon (allegorically Redcrosse, defeated by his vices, becomes a prisoner of them):

> Him to his castle brought with hastie forse,
> And in a Dongeon deepe him threw without remorse.[11]

Prince Arthur arrives to rescue Redcrosse, and Orgoglio attacks him:

Therewith the Gyant buckled him to fight,
Inflam'd with scornfull wrath and high disdaine,
And lifting vp his dreadfull club on hight
. . . .
Him thought at first encounter to haue slaine.
But wise and warie was that noble Pere,
And lightly leaping from so monstrous maine,
Did faire auoide the violence him nere;
It booted nought, to thinke, such thunderbolts to beare.

Ne shame he thought to shunne so hideous might:
The idle stroke, enforcing furious way,
Missing the marke of his misayméd sight
Did fall to ground, and with his heauie sway
So deepely dinted in the driuen clay,
That three yardes deepe a furrow vp did throw:
The sad earth wounded with so sore assay,
Did grone full grieuous underneath the blow,
And trembling with strange feare, did like an earthquake show.[12]

After a fierce battle, virtue triumphs and Arthur fells Orgoglio, of whom nothing then remains:

Such was this Gyaunts fall, that seemd to shake
The stedfast globe of earth, as it for feare did quake.
. . . .
That huge great body, which the Gyaunt bore,
Was vanisht quite, and of that monstrous mas[s]
Was nothing left, but like an emptie bladder was.[13]

Thus Spenser symbolizes the ultimate victory of Anglican Protestantism over the corruption he saw to be inherent in Roman Catholicism.

About the time that Edmund Spenser was getting *The Faerie Queene* ready for publication, William Shakespeare was

William Shakespeare, from *Mr. William Shakespeares comedies, histories, & tragedies*. Published according to the true original copies. London, printed by Isaac Iaggard and Ed. Blount, 1623. (Courtesy of Special Collections and Archives, Olin Library, Wesleyan University.)

writing *Romeo and Juliet*. There is no direct evidence of the year in which the play was published, but scholars have found references to it as early as 1595. A line in act 1, scene 3, provides an additional clue: Apparently alluding to the earthquake of 1580, Juliet's nurse recalls to Lady Capulet: "'Tis since the earthquake now eleven years, / And she was weaned. . . ."[14] This line, the only reference to a time frame within the play itself, supports the conclusion that Shakespeare wrote the play in the early 1590s.

Subsequently Shakespeare invoked earthquakes in other plays, primarily as phenomena associated with birth or death. In *Henry IV*, Part I, in the opening scene of act 3, Hotspur chides the Welsh prince Glendower for boasting that the earth quaked when he was born:

> ***Glendower*** . . . at my birth
> The frame and huge foundation of the earth
> Shaked like a coward.
> ***Hotspur***: Why, so it would have done at the same season if your
> mother's cat had but kittened, though you yourself had
> never been born.
> ***Glendower***: I say the earth did shake when I was born.
> ***Hotspur***: And I say the earth was not of my mind
> If you suppose as fearing you it shook.
> ***Glendower***: The heavens were all on fire, the earth did tremble.
> ***Hotspur***: Oh, then the earth shook to see the heavens on fire,
> And not in fear of your nativity.
> Diseasèd nature oftentimes breaks forth
> In strange eruptions; oft the teeming earth
> Is with a kind of colic pinched and vexed
> By the imprisoning of unruly wind
> Within her womb; which, for enlargement striving,
> Shakes the old beldam earth and topples down
> Steeples and moss-grown towers. At your birth
> Our grandam earth, having this distemperature,
> In passion shook.[15]

In *Macbeth*, in the crucial third scene of act 2, Macduff enters with the shocking news that Duncan, the king, was murdered during the preceding night. Immediately before Macduff's entrance, Macbeth and Lennox had been discussing the king's plans for the coming day. Lennox had described ominous events during the night, speculating that there might even have been an earthquake:

Lennox: The night has been unruly. Where we lay,
Our chimneys were blown down, and, as they say,
Lamentings heard i' the air, strange screams of death,
And prophesying with accents terrible
Of dire combustion. . . .
. . . .
. . . Some say the earth
Was feverous and did shake.
Macbeth: 'Twas a rough night.[16]

• • •

A powerful earthquake devastated the Caribbean island of Jamaica in June 1692. That far-off catastrophe resonated throughout England—psychologically if not physically—because only thirty-six years earlier Jamaica had become one of Britain's vital possessions in the New World. The quake virtually destroyed the island's largest city, Port Royal, most of which sank into the sea. Contemporary reports indicate that the convulsions lasted as long as seven minutes.

Most of the houses in Port Royal had been built upon sand. Occupying the tip of a sand spit, the city had grown around and between four forts designed to protect the bay and harbor behind the spit from enemy attack by sea. Unknown to those who built the houses, water-soaked sand like that beneath much of the city, when shaken, tends to liquefy. Individual grains no longer stick together but are separated by water, as in quicksand. And of course they no longer support the weight of buildings, or even people. Buildings sank straight down during the earthquake, and for years afterward their ruins were visible from boats sailing above them. People standing on that unstable ground during the quake sank out of sight. Most never resurfaced, but some did and managed to keep their heads above the muck. But when the shaking stopped, the sand firmed up and locked their bodies in place. Most of those people suffocated because, in their unforgiving molds, they could not expand their lungs to breathe. It has been estimated that twenty-five thousand people died in Port Royal.

Charles Lyell, the eminent nineteenth-century British scientist, devoted several pages of his groundbreaking book *Principles of Geology* to the Port Royal earthquake. Lyell wrote:

> In the year 1692 the island of Jamaica was visited by a violent earthquake, the ground swelled and heaved like a rolling sea, and was traversed by numerous cracks, . . . opening and then closing rapidly again. Many people were swallowed up in these rents; some the earth caught by the middle and squeezed to death; the heads of others only appeared above ground, and some were first engulphed, and then cast up again with great quantities of water. Such was the devastation, that . . . at Port Royal, then the capital, . . . three-quarters of the buildings . . . sank down with their inhabitants entirely under water.
>
> . . . the part of Port Royal described as having sunk, was built upon newly-formed land, consisting of sand in which piles had been driven, and the settlement of this loose sand, charged with the weight of heavy houses, may have given rise to the subsidences alluded to.[17]

From the mid-1600s until about 1680, Port Royal was a haven for pirates who preyed upon ships carrying treasures looted from the Spanish Main in Central and South America. Bound for the coffers of Spain, the treasure ships carried gold, silver, and jewelry. Centrally located Port Royal became the entrepôt where the plundered goods were stored and sold. Henry Morgan, probably the most notorious of the seventeenth-century buccaneers, even served as governor of Jamaica for a time, with Port Royal as his capital. Taverns and bordellos abounded in the rowdy city.

When news of the 1692 disaster reached England, not a few God-fearing people celebrated the demise of the city that had become known as "the Sodom of the Caribbean." The scoundrels who had lived there deserved their fate! Preachers in Britain and America, as well as in Jamaica, lost no time in attributing the earthquake to the wrath of God. One of them, the Reverend Emmanuel Heath, rector of St. Paul's Church in Port Royal, wrote to a friend in London, "I hope by this terrible Judgment, God will make them reform their Lives, for there was not a more ungodly People on the Face of the Earth."[18]

Hardly had the psychological and religious reverberations of the Jamaican catastrophe been assimilated in Britain than, in September 1692, a widely felt earthquake struck England itself. With a magnitude now estimated to have been 5.7, it originated across the channel in the Low Countries and was felt strongly throughout southeastern England. In London, according to one description:

> All the People were possessed with a Panick Fear; some Swooning, others Aghast with Wonder and Amaze; the Houses were deserted, and the Streets thronged with . . . confused Multitudes. . . . In houses in divers Parts, the Pewter and Brass were thrown from Shelves. . . . Many Persons were taken with Giddiness in their Heads. . . . These, and other Calamities, are occasioned by the Sins of this Nation.[19]

Though the two earthquakes occurred half a world apart, religious leaders in England lost no time in linking the two events, so close in time, to the will of an ever-vengeful God bent on punishing sinners. During the early 1700s this continuing religious fervor coincided with the evangelical preaching of John Wesley (1703–1791), his brother Charles (1707–1788), and their colleague George Whitefield (1714–1770), all of whom split from the Anglican Church and founded the religious movement that came to be known as Methodism. Whitefield and the Wesley brothers, darkly preaching that people were doomed without holiness, promised salvation through their new faith.

John and Charles Wesley, between them, wrote literally thousands of hymns that conveyed their message. Many are still sung today in Methodist churches around the world. The songs frequently allude to the rending of the earth and the destruction of mountains at the time of God's final judgment of sinners. Following is an excerpt from number 62 in John Wesley's *Collection of Hymns*:

Woe to the men on earth who dwell,
  Nor dread th' Almighty's frown;
When God doth all his wrath reveal,
  And shower his judgments down.
. . . .

Lo! from their seats the mountains leap,
  The mountains are not found,
Transported far into the deep,
  And in the ocean drowned.

Who then shall live and face the throne,
  And face the Judge severe?
When heaven and earth are fled and gone,
  O where shall I appear?

Now, only now, against that hour,
  We may a place provide;
Beyond the grave, beyond the power
  Of hell our spirits hide.

Firm in the all-destroying shock
  May view the final scene;
For lo! the everlasting Rock
  Is cleft to take us in.[20]

The Methodists' message spread rapidly throughout England. By the mid-1700s many people had taken it to heart and lived in fear of God's judgment. The year 1750 began with an especially vivid and, to many, frightening display of the aurora borealis, or northern lights. Like comets and other then-unexplained celestial phenomena, the shimmering streamers of light from the heavens were looked upon with awe, as mysterious messages from God. All through January and February people could not help but notice that many of the streamers had an ominous, deep red color—like blood. Then on February 4 the city of Bristol, 160 kilometers west of London and headquarters of a large Wesleyan group headed by George Whitefield, was struck by a terrifying thunderstorm. The wind uprooted trees, shook houses, and tore off roofs. Several people were killed. It seemed almost like an earthquake.

Signs of doom, then, were well established when, on February 8, an earthquake did strike southern England. It was a minor quake (the British Geological Survey estimates its magnitude to have been only 2.6), but its origin, directly beneath London, was shallow, and locally the shaking was frightening. John Wesley, in London at the time, described it this way in his journal:

> It was about quarter after twelve, that the earthquake began . . . in the southeast, went through Southwark, under the river, and then from one end of London to the other. . . . There were three distinct shakes, or wavings to and fro, attended with an hoarse, rumbling noise, like thunder. How gently does God deal with this nation! O that our repentance may prevent heavier marks of his displeasure![21]

A month later, to the day, another quake struck in the same area. This time the magnitude is thought to have been about 3. Wesley's journal entry for March 8 reads, "God rent the rocks again. I wondered at the words he gave me to speak. But he doeth whatsoever pleaseth him." John seems to have been still in London. Charles, however, apparently was in Bristol at Whitefield's headquarters in a converted metal foundry, for John went on to write:

> To-day God gave the people of London a second warning; of which my brother Charles wrote as follows:
>
> "This morning, a quarter after five, we had another shock of an earthquake, far more violent than that of February 8. . . . it shook the Foundery so violently, that we all expected it to fall

upon our heads. . . . I immediately cried out, 'Therefore will we not fear, though the earth be moved, and the hills be carried into the midst of the sea: for the Lord of hosts is with us; the God of Jacob is our refuge.' He filled my heart with faith, and my mouth with words, shaking their souls as well as their bodies."

The earth moved westward, then east, then westward again, through all London and Westminster. It was a strong and jarring motion, attended with a rumbling noise, like that of distant thunder. Many houses were much shaken, and some chimneys thrown down, but without any farther hurt.[22]

The Reverend Stephen Hales, who lived in central London, wrote a paper titled "Some Considerations of the Causes of Earthquakes," which he submitted to the Royal Society of London. In his paper Hales describes the March quake in these words:

> At about 20 Minutes before 6 in the Morning . . . I being then awake in Bed, on a Ground-floor, near the Church of St. Martin in the Fields, very sensibly felt the Bed heave, and consequently the Earth must heave too. There was a hollow, obscure, rushing Noise in the House, which ended in a loud Explosion up in the Air, like that of a small Cannon: The whole Duration, from the Beginning to the End of the Earthquake, seemed to be about 4 Seconds of Time. The Soldiers who were upon Duty in St. James's Park . . . saw a blackish Cloud, with considerable Lightning, just before the Earthquake began; it was also very calm Weather.[23]

Hales then went on to speculate on the causes of earthquakes:

> We find, in the late Earthquakes at London, and in the Accounts of many other Earthquakes, that, before they happen, there is usually a calm Air, with a black sulphureous Cloud: Which Cloud would probably be dispersed like a Fog, were there a Wind: Which Dispersion would prevent the Earthquake; which is probably caus'd by the explosive Lightning of this sulphureous Cloud; being both nearer the Earth than com-

> mon Lightnings; and also at a time when sulphureous Vapours are rising from the Earth in greater Quantity than usual. . . . In which combined Circumstances, the ascending sulphureous Vapours in the Earth may probably take Fire, and thereby cause an Earth-Lightning; which is at first kindled at the Surface, and not at great Depths, as has been thought: And the Explosion of this Lightning is the immediate Cause of an Earthquake.[24]

It is interesting to note that Hales felt compelled to preface his remarks with the following disclaimer:

> But I must first obviate an Objection of some serious well-meaning People, who are apt to be offended at any Attempts to give a natural Account of Earthquakes. . . . But it ought to be considered, that the ordinary Course of Nature is as much carried on by the Divine Agency, as the extraordinary and miraculous Events. God sometimes changes the Order of Nature, with Design to chastise Man for his Disobedience and Follies; natural Evils being graciously designed by him as moral Goods: All Events are under his Direction, and fulfil his Will.[25]

England was jolted by four other temblors in 1750, which became known as "the year of the earthquakes." All that seismic activity inspired the submission of more than 50 papers to the Royal Society. Most of the authors ascribed the quakes to supernatural causes or, like Hales, espoused some variation on the theme suggested by Aristotle so many centuries earlier.

Soon after the March 8 earthquake a British army officer named Mitchell took it upon himself to remind the people of London, in a series of well-publicized stump speeches, that the February and March earthquakes had occurred a month apart. He warned that a third shock should be expected after another month—that is, in early April. Preachers seized upon Mitchell's prophecy as a warning to sinners. People of means began leaving London to stay with relatives or friends in the country or to pay for lodgings in outlying towns. By early April the trickle of believers had become a torrent. Those who could not find or afford lodgings slept in the open. It has been estimated that a hundred thousand people fled the city.

When the first week of April came and went with no earthquake, the evacuees, somewhat sheepishly, began returning to the city. *The Gentleman's Magazine* published a satirical welcome "To the Fugitives on Account of the expected EARTHQUAKE":

Come—come out of your holes, for you've got a reprieve,
O ye Sons and ye daughters, of Adam and Eve;
Like that naughty *pair*, by your vices confounded,
Without quiet—without shame—without sorrow—surrounded,
You have fled from the call, unreform'd tho' afraid,
When *the voice of the Lord* was in earthquakes convey'd.
O wonderful work of a reasoning creature![26]

In Portugal only five and a half years later, on November 1, 1755, the city of Lisbon was destroyed by one of the most disastrous earthquakes in history. Like the earthquake in Jamaica sixty-three years earlier, the Lisbon earthquake profoundly affected religious people in England. If God could so punish Lisbon, why had he withheld such punishment from London in 1750? Was that quake merely a warning? Would Lisbon's fate be London's one day soon? John Wesley once again seized an opportunity to try and save sinners. In a pamphlet titled *Serious Thoughts occasioned by the late Earthquake at Lisbon*, he wrote:

Covetousness, ambition, various injustice, luxury and falshood in every kind, have infected every rank and denomination of people. . . . God . . . is not well pleased with this. . . . How many thousands . . . hath the earth opened her mouth and swallowed up? Numbers sunk at *Port-Royal*, and rose no more. . . .

And what shall we say of the late accounts from *Portugal*? That some thousand houses, and many thousand persons are no more! That a fair city is now in ruinous heaps. Is there indeed a God that judges the world? . . .

> It has been the opinion of many, that even this nation has not been without some marks of God's displeasure. . . . And although the earth does not yet open in *England* or *Ireland*, has it not shook, and reeled to and fro like a drunken man? And that not in one or two places only, but almost from one end of the kingdom to the other?[27]

Wesley then went on to expound his view of the causes of earthquakes:

> Alas! why should we not be convinced . . . that it is not chance which governs the world? Why should we not now, before *London* is as *Lisbon* . . . acknowledge the hand of the Almighty, arising to maintain his own cause? Why, we have a general answer always ready, to screen us from any such conviction: "All these things are purely natural and accidental; the result of natural causes." But there are two objections to this answer: first, it is untrue; secondly, it is uncomfortable. . . .
>
> Nay, what is nature itself but the art of God? Or God's method of acting in the material world?[28]

Wesley pointed out that even "men of fortune," if lacking faith, have no source of comfort during an earthquake:

> You may buy intelligence, where the shock was yesterday, but not where it will be tomorrow. . . . It comes! The roof trembles! The beams crack. The ground rocks to and fro. Hoarse thunder resounds from the bowels of the earth. And all these are but the beginning of sorrows. Now what help? . . . What money can purchase . . . an hour's reprieve? . . . If any thing can help, it must be prayer. But what wilt thou pray to? Not to the God of heaven: you suppose him to have nothing to do with earthquakes. . . . How uncomfortable the supposition . . . that all these things are the pure result of meerly natural causes![29]

Charles Darwin, during his epochal nineteenth-century voyage around the world in HMS *Beagle*, witnessed a devastating earthquake in central Chile near the city of Concepción.

After returning to England he speculated on how a similar quake would affect his native country. In his journal *Voyage of the Beagle* he wrote:

> Earthquakes alone are sufficient to destroy the prosperity of any country. If beneath England the now inert subterranean forces should exert those powers, which most assuredly in former geological ages they have exerted, how completely would the entire condition of the country be changed! What would become of the lofty houses, thickly packed cities, great manufactories, the beautiful public and private edifices? If the new period of disturbance were first to commence by some great earthquake in the dead of the night, how terrific would be the carnage! England at once would be bankrupt; all papers, records, and accounts would from that moment be lost. Government being unable to collect the taxes, and failing to maintain its authority, the hand of violence and rapine would remain uncontrolled. In every large town famine would go forth, pestilence and death following in its train.[30]

Fortunately Darwin's concerns have not materialized. But only about fifty years later, on April 22, 1884, a damaging earthquake did shake much of England. Centered in Essex, it had a magnitude that has been estimated to be 4.6. The *Essex Telegraph* of April 26 reported that the town of Colchester "was thrown into a state of indescribable panic and alarm," that the streets undulated like waves and buildings tottered, and that "women shrieked in their terror and alarm in the most piercing manner, and strong men were utterly unnerved and paralysed."[31] And in 1931 a major quake originated beneath the North Sea. Its magnitude has been estimated at about 6. Damage was reported from seventy places along England's eastern coast.

Great Britain may be far from the places where tectonic plates are colliding, but its crowded cities nevertheless remain at risk from earthquakes spawned by movements of the earth's crust along ancient fractures.

5 • The Great Lisbon Earthquake and the Axiom "Whatever Is, Is Right"

If this is the best of all possible worlds,
what can the rest be like?

Voltaire, *Candide*

ON NOVEMBER 1, 1755—ALL SAINTS' DAY—a powerful earthquake shook Europe's Iberian Peninsula as well as northwestern Africa. It did enormous damage throughout much of Portugal, southwestern Spain, and Morocco. It virtually destroyed the city of Lisbon and may have killed as many as ten thousand people outright. Two to three times that number were injured, and many of them died in the following weeks and months.

To this day, that earthquake is considered the most catastrophic in European history. Its importance was not limited to lives lost and physical destruction. The devastation wrought in Lisbon by the earthquake and ensuing fires caused educated people in western Europe, led by the French *philosophe* Voltaire, to question the philosophy of optimism espoused by such eighteenth-century thinkers as Leibniz, Pope, and Rousseau. Further, it served as a catalyst for scientific thinking as learned men strove to understand the forces of nature that had produced the quake. Moreover, the catastrophe greatly reduced the influence of church dogma, which attributed such disasters to the wrath of God rather than to natural causes.

Before the earthquake Lisbon was the queen of Iberian cities. About a quarter of a million people lived and worked there. Occupying a series of low hills near the mouth of the Tagus River, the city contained magnificent churches, monasteries, and palaces. But Lisbon was not a beautiful city. The houses where most people lived, built mainly of stone and often several stories high, were crowded together in a medieval warren of narrow, dark, dirty streets and alleys. Nevertheless the city was staggeringly rich, both in the contents of its palaces and churches and in its commercial enterprises, which brought in wealth from Portugal's worldwide colonies.

Lisbon had attained prominence in the 1500s, when Portuguese explorers undertook their great voyages of discovery. Vasco da Gama ushered in a "Golden Age" in 1498 when he sailed to India and provided Portugal with a virtual monopoly of the spice trade. Spices were then much in demand in Europe, primarily to render often-rancid meats palatable.

In 1493 Pope Alexander VI established a north-south line of demarcation in the Atlantic Ocean 100 leagues (480 kilometers) west of the Cape Verde Islands. Spain was given rights of exploration west of the line, and Portugal rights to the east, effectively dividing the world between the two powers. The following year Spain and Portugal signed the Treaty of Tordesillas, which reaffirmed Pope Alexander's division but moved the line some 1,300 kilometers farther west, to 60 degrees west longitude. The new line, as it turned out, bisected South America and ensured Portugal's possession of Brazil when that country was "discovered" by Pedro Alvares Cabral six years later, in 1500. By 1521 the vast natural resources of Brazil were being exploited and had begun to augment the wealth of Portugal.

Thus Portugal became the world's first maritime "great power." But the nation's dominance was challenged in the 1600s by Dutch and English traders, and by the early 1700s the power of Portugal had waned. The country was still fabulously rich, however, as gold and diamonds had been discovered in Brazil. The imported wealth had increasingly been concentrated in Lisbon.

In the early 1700s Joao V was king of Portugal. A devout Catholic, he contributed generously to the Roman Church, which had become extremely powerful in Portugal. The Society of Jesus—the Jesuits—had acquired great influence in Portuguese affairs, and its Inquisition was notoriously active in suppressing any hint of heresy. In 1749 Joao V appointed, as his minister for war and foreign affairs, one Sebastiao José de Carvalho e Mello, the son of a country squire. Joao V died in 1750, and his son José I ascended the throne. He confirmed the appointment of Carvalho, who soon came to dominate the new king's cabinet and, twenty years later, was given the title Marquês de Pombal.

When the earthquake struck Lisbon on November 1, 1755, the first shock, at 9:30 AM, reportedly lasted about three minutes. After a pause that may have been as long as fifteen minutes, shaking continued for another four or five minutes—an unusually long time, suggesting that there may have been a number of individual quakes. Contemporary reports on earth movements in a lead mine in Derbyshire, England, suggest five distinct jolts, of which the second was the most severe. In Lisbon a strong aftershock arrived about noon, and tremors continued for months. Major aftershocks also shook the city on November 18 and December 11.

Lisbon's citizens were not unfamiliar with earthquakes. At least four quakes had shaken the city during the fourteenth and sixteenth centuries. The people were unprepared for the massive onslaught in 1755, however. In observance of All Saints' Day, most had crowded into churches for services at 9:00 that morning. As church roofs collapsed and cascaded onto panicked worshippers throughout much of Portugal, the seismic waves caused church bells to ring throughout Spain and western France, as if proclaiming Portugal's agony. Damage was severe in Portugal as well as in southwestern Spain and northwestern Africa, especially Morocco, where the cities

FIGURE 5-1. Earthquake ruins in Lisbon. Horrified survivors pull compatriots from gaping cracks in soft ground near the city's waterfront. (From Boscowitz, *Earthquakes*, 181.)

of Fez and Casablanca were destroyed. But because Portugal was a world power in those days, Lisbon, its capital, became the focus of world attention.

The worst damage caused by the earthquake itself was done to facilities in Lisbon's harbor and buildings in low-lying areas bordering the estuary of the Tagus River. Those areas were underlain by unconsolidated sediments, which, unlike hard rock, greatly amplify seismic waves. Some buildings and stone quays slumped into the Tagus, disappearing beneath its turbulent waters. Figure 5-1 is one artist's impression of devastation in an area near the river. The great British geologist Charles Lyell, in his book *Principles of Geology*, quoted an eyewitness account:

> The most extraordinary circumstance which occurred at Lisbon during the catastrophe was the subsidence of the new quay, built entirely of marble. . . . A great concourse of people had col-

> lected there for safety, as a spot where they might be beyond the reach of falling ruins; but, suddenly, the quay sank down with all the people on it, and not one of the dead bodies ever floated to the surface. A great number of boats and small vessels anchored near it, all full of people, were swallowed up, as in a whirlpool.[1]

The destruction of the harbor led, in future years, to legends of the earth's opening to form an enormous chasm that swallowed the city. Even leading scientists nourished such legends. In the early 1800s Benjamin Silliman, a noted professor of natural history at Yale University, edited the American edition of *An Introduction to Geology* by British author Robert Bakewell. "In violent earthquakes," the text assured readers, "the chasms are so extensive, that large cities have, in a moment, sunk down and forever disappeared. . . ."[2]

Other parts of Lisbon were constructed on hills underlain by solid rock, some of sedimentary origin and some volcanic, and those areas should have withstood the seismic waves quite well. But the effects of earthquakes in 1531 and 1551 had been forgotten, and the buildings, mostly of masonry, had not been reinforced. The prolonged shaking caused many of them to collapse, sending billowing clouds of dust into the air.

The most widespread damage in Lisbon, however, resulted from fires that started as buildings collapsed upon hearths where the midday meal was being prepared. Wooden floors and beams caught fire. Small fires rapidly spread through closely spaced dwellings and blended into infernos that raged throughout the city for more than a week. At least twenty thousand houses were consumed. Virtually the whole of Lisbon became uninhabitable. The agony of Lisbon's surviving citizens was compounded by polluted drinking water, spoiled food, inability to treat the injured, and looting.

One J. Chase witnessed the events of November 1 and wrote the following account:

No place nor time could have been more unlucky for the miserable people! The city was full of narrow streets; the houses strong built and high, so that their falling filled up all the passages; the day of All Saints . . . —a great holiday, when all the altars of the churches were lighted up with candles, just at the time when they were fullest of people! Most of the churches fell immediately. The streets were thronged with people . . . , many of whom must have been destroyed by the mere falling of the upper parts of the houses. . . . Some . . . were imprisoned under the ruins of their dwellings, only to be burnt alive! . . .

Three times I thought myself inevitably lost! The first, when I saw all the city moving like the water; the second, when I found myself shut up between four walls; and, the third time, when, with the vast fire before me, I thought myself to be abandoned . . . ; and even in the square, . . . the almost continual trembling of the earth, as well as the sinking of the great stone quay adjoining to the square, at the third great shock at twelve o'clock . . . made me fearful lest the water had undermined the square, and that at every succeeding shock we should likewise sink. . . . Full of these terrors, . . . it more than once occurred to me that the Inquisition, with all its utmost cruelty, could not have invented half such a variety of tortures. . . .

As for the Portuguese, they were entirely employed in a kind of religious madness, lugging about saints without heads or limbs, . . . and if by any chance they espied a bigger, throwing their own aside, they hauled away the greater weight of holiness.[3]

Lisbon's harbor areas were devastated by three or four tsunamis that followed the earthquake by about half an hour. They were up to 6 meters high along Portugal's coast but increased to as much as 10 meters in narrow estuaries. Besides wreaking havoc ashore, the great waves sank ships and, as they withdrew, sucked people and debris into a maelstrom of death and destruction. They also washed enormous quantities of sand into harbors all along the coast of Portugal, causing many to become unusable to fishermen.

Elsewhere, especially along the southwest coast of Spain and in northwestern Africa, the tsunamis were even larger. Some are thought to have been more than 15 meters high. In Cadiz they topped the medieval seawalls and killed many people. In Africa they caused severe damage in many towns and cities, most notably Algiers and Tangier. The death toll attributable to tsunamis in those places probably equaled that of Lisbon, but the African deaths are ignored in most reports. The tsunamis crossed the Atlantic Ocean and were reported from several sites along America's eastern seaboard.

In many parts of Europe, standing waves called *seiches* disturbed the normally quiet surfaces of lakes, wells overflowed or dried up, and springs changed their behavior. In Scotland's Loch Lomond, almost 2,000 kilometers from Lisbon, the waters sloshed back and forth for almost two hours, the waves reaching heights of as much as a meter. And springs in the city of Teplice, a spa in Bohemia, suddenly became muddy about 10:30 AM on November 1. Some thirty minutes later they produced such a quantity of water that mineral baths ran over. Elsewhere in central Europe the opposite happened, and the output of springs declined or ceased altogether.

The Lisbon earthquake is thought to have been felt over an area of more than 15 million square kilometers. Disturbances in bodies of water were reported from as far away as Finland, more than 3,000 kilometers to the northeast, and tsunamis were recorded in the West Indies, almost 6,000 kilometers southwest.

Since no seismic instruments were available in 1755, it was impossible for anyone to know then where the shocks had originated. In Voltaire's satirical work *Candide*, published in 1759, the naive philosopher Pangloss exemplifies the scientific simplicity of the time when he says: "This earthquake is nothing new . . . ; the town of Lima in America experienced the same shocks last year. The same causes produced the same effects. There is certainly a vein of sulphur running under the earth from Lima to Lisbon."[4] Pangloss was right about the direction, however. Survivors of the earthquake agreed that the shocks had come from the southwest, somewhere in the Atlantic Ocean.

John Michell, a professor of geology at Cambridge University in England, analyzed reports of the 1755 quake and, in 1760, published a book titled *Conjectures concerning the Cause, and Observations upon the Phaenomena of Earthquakes,* in which he proposed a method for determining where earthquakes originated. He suggested that the directions of wave propagation at different locations be plotted as lines on a map and that the lines then be extended until they intersected. He thus confirmed that the Lisbon quake had originated in the eastern Atlantic. Michell is considered to be among the "fathers" of seismology.

It is known that the first tsunami arrived at Lisbon about thirty minutes after the quake struck. Since tsunamis travel at 400 to 500 kilometers per hour, the epicenter had to be 200 to 250 kilometers from Lisbon. There is indeed a tectonically active area at that distance southwest of Lisbon—near a relatively shallow area of banks, or uplifts, in the seafloor, that lie along the boundary between the Eurasian and African tectonic plates. That boundary starts at the Mid-Atlantic Ridge near the Azores archipelago and extends eastward into the Mediterranean Sea as shown in figure 5-2.

About 175 million years ago the African and North American plates began to separate along the Mid-Atlantic Ridge, opening the southern part of the North Atlantic Ocean. Farther north, however, Europe and North America remained connected for another 115 million years. As the African plate moved eastward during that time, it slipped past the Eurasian plate along a wide zone of crustal fracturing—the plate boundary depicted in figure 5-2.

About 60 million years ago the Eurasian plate also began

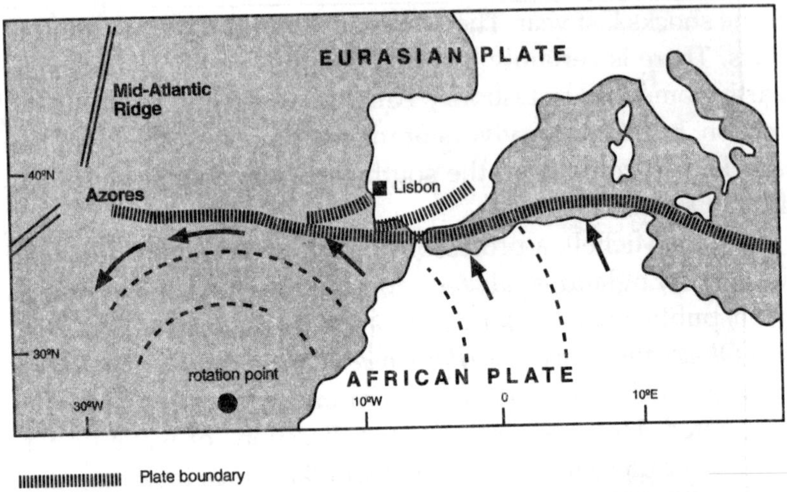

FIGURE 5-2. Boundary between the Eurasian and African plates. Both plates are moving eastward, but the African plate is also rotating counterclockwise around a point a short distance west of the coast of Africa. As a result there is crustal extension, hence fracturing and volcanism, in the Azores Islands. Offshore from Lisbon, compression of the crust has led to uplifting of the ocean floor in places.

moving eastward as North America and Eurasia finally began to separate, opening the northern part of the North Atlantic. Meanwhile the African plate has continued to move eastward, at a rate somewhat faster than the Eurasian plate, while simultaneously rotating counterclockwise as also shown in figure 5-2. This rotation has caused the earth's crust to be extended in the western part of the African-Eurasian plate boundary, near the Mid-Atlantic Ridge, and compressed farther east off the coast of Portugal. The extension has caused crustal fracturing, allowing molten rock (magma) to rise from the depths, leading to volcanism in the Azores. Compression of the crust, on the other hand, has led to the uplifting of areas to the east, such as the Gorringe and Ampere banks shown in figure 5-3.

Just in the fifty years between 1930 and 1980, many earthquakes were caused by the release of compressive stress along faults near the Gorringe Bank. Most were of relatively low magnitude, but five—in 1931, 1939, 1941, 1969, and 1975—had a

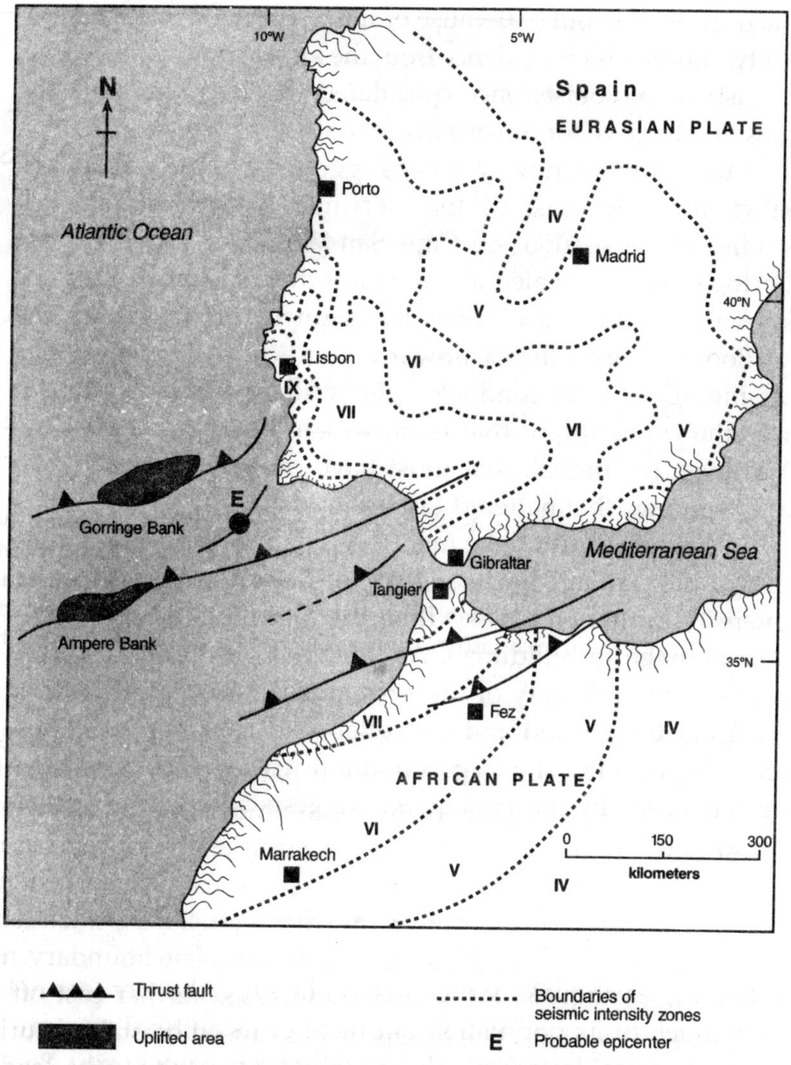

FIGURE 5-3. Major faults in the vicinity of Portugal and Morocco. The black dot off the southwestern tip of Portugal indicates the probable epicenter of the 1755 earthquake. Also shown are probable zones of equal seismic intensity resulting from that quake. Indicated values range from IV (felt indoors by many, outdoors by few) to IX (great damage, cracks in ground).

magnitude of about 7. Because of the history of this seismic activity, coupled with evidence from the arrival times of tsunamis in Lisbon, geologists once considered the Gorringe Bank the most likely place for the origin of the 1755 earthquake.

Recent work, however, has suggested an origin about 100 kilometers southeast of the Gorringe Bank. Seismological studies of the seafloor off Cape San Vicente, in southwestern Portugal, have revealed a major fault that was previously unknown.[5] Along a 200-kilometer segment of that fault, the seafloor has been thrust upward as much as 10 meters. The seismologists who conducted the studies concluded that it was the rupturing of that fault, which they named after the Marquês de Pombal, that must have caused the earthquake and tsunamis that battered Lisbon in 1755.

The 1969 earthquake mentioned above had a magnitude of 6.9, and damage in the vicinity of Lisbon indicates that its intensity in that area was VII on the Mercalli scale (considerable damage to buildings). As illustrated in figure 5-3, estimates of the intensity of the 1755 quake, based on reports of cracks in the ground and the collapse of masonry buildings, are as high as IX. The large amount of energy that must have been released by the 1755 quake suggests a magnitude possibly as high as 8.5.

• • •

When the earthquake struck Lisbon in 1755, the city lost not only much of its population but most of its cultural heritage. Libraries were destroyed, along with charts of the great Portuguese voyages of discovery. Lost, too, were important works of art, including paintings by such masters as Correggio, Rubens, and Titian. Also destroyed were administrative and commercial centers. In the chaos that followed, the king, an indecisive leader, sought the advice of his ministers. The pragmatic Pombal is said to have replied, with blunt common sense: "Bury the dead and feed the living."[6] José gave him absolute authority, and Pombal used it well. He had the dead collected and their bodies buried at sea to prevent plague. He stationed soldiers throughout the ruins to stop looting, had camps set up to house the homeless, and established centers for the distribution of food and unpolluted water. His architects drew up plans for rebuilding Lisbon with wide thoroughfares.

Pombal's efforts at reconstruction, however, were strongly resisted by the clergy, especially the Jesuits. They opposed his initiatives because they believed the earthquake to have been God's punishment of sinful people who had become too worldly. To them, the first and most pressing duty of the survivors was to pray and make their peace with God, not to waste time rebuilding the ruined city. Basically, the clergy feared losing their grip on the people, and they fiercely attacked Pombal's authority. Most vocal among his critics was a Jesuit named Gabriel Malagrida, who wrote:

> Learn, O Lisbon, that the destroyers of our houses, palaces, churches, and convents, the cause of the death of so many people and of the flames that devoured so many treasures, are your abominable sins, and not . . . natural phenomena. . . . It is scandalous to pretend the earthquake was just a natural event, for if that be true, there is no need to repent and to try to avert the wrath of God. . . . It is necessary to devote all our strength and purpose to the task of repentance.[7]

Lisbon's surviving sinners, Malagrida said, should recognize an obligation to retreat for at least six days in Jesuit monasteries, wherein they could be properly "cleansed." Above all, they should not participate in reconstruction efforts. Instead, they should spend their time in prayer. The clergy also suggested self-immolation, and their Inquisition condemned many people to be burned at the stake in the religious ceremonies known as autos-da-fé (acts of the faith). As Voltaire later wrote, scathingly, in *Candide*, "the authorities . . . could find no surer means of avoiding total ruin than by giving the people a magnificent auto-da-fé." And "the sight of a few people ceremoniously burned alive before a slow fire was an infallible prescription for preventing earthquakes."[8]

A number of religious myths arose out of the earthquake, many of them no doubt fostered by the clergy to support their belief in the supernatural origin of the disaster. A young girl was said to have been found alive in the ruins nine days after the earthquake, clutching an image of St. Anthony. The bodies of officiating priests supposedly were found miraculously well preserved after months of burial beneath the rubble. Thus, the thinking went, innocence had been rewarded. And in one church a statue of Our Lady is reported to have cried aloud, "It is enough, my Son, it is enough!"

There were reports, too, that God had provided warnings of the earthquake. A nun named Maria Joanna claimed that Jesus, in a vision, had told her of his displeasure at the sins of Lisbon and that the people would be punished. And in 1752 a Sebastianist had predicted a terrible event on All Saints' Day. When nothing out of the ordinary occurred that year, he repeated his prediction for 1753, and again for 1754. When the earthquake finally happened in 1755, the prophecy was recalled and given credence, leading to a surge of converts to Sebastianism.

Many people believed that another earthquake would obliterate Lisbon on the first anniversary of the 1755 quake. By late October of 1756 the belief was so widespread that a proclamation was issued forbidding anyone to leave Lisbon, and troops surrounded the city. A minor aftershock on October 29 seemed to confirm the rumor. It was not unknown for such rumors to be spread by robbers, who sought to frighten people into abandoning their homes. It has been suggested, too, that they were spread by church officials, anxious about maintaining their influence over the people.

Pombal used the Lisbon earthquake as a springboard for a campaign to reduce the influence of the church, and especially the Jesuits, in Portugal and its colonies. In part he resented their efforts to interfere with his plans to rebuild Lisbon, and in part he thought the Jesuits were supporting native resistance to Portugal's control of a profitable colony in Paraguay. Indeed, Malagrida had been a missionary in neighboring Brazil, and he became the leader of Jesuit-sponsored efforts to overthrow Pombal. Pombal countered by persuading King José to issue a decree forbidding the Jesuits to hear confessions or to preach. Moreover, he closed their famous university at Coimbra.

In addition to the Jesuits, many aristocrats among the noble families in Portugal resented the power of the lowborn Pombal, especially his influence over King José. As it happened, there was an attempt on José's life one night in September 1758, and Pombal attributed the attack to the Jesuits and a group of nobles. Accordingly he had leading Jesuits, including Malagrida, arrested, along with suspected members of the nobility. Several of the prisoners were executed, and the rest languished in jail for years. Malagrida was finally brought to trial in 1760, and in 1761 he was strangled and his body burned. Eventually all Jesuit property in Portugal was confiscated, and the Jesuits themselves were exiled. Moreover, the government took control of the Inquisition and made it a public tribunal. Thus Pombal, who had attained dictatorial power as a result of the Lisbon earthquake, succeeded in weakening the authority of both church and nobility in Portugal.

In 1777 King José died, and his daughter Maria became queen. Sympathetic to the church and the nobility, she reinstated the Inquisition as it had been and ordered the release of Pombal's political prisoners. Meanwhile Pombal's popularity had declined because of his anticlericalism and his autocratic methods. The queen dismissed him and declared him an "infamous criminal." He died in disgrace five years later.

Portugal never regained its sixteenth- and seventeenth-century prominence. To a large degree, however, the country retained many of the social changes brought about by the earthquake, and by the Marquês de Pombal.

• • •

The early eighteenth century in Europe was an age of optimism. Intellectuals, for the most part, subscribed to the doctrine of "universal good." Evil was relegated to the background, disagreeable but necessary. Rousseau, for example, believed that mankind is essentially good, though corrupted by society. Leibniz believed that the world had been created with inherent evils but that God could not intervene, because such intervention would show that his creation was imperfect—an obvious impossibility. Thus the world experienced by mankind was, as Leibniz wrote, "the best of all possible worlds." In England Alexander Pope published his *Essay on Man* in 1733, expounding on Leibniz's fatalistic concept as follows:

> Who finds not Providence all good and wise,
> Alike in what it gives, and what denies?
> . . . .
> All Nature is but Art, unknown to thee;
> All Chance, Direction which thou canst not see;
> All Discord, Harmony, not understood;
> All partial Evil, universal Good:
> And, in spite of Pride, in erring Reason's spite,
> One truth is clear, "WHATEVER IS, IS RIGHT."[9]

Voltaire, though an early disciple of Pope (he even wrote an imitative work called *Discours sur l'homme*), became disenchanted with the visionary notion of "universal good." The Lisbon earthquake confirmed his skepticism, for he saw no "right" in the indiscriminate nature of that catastrophe. Voltaire recognized the presence of gratuitous evil in the world, and he felt that Pope's thinking, and especially the words *whatever is, is right*, "only insult us in our present misery."[10]

Thus, in 1756, Voltaire was inspired to write his masterful *Poème sur le désastre de Lisbonne.* In the preface he wrote:

> If, when Lisbon . . . and other cities were swallowed up with a great number of their inhabitants . . . , philosophers had cried

> out . . . , "all this is productive of general good; the heirs of those who have perished will increase their fortune; masons will earn money by rebuilding the houses, beasts will feed on the carcasses buried under the ruins; it is the necessary effect of necessary causes; your particular misfortune is nothing, it contributes to the universal good," such a harangue would doubtless have been as cruel as the earthquake was fatal.

And in the poem itself he wrote:

> Oh wretched man, earth-fated to be cursed;
> Abyss of plagues, and miseries the worst!
> Horrors on horrors, griefs on griefs must show,
> That man's the victim of unceasing woe,
> And lamentations which inspire my strain,
> Prove that philosophy is false and vain.
> Approach in crowds, and meditate awhile
> Yon shattered walls, and view each ruined pile,
> Women and children heaped up mountain high,
> Limbs crushed which under ponderous marble lie;
> Wretches unnumbered in the pangs of death,
> Who mangled, torn, and panting for their breath,
> Buried beneath their sinking roofs expire,
> And end their wretched lives in torments dire.
> . . . .
> Whilst you these facts replete with horror view,
> Will you maintain death to their crimes was due?
> And can you then impute a sinful deed
> To babes who on their mothers' bosoms bleed?
> Was then more vice in fallen Lisbon found,
> Than Paris, where voluptuous joys abound?
> Was less debauchery in London known,
> Where opulence luxurious holds her throne?
> . . . .
> Look round this sublunary world, you'll find
> That nature to destruction is consigned.
> . . . .

All *may* be well; that hope can man sustain,
All now *is* well; 'tis an illusion vain.[11] [italics added]

Rousseau responded to Voltaire's poem with a personal letter reiterating his belief that human misery is the result of human faults, and he rigidly maintained that the Lisbon earthquake was proper punishment for man's abandoning the natural life and crowding into cities. He insisted that Leibniz was right—that since God had created the world, evils and all, it must all be for the best. Indeed, he claimed that the optimism ridiculed in the poem helped mankind cope with misfortune. The letter was published and was hailed by the intelligentsia as an apt reply to the pessimistic views expressed in Voltaire's poem.

Then in 1759 Voltaire published *Candide,* his brilliant satire on the state of the eighteenth-century world and its dominant philosophy of optimism. Whereas his poem had been written primarily for the intellectuals and the ruling classes of Europe, *Candide* was written for the masses, and it was read widely. It immediately made optimism appear foolish. At one point in the story, for example, Candide and the Rousseauian philosopher Pangloss are marooned in Lisbon on that fatal All Saints' Day. Although Candide was injured, they worked to help other victims of the earthquake. Wrote Voltaire:

> Some of the citizens whom they had helped gave them as good a dinner as could be managed after such a disaster. The meal was certainly a sad affair, and the guests wept as they ate; but Pangloss consoled them with the assurance that things could not be otherwise:
>
> "For all this," said he, "is a manifestation of the rightness of things, since if there is a volcano at Lisbon it could not be anywhere else. For it is impossible for things not to be where they are, because everything is for the best."

Candide and Pangloss were subsequently imprisoned by the Inquisition, Pangloss for maintaining that "the fall of

Man" was of necessity part of "the best of all possible worlds," and Candide "for listening with an air of approval." A few days later they were "marched in procession . . . to hear a moving sermon followed by beautiful music in counterpoint. Candide was flogged in time with the anthem . . . and Pangloss was hanged":

> The terrified Candide stood weltering in blood and trembling with fear and confusion.
>
> "If this is the best of all possible worlds," he said to himself, "what can the rest be like?"[12]

• • •

Thus the Lisbon earthquake of 1755 had implications far beyond its geological significance. It led to the rise of the Marquês de Pombal to be virtual dictator of Portugal, and hence, despite Pombal's ultimate fall, to the weakening of the nobility and the influence of the Catholic Church in that country. In both Europe and America the earthquake encouraged the search for scientific reasons for natural phenomena. And, primarily through Voltaire's writings, it ushered in the end of "the age of optimism."

Today, the trauma of 1755 echoes in the mournful fado songs of Portugal. (*Fado* means "fate" in Portuguese.) Those traditional songs speak of mankind's fragile existence, always at risk because of destructive powers beyond human control.

THE WONDERFUL "ONE-HOSS-SHAY"

During 1857 and 1858 Oliver Wendell Holmes wrote, for the then-new *Atlantic Monthly* magazine, a series of humorous, rambling monologues collectively called "The Autocrat at the Breakfast Table," ostensibly recited to a group of boarders in a rooming house. The monologues often included poems. One of them, presented as a "rhymed problem," invoked the Lisbon earthquake of 1755. Titled "The Deacon's Masterpiece, or The Wonderful 'One-Hoss-Shay'—a Logical Story," it includes the following whimsical lines:

> Have you heard of the wonderful one-hoss-shay,
> That was built in such a logical way
> It ran a hundred years to a day,
> And then, of a sudden, it—ah, but stay,
> I'll tell you what happened without delay,
>
> . . . .
>
> Seventeen hundred and fifty-five,
> *Georgius Secundus* was then alive, —
> Snuffy old drone from the German hive;
> That was the year when Lisbon-town
> Saw the earth open up and gulp her down,
>
> . . . .
>
> It was on the terrible earthquake-day
> That the Deacon finished the one-hoss-shay.
>
> . . . .
>
> She was a wonder, and nothing less!
> Colts grew horses, beards turned gray,
> Deacon and deaconess dropped away,
> Children and grand-children—where were they?
> But there stood the stout old one-hoss-shay
> As fresh as on Lisbon-earthquake day!
>
> EIGHTEEN HUNDRED; —it came and found
> The Deacon's masterpiece strong and sound. . . .
> Eighteen hundred and twenty came; —
> Running as usual; much the same.
> Thirty and forty at last arrive,
> And then come fifty, and FIFTY-FIVE.

. . . .

FIRST OF NOVEMBER, —the Earthquake-day. —
There are traces of age in the one-hoss-shay.

. . . .

First of November, 'Fifty-five!
This morning the parson takes a drive.

. . . .

All at once the horse stood still,
Close by the meet'n'-house on the hill.
—First a shiver, and then a thrill,
Then something decidedly like a spill, —
And the parson was sitting upon a rock,
At half-past nine by the meet'n'-house clock, —
Just the hour of the Earthquake shock!
—What do you think the parson found,
When he got up and stared around?
The poor old chaise in a heap or mound,
As if it had been to the mill and ground.

. . . .

End of the wonderful one-hoss-shay.
Logic is logic. That's all I say.[1]

Holmes, who lived in Boston, Massachusetts, might well have chosen the anniversary of another earthquake as the time for his wonderful horse-drawn chaise to disintegrate. On November 18, 1755, only about two weeks after the Lisbon quake, a strong temblor struck much closer to home. Its epicenter was in the Atlantic Ocean about 100 kilometers southeast of Boston, and it shook the East Coast of North America from Nova Scotia to South Carolina. With a magnitude estimated to have been as high as 6.3, it caused enough damage in Boston to provide ammunition for Puritan preachers in their warnings of divine punishment for sinners.

6 • New Madrid, Missouri, in 1811: The Once and Future Disaster

This district, formerly so level, rich, and beautiful, had the most melancholy of all aspects of decay, the tokens of former cultivation and habitancy, which were now mementos of desolation and desertion. Large and beautiful orchards, left uninclosed, houses uninhabited, deep chasms in the earth, obvious at frequent intervals—such was the face of the country.

Timothy Flint, *Recollections of the Last Ten Years* (1826)

A SERIES OF devastating earthquakes shook America's heartland during the winter of 1811–1812. Among the strongest ever recorded in North America, the quakes were focused in the central Mississippi Valley. The town nearest the epicenters was New Madrid (locally pronounced New *Mad*rid), on the Mississippi River just north of what today is called the "Bootheel" of Missouri, where a small, heel-shaped area of that state protrudes southward into Arkansas. The first major earthquake was on December 16, 1811, the second on January 23, 1812, and the third on February 7. Each began with a powerful shock followed by prolonged aftershocks, some very strong. The ground shook incessantly until March 1812, there were small quakes every few days for the rest of the year, and noticeable vibrations continued intermittently for several years. In Louisville, Kentucky, 300 to 400 hundred kilometers from the epicenters of the various quakes, a surveyor named Jared Brooks, using homemade instruments consisting of pendulums and springs, counted 1,874 shocks over a period of three months after the initial earthquake on December 16.

The earthquakes killed few people, as the region was sparsely populated in the early 1800s. Fissuring, uplift, and subsidence, however, disrupted the landscape over as much as 20,000 square kilometers of the Mississippi and Ohio River valleys, and there were lesser effects over a much larger area. Included were parts of the present states of Missouri, Illinois, Indiana, Kentucky, Tennessee, Mississippi, and Arkansas.

Movements of the ground were felt as far away as the East Coast of the United States, including New England, and from the Gulf of Mexico to the Great Lakes (see figure 6-1). The quakes rang church bells in Richmond, Virginia. The earth trembled, though slightly, as far away as Quebec, Canada, almost 1,900 kilometers from New Madrid. There are no records of disturbances west of the Mississippi Valley, as that region was largely unexplored by Europeans at the time of the quakes. It is not unlikely, however, that the earth shook throughout the Great Plains.

It all started shortly after 2:00 in the morning on Monday, December 16, 1811. Inhabitants of New Madrid and the surrounding area were rudely awakened when the earth shook violently, furniture was upset, the timbers of their houses and log cabins groaned and cracked, and chimneys crashed to the ground. Terrified people fled outdoors. They shivered in the winter darkness, afraid, with the continual aftershocks, to return to their weakened dwellings. Morning brought no relief, as at 8:15 AM another violent shock, almost as powerful as the first, tore through the region.

A century later, in 1912, Myron L. Fuller, a geologist with the U.S. Geological Survey, published the first scientific account of the earthquake. He described the events of 1811 and 1812 as follows:

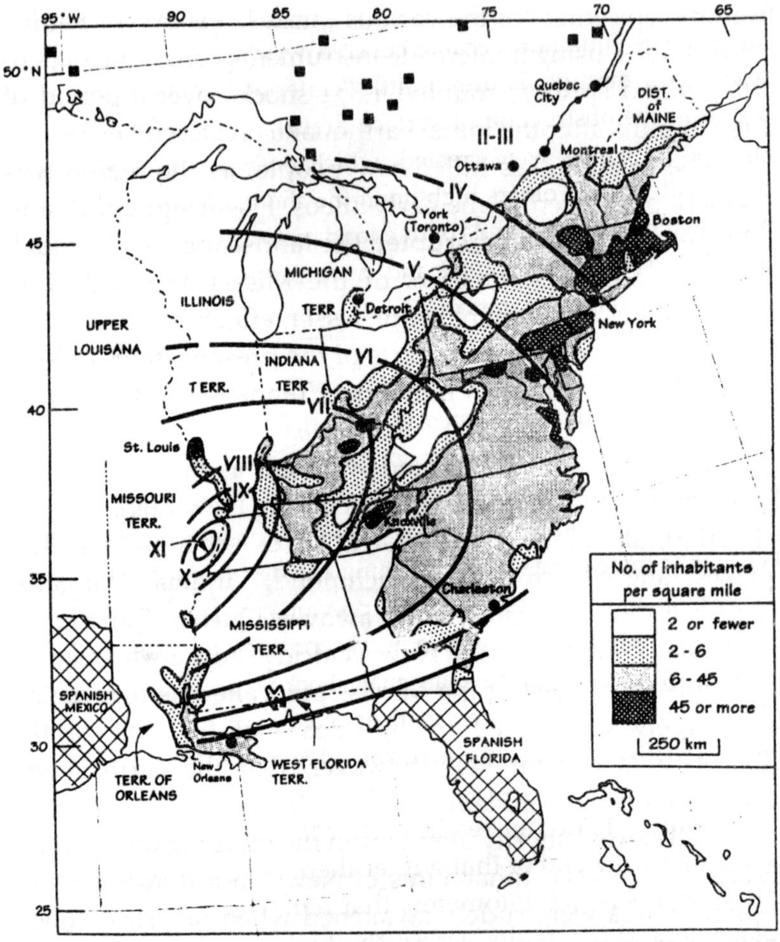

FIGURE 6-1. Zones of equal seismic intensity resulting from the earthquake of December 16, 1811. Shown are values on the Mercalli scale, ranging from II in New England and southeastern Canada (felt by few people) to XI at the quake's epicenter (widespread destruction). (After Johnston and Sweig, "Enigma," 343.)

The ground rose and fell as earth waves, like the long, slow swell of the sea, passed across its surface, tilting the trees until their branches interlocked and opening the soil in deep cracks as the surface was bent. Landslides swept down the steeper bluffs and hillsides; considerable areas were uplifted, and still

> larger areas sunk and became covered with water emerging from below through fissures or little "craterlets" or accumulating from the obstruction of surface drainage. On the Mississippi great waves were created, which overwhelmed many boats and washed others high upon the shore, the return current breaking off thousands of trees and carrying them out into the river. High banks caved and were precipitated into the river, sand bars and points of islands gave way, and whole islands disappeared.
>
> During December 16 and 17 shocks continued at short intervals but gradually diminished in intensity. They occurred at longer intervals until January 23, when there was another shock, similar in intensity and destructiveness to the first. This shock was followed by about two weeks of quiescence, but on February 7 there were several alarming and destructive shocks, the last equaling or surpassing any previous disturbance, and for several days the earth was in nearly constant tremor.
>
> For fully a year from this date small shocks occurred at intervals of a few days, but as there were no other destructive shocks the people gradually became accustomed to the vibrations.[1]

Virtually all the houses in New Madrid ultimately collapsed, and by the end of that winter there were few buildings within a radius of 400 kilometers that remained undamaged. Displacement along faults across the bed of the Mississippi River created temporary dams that locally caused the "Father of Waters" to appear to flow backward for a time. And east of the river, in the northwestern corner of Tennessee, a low, swampy area sank lower and filled with water to form Reelfoot Lake, supposedly named after an Indian chief who had a clubfoot, thus a reeling gait. The lake was almost 30 kilometers long, about 8 kilometers wide, and as much as 6 meters deep. Today that lake, somewhat smaller, is a scenic resort noted for its fishing.

In terms of the number of shocks, their severity, the area affected, and the length of time involved, the New Madrid earthquakes of 1811 and 1812 far surpass any other seismic event in North American history. In comparison, the San Francisco earthquake of 1906, though it had an estimated magnitude of 7.9, was felt no farther than 560 kilometers away, in central Nevada. Earthquakes in the eastern and midwestern United States typically affect larger areas than comparable quakes in the West because rock formations in the West tend to be less dense than those in the East. As a result, they tend to absorb seismic energy, whereas seismic waves are more readily transmitted through the denser eastern formations.

The New Madrid earthquakes, in fact, are thought to have been the strongest ever recorded in the interior of a continent. Because the New Madrid region was largely unsettled in 1811, however, the devastation there was known to relatively few people. There was little communication between the western frontier on the Mississippi River and eastern population centers. Moreover, the citizens of the young United States were preoccupied with the rapidly deteriorating relations with England that led to the War of 1812. Thus the quake received little national publicity. In later years it was all but forgotten except for an occasional paper published in the scientific literature.

• • •

Although Hernando de Soto, a Spanish explorer, is credited with the European discovery of the Mississippi River in the mid-1500s, it was France that first laid claim to the territory in 1682 when Robert Cavelier, Sieur de la Salle, came down the river from French possessions in what is now Canada. La Salle named the area Louisiana in honor of King Louis XIV. France transferred the territory to Spain in 1762, and in 1763 Spain ceded the area east of the Mississippi to Great Britain. In 1795, after the American Revolution, Spain recognized the Mississippi as the western boundary of the United States. Three years later, in 1800, the Louisiana Territory reverted to France, and in 1803 the French, under Napoleon Bonaparte, sold it to the United States to raise money for Bonaparte's long-lasting war with England.

The New Madrid earthquakes happened at a time when the young nation was concerned not only about becoming involved, itself, in war with England but also about the threat of fighting on its own western frontier. A visionary Shawnee Indian chief named Tecumseh was striving to unite the Native American tribes of the Midwest in an effort to stop the westward encroachment of white settlers. (It was one of those tribes, the Ojibway, who gave the river the name Misi Sipi, or "Great Water.") More and more of North America's interior—the great hunting ground of Native Americans—was being appropriated and settled by Europeans in the early 1800s.

The Mississippi already had become a highway of commerce as flatboats, keelboats, and barges floated downstream to the thriving ports of Natchez, in what was then the territory of Mississippi, and New Orleans, in what is now the state of Louisiana. A number of small villages and trading posts dotted the riverbanks, but settlements farther west were few. The only states bordering the Mississippi in those days were Kentucky and Tennessee. River traffic was virtually all one-way: Rafts and small boats without sails drifted south with the current. There was no practical way to haul them back upstream for reuse.

The town of New Madrid, named after the capital city of Spain, was founded in the 1780s on the west bank of the Mississippi in what was then Spanish territory. The location, on the outside of a large, looping bend in the river, seemed to have many advantages. It commanded a view for a great distance both upstream and down, and the river's current, as it swept around the bend, brought all boat traffic close to shore at the town site. Moreover, the town was situated on a high bluff, apparently safe from any flood. New Madrid soon became an important landing place, second only to Natchez as a port for Mississippi River traffic between the Ohio River junction and New Orleans. Possibly as many as a thousand people lived there in 1811, fully expecting their village to one day become the gateway to the American West.

As early as 1796, however, it was becoming apparent that the high riverbank was subject to erosion. The river's powerful current carried away large sections of the bluff from time to time, eventually eating into the town site itself.

• • •

Most severe earthquakes occur near the boundaries of colliding tectonic plates. Thus the New Madrid quakes, focused near the center of the North American plate, appear to have been anomalous. Long-lasting sequences of earthquakes are not normally expected in continental interiors, because of the apparent absence of plate boundaries.

The origins of the New Madrid quakes were not understood until the late 1970s, when increasing interest in seismic hazards, especially with regard to nuclear power generation, led the U.S. Geological Survey to undertake seismic and gravity studies in the region. The work revealed an ancient north-northeast-trending rift zone beneath thick layers of sedimentary rock in the Mississippi Valley. The eastern and western boundaries of the zone, as revealed by seismological studies, are faults between which ancient formations of igneous and metamorphic rock, the so-called basement complex, sank while thick layers of sediment accumulated on top of them. The basement rock sank as much as 1,500 meters.

Formed more than 500 million years ago, the zone is about 80 kilometers wide and 320 kilometers long. It is known today as the Reelfoot rift zone, named after Reelfoot Lake. Deformation within the zone is most likely related to crustal stresses associated with the westward movement of the North American plate.

Geologists surmise that this weakened zone of the earth's crust gave way in 1811 as several ancient faults were reactivated. The central Mississippi Valley has remained seismically active since then, and tremors are common in the area, though most of them are detectable only with instruments. In 1843, however, and again in 1895, the New Madrid region suffered powerful earthquakes. Each had an estimated magnitude greater than 6.

The Reelfoot rift zone lies within a geologic structure known as the Mississippi embayment, a large downwarp, or syncline, in the earth's crust that extends north-northeast from the Gulf of Mexico into Missouri, western Kentucky, and southern Illinois. The rate of downwarping, or subsidence, originally was slow, but it accelerated sharply between 70 and 40 million years ago and then ceased. Subsidence has begun anew during the last few million years, possibly because of loading by large volumes of sediment brought in from glacial erosion of the Canadian Shield.

During glaciation north of the embayment, the ancestral Mississippi and Ohio rivers were wide, shallow, meandering streams that left thick deposits of unconsolidated, water-soaked sand and silt over wide areas. When an earthquake strikes, this inherently unstable material tends to liquefy and quiver like gelatin, intensifying the effect of seismic waves.

Winds scouring the barren, glaciated plains picked up particles of silt and, over the centuries, dropped them in thick, unstratified deposits known as loess, from the German *löss*, meaning "loose." About six thousand years ago the meandering streams slowly evolved into the river systems of today, and the Ohio and Mississippi began to cut into and rework earlier deposits. It is where those rivers have cut into the unconsolidated loess that their banks are most subject to rapid erosion.

While regional subsidence appears to have been predominant in the region affected by the earthquakes, there were local uplifts. An ancient structural basin along the axis of the Reelfoot rift zone in Missouri, for example, was uplifted to form the Blytheville arch. As shown in figure 6-2, the

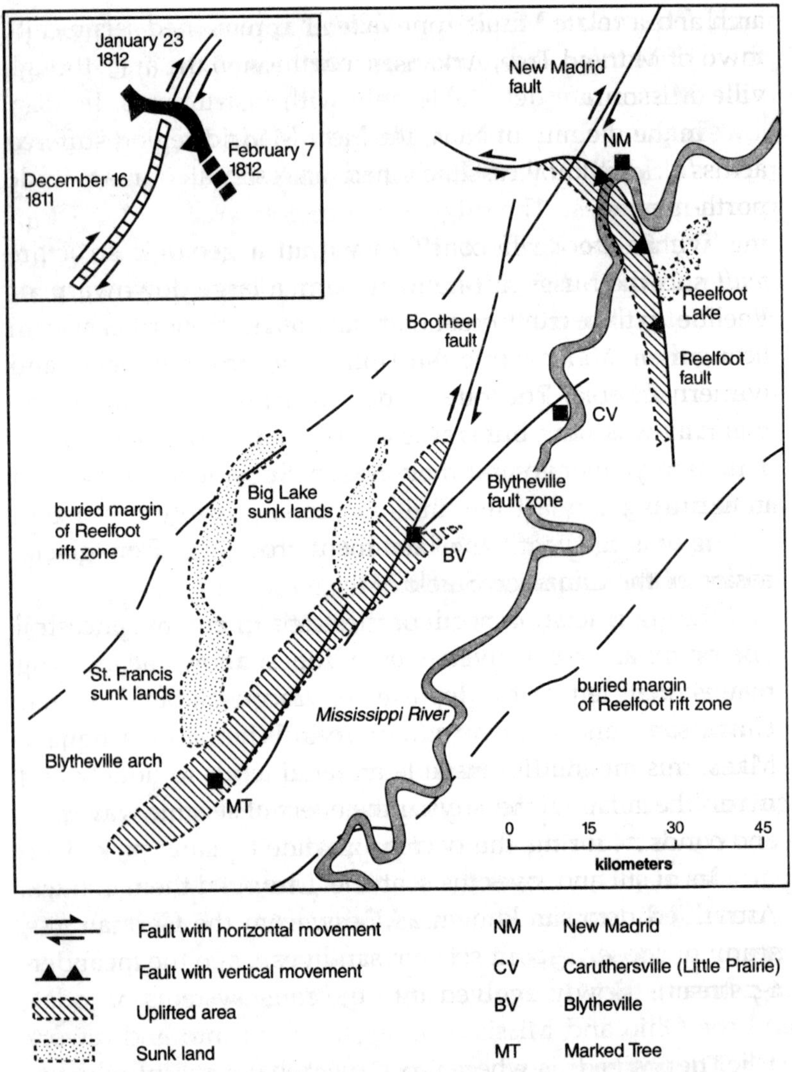

FIGURE 6-2. Tectonic setting of the Reelfoot rift zone, showing major faults as well as areas of uplift and subsidence related to the earthquakes of 1811 and 1812. The inset illustrates three sequences of seismic activity as described in the text: December 1811 (bottom left), January 1812 (top right), and February 1812 (heavy line between). (Adapted from Johnston and Schweig, "Enigma," 344, 374.)

arch and a related fault zone extend approximately from the town of Marked Tree, Arkansas, northeastward to Caruthersville, Missouri.

In the vicinity of New Madrid the Mississippi River cuts across a ridge known as the Tiptonville "dome," which trends north-northwest. The ridge was formed above a zone of faulting, within the Reelfoot rift zone, that includes the Reelfoot *fault* shown in figure 6-2. Rock formations northeast of the Reelfoot fault were thrust beneath strata to the southwest, uplifting them and creating the Tiptonville structure. The southwestern shore of Reelfoot Lake is bordered by an escarpment that is as much as 3 meters high, which gave the fault its name. That escarpment is shown by the closely spaced contour lines in figure 6-3.

It was not until the late 1960s that geologists became aware of the unique character of the New Madrid earthquakes and the enormous consequences related to the reactivation of one or more of the ancient fault zones. Most influential in reawakening interest in the events was the work of St. Louis University seismologist Otto W. Nuttli from 1973 to 1987. Many seismic studies have been conducted since then, primarily because of the construction of nuclear power plants and concerns for the safety of population centers.

In 1996 two geologists at the University of Memphis, Arch C. Johnston and Eugene S. Schweig, published a detailed study of the 1811–1812 seismic activities.[2] As shown in figure 6-2 (inset), they distinguished three sequences:

- The first sequence began on December 16, 1811, at 2:15 AM, with an earthquake with a magnitude estimated to have been 8.1. The most likely cause was slippage along a fault within the Blytheville arch and along the Bootheel fault, which cuts through the arch. The length of the reactivated fault segments together probably was about 140 kilometers. Horizontal slippage would have been about 10 meters, the eastern block moving southward. That earthquake was fol-

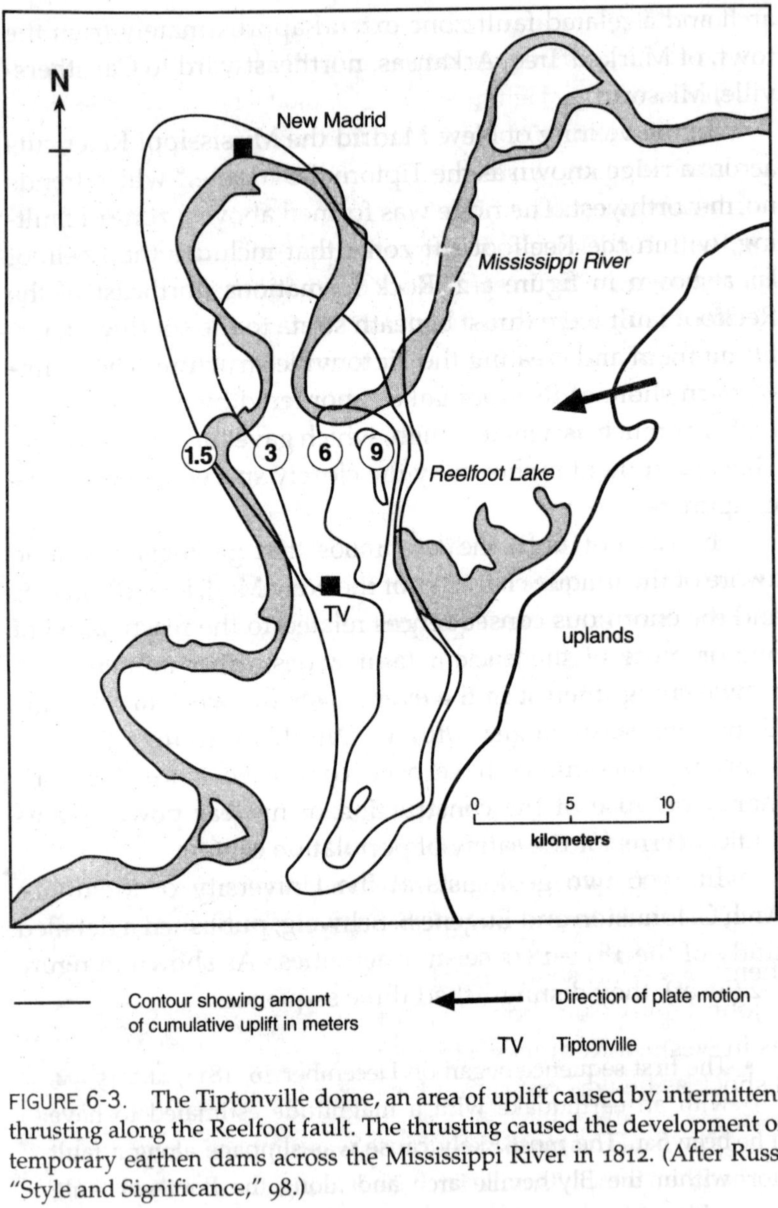

FIGURE 6-3. The Tiptonville dome, an area of uplift caused by intermittent thrusting along the Reelfoot fault. The thrusting caused the development of temporary earthen dams across the Mississippi River in 1812. (After Russ, "Style and Significance," 98.)

lowed the same day by four aftershocks with magnitudes of 5.9 to 7.2. At noon on December 17 there was yet another shock, with a magnitude of 7.1. A moderate shock, with a magnitude of 5.8, followed at 11:00 PM on January 16, 1812. In addition, this first sequence included 63 events with magnitudes of 4.7 to 5.

- The second seismic sequence began on January 23, 1812, at 9:00 AM, with an earthquake that had an estimated magnitude of 7.8. The most likely cause of this quake was rupturing of the New Madrid fault, which trends northeast-southwest near New Madrid. Maximum slippage probably was about 8 meters, with the eastern block moving southward. It was followed by three aftershocks, on January 23 and 27 and February 4, with magnitudes of 5.5 to 6.3. In total there were 31 events with magnitudes greater than 4.7.
- The third sequence began with an earthquake at 3:45 AM on February 7, 1812, with a magnitude that is thought to have been 8.0. It was followed on February 7, 10, and 11 by four aftershocks with magnitudes of 6.3 to 7.0. These quakes probably were caused by rupturing of the Reelfoot fault. Slippage was as much as 10 meters, with both horizontal motion (the northeastern block moving westward) and thrusting motion (the northeastern block being pushed beneath the southern). In all, there were 113 events in this sequence with magnitudes greater than 4.7.

When the second sequence of earthquakes struck on January 23, John James Audubon, the naturalist and painter of birds, was in western Kentucky. He described the onset of a powerful shock as he was out riding his horse that morning:

> I heard what I imagined to be the distant rumbling of a violent tornado, on which I spurred my steed, with a wish to gallop as fast as possible to a place of shelter; but it would not do, the animal knew better than I what was forthcoming, and instead of going faster, so nearly stopped that I remarked he placed one foot after another on the ground, with as much precaution as if

> walking on a smooth sheet of ice. I thought he had . . . foundered, and . . . was on the point of dismounting and leading him, when he all of a sudden fell a-groaning piteously, hung his head, spread out his four legs, as if to save himself from falling, and stood stock still, continuing to groan. . . . at that instant all the shrubs and trees began to move from their very roots, the ground rose and fell in successive furrows, like the ruffled waters of a lake, and I became bewildered . . . as I too plainly discovered that all this awful commotion in nature was the result of an earthquake.[3]

The noise Audubon heard was more than the rumbling of the quaking earth. It was a cacophony of caving riverbanks, falling trees, frightened calls from multitudes of birds that had been roosting in the trees, and explosions that sounded like artillery fire. The explosions probably were caused by the violent ejection of water, subsurface gases, and air as earthquake fissures opened and snapped shut in the undulating ground. An enormous quantity of water was exuded, in some places accumulating to a depth of a meter or, in some cases, much more. Strong currents were created as water flowed over the ground toward open fissures or related depressions. It has been estimated that some 10,000 square kilometers subsided and were flooded. As described by Louis Bringier, a New Orleans surveyor who, like Audubon, happened to be on horseback near New Madrid at the time:

> Water . . . rushed out in all quarters, bringing with it an enormous quantity of carbonized wood . . . which was ejected to the height of from ten to fifteen feet [3 to 4.5 meters], and fell in a black shower, mixed with . . . sand . . . ; at the same time, the roaring and whistling produced by the impetuosity of the air escaping from its confinement, seemed to increase the horrible disorder. . . . In the mean time, the surface was sinking and a black liquid was rising up to the belly of my horse, who stood motionless, struck with . . . terror. . . . The whole surface of the country remained covered with holes, which . . . resembled so many craters.[4]

Not only water and air were driven out but also odorous gases that had accumulated in the sediments of the river valley. According to an observer named S. P. Hildreth:

> The sulphurated gases that were discharged during the shocks tainted the air with their noxious effluvia and so strongly impregnated the water of the river to the distance of 150 miles [240 kilometers] below that it could barely be used for any purpose for a number of days.[5]

Both hydrogen sulfide and methane had been formed over the ages from decomposing organic matter buried in the wetlands bordering the Mississippi.

The sand mentioned by Bringier came mostly from water-soaked sediments buried beneath layers of peat and clay. The shaking liquefied lenses of sand, which contained much groundwater. The weight of overlying deposits forced the sandy liquid upward into earthquake fissures. Where the mixture reached the surface it erupted in fountains, or "sand blows," which produced cratered mounds of sand as much as 30 meters across and a meter high—Bringier's "craters" (see figure 6-4). One sand blow spit out the fossilized skull of an extinct musk ox. Many of those features are visible in local farmland today, only slightly modified by years of plowing.

The area affected by liquefaction and the development of sand blows lies mainly west of the Mississippi River, extending northeastward in a belt as much as 80 kilometers wide and some 210 kilometers long, from northeastern Arkansas through the "Bootheel" of Missouri almost as far as Cairo, Illinois. It coincides with the area of greatest activity in the New Madrid seismic zone.

Few features created by the New Madrid earthquakes are as striking as the topographic depressions called "sunk lands," caused by the compaction of unconsolidated sediments (see figure 6-2). Swamps and lakes presently occupy most of those areas. The largest is Reelfoot Lake in northwestern Tennessee, which was formed partly by subsidence and

FIGURE 6-4. Drawing of an earthquake fissure along which liquefied sand erupted and covered the surrounding soil. (From Montessus de Ballore, *Science Séismologique*, 82.)

partly by the ponding of Reelfoot Creek. The ponding resulted from uplift related to formation of the Tiptonville dome, discussed above. Almost all the sunk lands trend southward and may represent former stream courses. Most of them contain the stumps of dead trees, killed by the rising waters. A local fur trapper named A. N. Dillard wrote:

> There is a great deal of sunken land caused by the earthquake of 1811. There are large trees of walnut, white oak, and mulberry, such as grow on high land, which are now seen submerged 10 and 20 feet [3 to 6 meters] beneath the water. In some of the lakes I have seen cypresses so far beneath the surface that with a canoe I have paddled among the branches.[6]

In 1846 the eminent British geologist Charles Lyell visited the New Madrid area. As a proponent of the theory of uniformitarianism—the concept that processes at work today on the earth can explain geological phenomena of past ages—he had great interest in earthquakes and especially their aftereffects.

In his seminal book *Principles of Geology* he wrote about the earthquakes of 1811 and 1812 as follows:

> the largest area affected by the great convulsion . . . is called "the sunk country," and is said to extend . . . between 70 and 80 miles [110 and 130 kilometers] north and south, and 30 miles [50 kilometers] east and west. . . . In March 1846 I skirted the borders of the "sunk country" nearest to New Madrid, . . . where dead trees of various kinds, some erect in the water, others fallen and strewed in dense masses over the bottom, in the shallows, and near the shore, were conspicuous. I also beheld countless rents in the adjoining dry alluvial plains, caused by the movements of the soil in 1811–12, still open, though the rains, frost, and river inundations have greatly diminished their original depth.[7]

Some of the "rents" reported by Lyell were several kilometers long and as much as 9 meters wide. One Godfrey Le Sieur, who as a boy survived the earthquakes, later wrote:

> The earth was observed to be rolling in waves a few feet in height, with a visible depression between. By and by these swells burst, throwing up large volumes of water [and] sand. . . . When the swells burst, wide and long fissures were left.[8]

University of Chicago history professor James Lal Penick Jr., in his book *The New Madrid Earthquakes*, writes:

> Of all the phenomena of the earthquakes none filled people with more fascinated horror than . . . the dread of being swallowed by the earth and buried alive. . . . Despite the terror engendered by fissures, however, only one firsthand account described someone actually falling into one. . . . "The fissure was so deep as to put it out of his power to get out at that place. He made his way along the fissure until a sloping side offered him an opportunity of crawling out."[9]

Many of the fissures paralleled buried and reactivated faults. Generally they trended northeast-southwest, but near

New Madrid they trended northwest-southeast, parallel to the Reelfoot fault, which connects the margins of the Reelfoot rift zone (see figure 6-2). Sand brought to the surface through the fissures created elongated ridges that remain visible on the ground to this day.

Undoubtedly many fissures opened in the riverbed of the Mississippi, just as they did in the nearby countryside. Fissures also developed in the natural levees along the river's banks, causing enormous chunks of the banks to slump into the stream. Some of them, many hectares in size and held together by dense forests, left the tops of trees sticking out of the water. The crashing of such masses into the river, along with the opening and closing of fissures beneath the water, caused great waves. Many of these waves overtopped the riverbanks, dragging much debris into the river as the water flowed back. The waves swamped a number of riverboats. No one knows how many lives the quakes claimed in the Mississippi River. Mute testimony to the toll was offered by boats later seen drifting downstream, ominously unoccupied.

S. P. Hildreth, quoted above, wrote about the experience of one eyewitness aboard a boat about 65 kilometers south of New Madrid when the first quake struck:

> In the middle of the night there was a terrible shock and a jarring of the boats. . . . Directly a loud roaring . . . was . . . accompanied by the most violent agitation of the shores and tremendous boiling up of the waters of the Mississippi in huge swells, . . . tossing the boats about so violently that the men with difficulty could keep upon their feet. . . . The water became thick with mud thrown up from the bottom, while the surface, lashed violently by the agitation of the earth beneath, was covered with foam. . . . From the temporary check to the current by the heaving up of the bottom [and] the sinking of the banks . . . into the bed of the stream, the river rose in a few minutes 5 or 6 feet [almost 2 meters], and . . . rushed forward . . . , hurrying along the boats, now set loose by the horror-stricken boatmen,

> as [they were] in less danger on the water than at the shore where the banks threatened to destroy them. . . . Many boats were overwhelmed in this manner, and their crews perished with them.[10]

A resident of New Madrid named Eliza Bryan described the earthquakes' effects on the river as follows:

> At first the Mississippi seemed to recede from its banks, its waters gathered up like mountains, leaving boats high upon the sands. The waters then moved inward with a front wall 15 to 20 feet [4.5 to 6 meters] perpendicular and tore boats from their moorings and carried them up a creek closely packed for a quarter of a mile. The river fell as rapidly as it had risen and receded within its banks with such violence that it took with it a grove of cottonwood trees. A great many fish were left upon the banks. The river was literally covered with wrecks of boats.[11]

The seismic waves also squeezed old, sunken tree trunks out of the river-bottom mud. Thus the river became choked with debris and the caving banks, forcing the current to find new channels in its meandering path, created new shoals. One result of the shifting channels was more rapid erosion along the banks of some meanders and more rapid sedimentation in others. Over the years these changes progressively worked their way downstream as far as New Orleans.

A number of low, sandy islands, previously charted in the river, disappeared during the earthquakes, the sand presumably liquefied by the tremors. Thus the quakes created serious problems for river navigation, both because of the debris and because boatmen had to learn the river anew.

Upthrusting of the riverbed during the earthquakes of February 7, when the epicenters were nearer New Madrid than previously, created two areas of rapids in the Mississippi. One was almost a kilometer above New Madrid, the other about 13 kilometers below the town. The uplift interrupted the river's flow in that area, causing the current to flow back upon itself for several hours. Thus the quake is sometimes said to have "reversed" the flow of the Mississippi River. The sand and mud of the riverbed soon eroded, however, and the current flowed south again. Within a few days the rapids had disappeared entirely.

As mentioned earlier, a considerable amount of forest land was thrown into the Mississippi with the caving of riverbanks, and large areas of upland forest became sunk lands, drowning the trees. Forests throughout the earthquake zone were severely shaken, with the violent motion breaking off many tree branches and even ripping tree trunks from their roots. Fissuring of the earth through root systems split some trees up the middle. Trees fell by the thousands, not only in forests but in orchards as well. An estimated 650 square kilometers of forests were laid waste.

There were two towns on the Mississippi River near the epicenters of the 1811 and 1812 earthquakes—New Madrid and, about 50 kilometers south, Little Prairie, near present-day Caruthersville. There may have been a thousand people living in New Madrid, and Little Prairie had perhaps only a hundred residents. Both towns were destroyed.

In New Madrid almost everybody fled after the first quake in December 1811. They passed the winter in tents or temporary huts in open fields nearby, gradually becoming accustomed to daily tremors. During the biggest shock on February 7, the bank on which the town stood slumped perhaps 6 meters toward the river, and spring floods in 1812 carried the town site away. This was the end of New Madrid's aspiration to become the new country's "gateway to the West." The town was later rebuilt and today occupies a site about 2 kilometers north of its former location, which now lies beneath the waters of the Mississippi.

The people in Little Prairie fared even worse than those in New Madrid. The epicenters of the earliest earthquakes were closer to Little Prairie, and the shaking and liquefaction there were more devastating. The first shock, at 2:15 AM on December 16, threw people from their beds. Some were injured and bleeding, others knocked unconscious. The ground shook so violently that many were unable to stand. Houses collapsed or sank into liquefying ground. Wide cracks opened in the earth, and when they slammed shut they spurted groundwater as high as the tops of trees. Much of the area became flooded. No one dared stay in the town or anywhere near it.

Led by a townsman named George Roddell, the hundred or so residents of Little Prairie struck out for higher ground. For about 13 kilometers they slogged through water, up to their waists in places, carrying small children, some food, and a few belongings. Fortunately, groundwater that had been forced to the surface was warmer then the winter air. The refugees tripped over submerged tree trunks and were terrified of stumbling into hidden earthquake crevices. As they waded, the water churned with sand and nauseating gases. Sometimes fountains of muddy water erupted from the trembling ground beneath their feet. All around them possums, raccoons, snakes, even wolves and coyotes, swam in panic.

In late afternoon on the sixteenth, Roddell's group succeeded in reaching dry ground near where the town of Hayti, Missouri, is today, a short distance west of a bend in the Mississippi River. After a cold night of fitful, shivering sleep, they began the long trek through the woods toward New Madrid. They climbed over downed trees and struggled through tangles of fallen branches. The ground quaked all day every day and was pitted with sand blows. Fissures were everywhere. They had to watch for bogs of quicksand created by local liquefaction. Finally, on Christmas Eve, eight days after they had left Little Prairie, the weary refugees straggled into New Madrid—only to find the town in ruins, the residents in their tent camps able to offer little help. But Roddell had led the people of Little Prairie to safety, and all survived their ordeal.

In March 1812 a merchant named George McBride, en route to New Orleans with two flatboats loaded with merchandise, arrived at the site of Little Prairie. Mooring his boats, he found that they floated over part of the town. The rest was a shambles. Coffins protruded from a nearby riverbank, their burial ground eroded away.

Compared with other earthquakes of similar magnitude, the New Madrid quakes claimed few human lives. No one knows the total, but because most of the region was wilderness, it was probably in the low hundreds. Coincidentally, in March 1812 in Venezuela, an earthquake destroyed the cities of Caracas and La Guaira, and more than twenty thousand people died in the crash of falling buildings. There is no record of collapsing houses killing anyone in the New Madrid region. Most of the known deaths were from drowning in the Mississippi River or, in fewer cases, on flooded ground.

On the other hand there are no records, either, of deaths among the Native American population of the region. Indians outnumbered white settlers by possibly two to one, and they often camped along the treacherous banks of the Mississippi. If their losses could be counted, the known death toll would be considerably higher.

After the Venezuelan earthquake the U.S. government appropriated $50,000 to aid needy people in that country. But victims of the American quake were ignored. Finally, in January 1814, two years after the quake, the Missouri territorial assembly petitioned Congress to demonstrate equal concern for U.S. citizens. Eventually a law was passed that enabled people whose land had been destroyed by the New Madrid event to claim an equal area of publicly owned land elsewhere. The quakes had stopped by the time the law was enacted, however, and most qualified victims had already begun a new life where they were. Reluctant to go to the expense and trouble of moving, they sold their claim certificates, mostly to land speculators, at very low prices. The speculators, armed with the certificates, immediately claimed the most valuable land they could find. Forgery was rampant, and the term *New Madrid claim* soon became a synonym for fraud. Years later the U.S. Supreme Court was still trying to untangle the legal mess.

• • •

A blazing comet was visible in the North American skies from about September 6, 1811, until January 16, 1812. Superstitious people took the comet as a sign from heaven, a portent of catastrophe about to happen—and when the earthquakes began on December 16, their apprehensions seemed to be confirmed. The *Pittsburgh Gazette* of April 19, 1812, quoted a Connecticut newspaper as follows:

> The period is portentous and alarming. We have within a few years seen the most wonderful eclipses, the year past has produced a magnificent comet, the earthquakes within the past . . . months have been almost without number—and . . . we constantly "hear of wars and summons of wars." . . . "Can ye not discern the signs of the times."[12]

Eclipses, comets, earthquakes, wars—fearful people of all faiths gathered in prayer. Backsliding Christians flocked to church services. Zealous preachers seized upon this God-given opportunity to increase the size of their congregations. "Consternation sat on every countenance, especially upon the wicked," intoned one. "It was a time of great terror to sinners," affirmed another.[13] The number of converts was great. Within the region most affected by the earthquakes, much of it sparsely populated, the Methodist Church is said to have gained more than fifteen thousand members.[14]

As the quakes began tapering off within a year or two, many churches saw their congregations shrink back to something like the number of worshippers they had before December 1811. Disconsolate preachers called the backsliders "earthquake Christians."

A singularly horrifying event began to unfold the night of December 15, just before the quakes began. Lilburne Lewis, a nephew of Thomas Jefferson and the owner of a plantation in western Kentucky, made terrified slaves watch as he took an ax and killed a recaptured runaway as an object lesson. As recounted in 1981 by James Lal Penick Jr. in *The New Madrid Earthquakes*:

> One of their number was handed the ax and told to dismember the corpse. Piece by piece, the bloody fragments were consigned to the fire . . . but before the work was finished, the ground quaked . . . and the fireplace collapsed. . . . The unburnt fragments of bone were hidden in the masonry when the fireplace was rebuilt, but the quakes continued, and on 7 February the fireplace collapsed again. This time a dog arrived before the repair crew. A neighbor later found it gnawing on the charred head of the victim and the dreadful secret was out.[15]

Twenty-eight years earlier, in 1953, Robert Penn Warren had published a dramatic narrative poem, *Brother to Dragons*, about this atrocious event and its racial overtones:

> Yes, God shook out the country like a rug,
> And sloshed the Mississippi for a kind of warning—
> Well, if God did, why should he happen to pick out
> Just Lilburne's meanness as excuse?[16]

Lilburne Lewis later killed himself, done in by the poetic justice of a trembling earth.

• • •

Seeking justice, too, the Shawnee Indian chief Tecumseh was striving to unite Native American tribes of mid-America and stop white settlers from taking their lands. In describing the plight of the Indians at that time, historian James Lal Penick Jr. wrote:

> The sun had almost set for the native peoples. . . . A brooding misery had settled upon the tribes in the years before the

> earthquakes. Yet beneath the surface, vague, often shapeless movement could be detected. Never united, long dependent on white technology and trade goods, the Indians were implicated in their own downfall. . . .
>
> Many Indians believed that they had betrayed the old ways of their fathers. Convulsive attempts to achieve purification sometimes afflicted entire villages in a consuming fury. The Delawares and Shawnees on the St. Francis River [which today forms the boundary between Arkansas and the "Bootheel" of Missouri] experienced such an outbreak. Numerous victims were executed by fire for obscure reasons in a frenzy that puzzled white observers, and the burnings only ceased . . . with the arrival of Tecumseh, . . . who had the qualities needed to give direction to formless yearning. This Shawnee chief was the equal in nobility and inherent ability of the greatest statesmen of the age. He ranged over astonishing distances conveying a message with all the force and eloquence at his command: Only national and cultural unity among the tribes could prevent further white encroachments.[17]

Born in 1768 at Old Piqua, an Indian settlement near what is now Greenville, Ohio, Tecumseh was the third son of the Shawnee chief Puckeshinwa and his wife, Methoataske. His name meant "I cross somebody's path" or, alternatively, "panther ready to spring." After Tecumseh became a chief in his own right, white men interpreted *panther* to mean "celestial tiger," which in time became "meteor" or "comet." In America the great comet of 1811 was known as "Tecumseh's Comet."

White men killed Tecumseh's father one day when he was out hunting. Tecumseh's mother, Methoataske, was pregnant at the time and later gave birth to triplets, one of whom died. One of the survivors, named Lalawethika ("noisemaker") eventually became a celebrated prophet among the Indians. Survivors of multiple births were believed to have mystical powers and usually became medicine men.

Methoataske moved her growing family to Chillicothe, a

larger Indian village not far from Old Piqua. She raised Tecumseh to become a warrior, and Lalawethika to become a mystic. Tecumseh was adopted by a warrior chief named Blackfish, who trained him in the arts of war and the hunt. Tribal medicine men trained Lalawethika in the mystical arts. Both brothers married, and in 1803, when Ohio became a state, they moved their families west, into the territory of Indiana.

Lalawethika unfortunately acquired a taste for the white man's whiskey and descended into alcoholism. One day in 1805 he collapsed and appeared to be dead. He was not breathing, and there was no apparent heartbeat. But later, as his body was being prepared for burial, he suddenly revived and sat up. He told astonished onlookers of a mystical near-death experience. The episode changed him forever. He swore off liquor and changed his name to Tenskwatawa, "the one who opens the door." He had mystical visions and delivered messages from the Great Spirit. Soon Indians from all over the Midwest flocked to his tepee for blessings from this man who talked with the Great Spirit and had risen from the dead.

Tenskwatawa, who became known as the Prophet, attracted thousands of followers. He preached that if Indians led pious lives and returned to the lifestyle of old, the Great Spirit would drive out the white men—the "long knives," so called because their soldiers carried long rifles, often with a bayonet affixed to the business end. He created a unity, based on religion, that far surpassed any previous alliance ever achieved among the American Indian tribes. Tecumseh became Tenskwatawa's most trusted adviser, and he traveled throughout the Midwest carrying the Prophet's message.

William Henry Harrison, then governor of Indiana Territory, sought to discredit this Indian prophet, whom he rightly saw as a threat to the white man's supremacy and further westward expansion. Early in 1806 he sent notices throughout the territory denouncing Tenskwatawa as a charlatan and a fraud. He taunted the Prophet, challenging him to demonstrate his influence with the Great Spirit by making the sun stand still.

As luck would have it, Tenskwatawa (but apparently not Harrison) had heard about astronomers in the area who were preparing to observe a solar eclipse on June 16. Knowing that Native Americans feared eclipses and viewed them with awe, he readily accepted Harrison's challenge and publicly declared that he would cause the sun to darken on June 16. Sure enough, about noon on the appointed day, sunlight faded into twilight. The Prophet assuaged the fears of his followers by promising that, just as he had dimmed the sun, he would make it brighten again—and of course the sun did brighten. He became even more famous after that; indeed, we might say his influence increased astronomically.

In 1808 Tenskwatawa and Tecumseh established a new settlement called Prophet's Town near where the Tippecanoe River joins the Wabash a short distance northeast of present-day Lafayette, Indiana. Prophet's Town was a thriving community, a mecca for hundreds of followers of Tenskwatawa, and the headquarters of his movement. By then it had become apparent that if their way of life was to survive, the Indians could not live in peace with the ever-growing numbers of white men who were settling on what had been Indian land. Somehow the long knives would have to be driven out. Gradually Tenskwatawa's religious movement metamorphosed into a military alliance, and Tecumseh, the warrior chieftain, became its leader.

Tecumseh traveled throughout the Midwest and the South in a crusade to rally the various Indian tribes and unite them in a war against the long knives. His charisma, his qualities as a leader, and his actions were of great concern to U.S. government officials. To gain intelligence about his plans, they sent men to follow him around the country and record his speeches. Early in 1811, in a highly publicized appeal to the Osage Indians of Missouri, he made a prediction:

> The white men are not friends to the Indians. . . . The red men all wish for peace. But where the white people are, there is no peace. . . . The Great Spirit is angry with our enemies. He speaks in thunder, and the earth swallows up their villages, and drinks up the Mississippi. The great waters will cover their lowlands, and their corn cannot grow.[18]

The spring of 1811 saw the greatest floods known to that time on the Ohio and Mississippi rivers, and during the following winter, of course, came the great earthquakes.

Early that October, two months and a few days before the onset of the earthquakes, Tecumseh uttered another prophecy, which, like the first, was recorded by government witnesses. He was in Alabama, in a Creek Indian town named Tuckhabatchee. In a speech delivered before the local chieftain, who was of mixed blood, half white, Tecumseh explained his mission. He talked of war and symbolically presented the chieftain with a bundle of medicine sticks, a piece of wampum, and a war hatchet. But he was not convinced of the man's loyalty to his cause. Angry, Tecumseh pointed at the chieftain and cried:

> Your blood is white! You have taken my talk and the sticks and the wampum and the hatchet, but you do not mean to fight. I know the reason. You do not believe the Great Spirit has sent me. . . . You will know that the Great Spirit has sent me. I leave and go directly to Detroit. When I arrive there, I will stamp on the ground with my foot and shake down every house in Tuckhabatchee.[19]

He then left Alabama and made his way northward.

The Creeks did not forget Tecumseh's threat, and word of it spread quickly among other tribes, including those in the central Mississippi Valley. Anxiously the Creeks counted the days until mid-December—the time when they calculated Tecumseh would reach Detroit. And on December 16, early in the morning, the earth shook. Terrified Indians rushed outdoors, and every house in Tuckhabatchee collapsed upon the ground.

After Tecumseh's two prophecies came true, more and more Indians rallied to his cause. But by then, alas! It was too late. On November 7 the governor, William Henry Harrison, had sent an army into Prophet's Town. In Tecumseh's absence the Indian alliance had been crushed in what white men celebrated as the Battle of Tippecanoe. The town was destroyed, the Indians dispersed, and Tecumseh's dream of stopping white encroachment.ended. Harrison became a national hero. Subsequently he became a major general in the U.S. Army and president of the United States. Some historians consider Tippecanoe the opening battle in the War of 1812, as the British were sympathetic to the Native American cause.

Tecumseh, disillusioned, joined British forces in Canada. He was commissioned a brigadier general in the British army and, in 1813, was killed fighting against General Harrison in the Battle of the Thames, in Ontario. Tenskwatawa died in 1834. Harrison and his running mate, John Tyler, won the presidential election of 1840 with the slogan "Tippecanoe and Tyler too!" Inaugurated on March 4, 1841, Harrison died of pneumonia only a month later.

• • •

Seismological studies seem to verify Native American legends concerning earthquakes that devastated the central Mississippi Valley many years ago. In addition to the nineteenth-century New Madrid quakes, powerful quakes shook the region in the ninth or tenth century and again in the fifteenth. There may have been an earlier quake in the fourth or fifth century as well, suggesting that the recurrence period for major earthquakes in the Mississippi Valley is several centuries. This periodicity may characterize only postglacial times, however. Earlier events could have been separated by thousands of years. Less intense quakes, with magnitudes of 6 to 7, appear to have happened about once a century.

But it is the great series of earthquakes that began in December 1811 that resonates in American history. The ground shook throughout the central Mississippi Valley for at least six months. No one knows how many people were killed in that remote frontier region, but many villages were destroyed. Shock waves were felt as far away as the East Coast. And lesser vibrations continued for years.

That such earthquakes could occur near the stable middle of a tectonic plate was a mystery to geologists until the 1970s, when seismological surveys revealed the existence of the deeply buried Reelfoot rift. Reactivation of ancient faults within the rift zone ravaged the landscape over thousands of square kilometers. Whole forests were destroyed. Fissures opened in the ground. Some land was uplifted while other land sank and became swampland, or was flooded to form lakes. Reelfoot Lake, created virtually overnight, remains a popular resort in northwestern Tennessee. Even the Mississippi River locally flowed back upon itself for several hours. New Madrid's earthquakes also immortalized Tecumseh, and they exposed the plight of the American Indian during the westward expansion of colonial America.

Other earthquakes have gained more notoriety in American history—Charleston in 1886, San Francisco in 1906—but they ripped through densely populated areas and devastated large cities. The Mississippi Valley was largely unsettled in the early 1800s, communications were primitive, and news of damage caused by the great quake was slow to spread. But the New Madrid earthquakes of 1811 and 1812 were among the most powerful of them all.

A DISASTROUS REPRISE?

In October 1989 a scientist named Iben Browning predicted that the New Madrid area would suffer a catastrophic earthquake on December 2 or 3, 1990. Browning had a reputation for making accurate long-term weather forecasts. In addition, he reputedly predicted the eruption of Mount St. Helens in 1980 and California's Loma Prieta earthquake in 1989. His guess about a reprise of the New Madrid earthquake was based on the not-unrealistic notion that the gravitational pull resulting from an alignment of the sun and moon in early December of 1990 would cause exceptionally strong tides on earth. The U.S. Geological Survey, in fact, confirmed that tidal forces would indeed be unusually strong at that time. But Browning assumed, unrealistically, that the tidal forces would be powerful enough to cause renewed movement along faults in the New Madrid area.[1]

Tidal forces can indeed create stresses in the earth's crust, but they are barely measurable. There was, of course, no quake in December 1990—but the preceding September a temblor did shake the town of New Hamburg, about 60 kilometers north of New Madrid. Browning's 1989 prediction had received wide publicity. The jolt in September 1990 convinced thousands of people that Browning must be right. Newspapers and radio talk shows discussed the coming disaster. Local government agencies published pamphlets on earthquake preparedness. Schools were closed in early December. The National Guard conducted emergency drills. People stocked up on food, gasoline, flashlight batteries, and electrical generators. The New Madrid Chamber of Commerce even sold T-shirts emblazoned "Visit New Madrid—While It's Still There."

Such marketing foolishness aside, the publicity and the preparations were not all in vain. For years, many (perhaps most) people living in the New Madrid region—even in the very town that gave its name to the greatest earthquakes in North American history—were unaware that they lived in a region of seismic danger. In the cities of mid-America, unlike cities in more obviously quake-prone regions like California and Japan, architects had given little thought to earthquake resistance in designing buildings and bridges.

That is changing, however. Geological work since the 1970s has revealed much about the tectonic character of the lower Mississippi Valley. Publicity like the earthquake scare induced by Iben Browning has made people aware of the danger. Today the New Madrid region is among the world's most intensively studied seismic zones. The social and economic threat to mid-America is recognized, though much still needs to be done to ensure minimal loss of life and property when the next series of earthquakes strikes.

There can be no question that another earthquake, or series of quakes, of the order of magnitude of those in 1811 and 1812 would be truly catastrophic in mid-America. Where very few people lived in the early nineteenth century, millions live today. Where there were no cities then, now there are metropolises—St. Louis, Cincinnati, Memphis—as well as sizable cities such as Little Rock, Nashville, and Evansville. Today there is a complex infrastructure of highways, railroads, bridges, electric power lines, and telephone lines, as well as gas and oil pipelines and high, wire-guyed towers for broadcasting radio and TV programs (and disaster instructions)—all vulnerable to destruction in moments. Farming would be disrupted and water supplies polluted. Another major earthquake could occur in this unstable region at any time. The potential for death and devastation is mind-boggling.

7 • Earthquake, Fire, and Politics in San Francisco

San Francisco has violated all underwriting traditions and precedents by not burning up.

National Board of Fire Underwriters, October 1905

IN 1906 SAN FRANCISCO was a bustling and bawdy cosmopolitan city, the premier seaport on the West Coast of the United States. Nobody understood then that the city lies within the California fault belt, a zone of crustal fracturing that extends from northern Mexico to northern California and marks the boundary between the Pacific and North American tectonic plates. San Francisco is wedged between the notorious San Andreas fault to the west and another major fault, the Hayward, to the east across San Francisco Bay. Those and other major faults in the Bay Area are identified in figure 7-1.

Early on the morning of April 18, 1906, stresses that had been building in the San Andreas fault zone for many decades were abruptly released. Some 470 kilometers of the fault ruptured, from Cape Mendocino in northern California to San Juan Bautista, 120 kilometers south of San Francisco. Movement along the fault was clearly shown by the offsetting of streams, roads, and fences. Measured offsets range from 2 meters at San Juan Bautista to almost 9 meters at Shelter Cove, a few kilometers south of Cape Mendocino. At Colma, a town 3 kilometers south of San Francisco itself, geologists have measured 4 meters of offset.

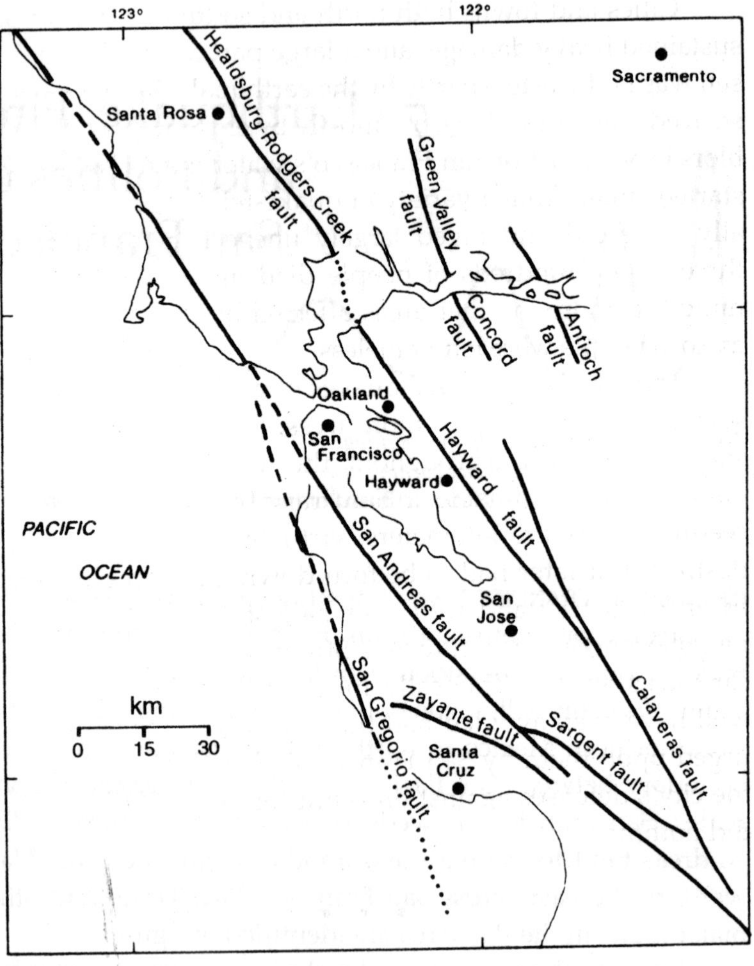

FIGURE 7-1. Major faults in the San Francisco area within the wide boundary zone between the Pacific and North American tectonic plates.

Estimates of the rupture velocity range from 2.7 to 3.2 kilometers per second. Assuming an average of 3 kilometers per second, the entire 470-kilometer rip took only about two and a half minutes. The resulting earthquake had a magnitude later estimated to have been about 8. Its epicenter was in the ocean about 15 kilometers southwest of San Francisco.

Cities and towns both north and south of San Francisco sustained heavy damage, and a large part of San Francisco itself was laid waste—partly by the earthquake itself, which destroyed many buildings, but mostly by ensuing fires. The temblors broke most of San Francisco's water mains, so fires that started small, from a variety of quake-related causes, eventually coalesced and raged largely unchecked for more than three days. Hundreds of people died in San Francisco, and hundreds more in other areas affected by the event. At least 250,000 people were left homeless.

There have been earthquakes of greater magnitude, and several have cost many more lives. but few have wreaked such devastation. Throughout the affected area, property damage was inestimable. In San Francisco itself, in an area exceeding 10 square kilometers, virtually every building was destroyed or later had to be torn down, including the entire business district and well over half of the city's residential neighborhoods (see figure 7-2). Streets were buckled and railcar tracks twisted. Tragically, much of the fire damage might well have been avoided had the city fathers taken measures urged upon them by San Francisco's fire chief to strengthen the city's defenses against fire—but for political reasons they did nothing.

• • •

San Francisco was, and is, a city of picturesque hills—some quite steep—and of beautiful vistas overlooking San Francisco Bay. Early settlers laid out the streets in rigid grid patterns with little regard for topography, and for the most part those patterns were followed as the city grew. For public transportation, precipitous inclines on many streets dictated the use of railcars pulled by underground cables instead of by horses. Today bus lines have replaced most of the original railcar routes. In 1906, however, their tracks traversed most of the city.

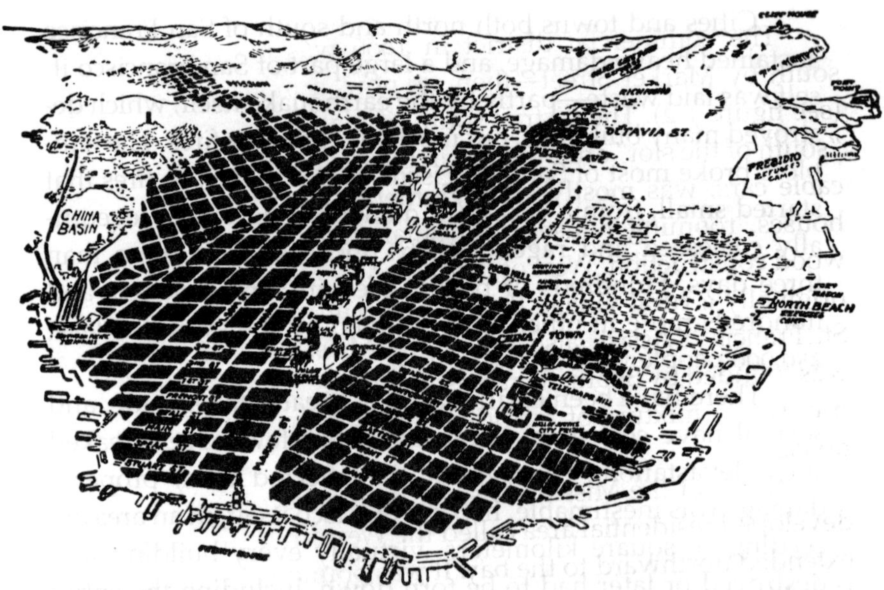

FIGURE 7-2. The devastated area of San Francisco, shown in black—a bird's-eye view looking toward the southwest, as depicted in an early book written about the earthquake. (From Morris, *Great Earthquake*, 185.)

By then the city's population had grown to some four hundred thousand. San Francisco's boom years started with the California gold rush of 1849, when the city's waterfront was crowded with sailing ships that brought prospectors from the eastern states, Europe, and elsewhere in the world. The boom continued with the discovery, ten years later, of gold and silver in the Comstock Lode in western Nevada.

San Francisco's prosperity in 1906, however, came less from the mines than from the huge truck farms in California's interior valleys and from the city's importance as a seaport for trade with Asia. The city's commercial district boasted many multistory brick and masonry buildings. Though many of those buildings were considered fireproof, few were reinforced to withstand the shaking of an earthquake. Wooden buildings predominated outside the commercial district, especially in residential areas.

The commercial district in 1906 was bounded on the south by Market Street—then, as now, a main thoroughfare (see figure 7-2). The district south of Market Street, known as "south of the slot" after the slot in the pavement for the street's cable cars, was mostly an agglomeration of factories, warehouses, rooming houses, and small hotels—virtually all of wood construction. West of that area was the Mission District, originally a rural village that grew up around the Mission of St. Francis d'Assisi, also known as Mission Dolores, which was founded by Spanish Franciscans in 1776. The Mission District was a mixture of factories, railroad yards, and wooden houses.

North of the Mission District there was a large, recently developed residential area called the Western Addition, which extended northward to the bay. It was bounded on the east by Van Ness Avenue, a wide boulevard lined with expensive houses, and on the west by Golden Gate Park and the military reservation known as the Presidio. East of Van Ness Avenue and north of the commercial district were Nob Hill, Chinatown, Russian Hill, North Beach, and Telegraph Hill—all primarily residential, all built mostly of wood. San Francisco was an enormous tinderbox.

Fires consumed large areas of San Francisco six times during the early, boisterous gold-rush years. The city was rebuilt each time, almost entirely of wood. It was only after the sixth fire, in 1851, that brick and stone buildings became common in the commercial district. By that time the city's well-tried Fire Department was considered one of the best in the world, its horse-drawn, steam-powered pumping engines racing through the streets to quench all-too-frequent fires before they could spread. The proficiency of the firefighters was enhanced by the completion of pipelines for distributing water throughout San Francisco from several reservoirs, and also by the construction of a number of large storage cisterns beneath downtown streets.

By 1906, however, the excellent reputation of the Fire Department apparently had led to complacency. Despite the fact that San Francisco was still a city built mostly of wood, the cisterns had been allowed to deteriorate, and the city fathers had ignored repeated pleas by San Francisco's fire chief, Dennis Sullivan, to provide money for an auxiliary saltwater system. Sullivan wanted to be able to pump water from the bay if the freshwater system should fail during a large fire. He also wanted money for training his men in the use of dynamite to create firebreaks, but that request was refused as well.

In October 1905 the National Board of Fire Underwriters published a report stating that "San Francisco has violated all underwriting traditions and precedents by not burning up. That it has not already done so is largely due to the vigilance of the Fire Department, which cannot be relied upon indefinitely to stave off the inevitable."[1] The report was ignored by a city administration steeped in corruption.

Political power in San Francisco was wielded by a lawyer named Abe Ruef, who had handpicked the mayor, Eugene Schmitz, to head a city government that openly took bribes from utilities, transportation companies, developers, and anyone else who wanted favors from city hall. The city was "wide open," with Ruef, Schmitz, and members of the board of supervisors regularly receiving payoffs from all-night saloons, dance halls, and houses of prostitution, most of which were in the notorious waterfront district known as the Barbary Coast, at the foot of Telegraph Hill. Chinatown, too, was infamous for its prostitutes, many of whom had been smuggled into the country as slave girls. Also in Chinatown were a good many opium dens. All contributed to the coffers of city hall, and the city fathers were more interested in collecting graft than in spending money for fire protection—especially when the Fire Department, for years, had been quite capable of protecting the city with the facilities at its disposal.

Nor were the politicians or the people of San Francisco particularly worried about earthquakes, the other threat to their city. They had not experienced a serious quake in thirty-eight years. The city had been rocked in 1836, 1838, and 1868, but there had been only minor temblors since then. Those earlier quakes were strong enough to have provided a warning, however. Mark Twain was in San Francisco, strolling down Third Street, when the 1868 temblor struck. In his book *Roughing It* he wrote:

> There came a really terrific shock . . . and there was a heavy grinding noise as of brick houses rubbing together. . . . As I reeled about on the pavement trying to keep my footing, I saw a sight! The entire front of a tall four-story brick building . . . sprung outward like a door and fell sprawling across the street. . . . Every door of every house . . . was vomiting a stream of human beings; and . . . there was a massed multitude of people stretching in endless procession down every street.[2]

But the 1868 shock apparently was forgotten. In 1906, on the fine spring evening of Tuesday, April 17, the people of San Francisco were comfortable in their homes, out strolling, or perhaps carousing in the city's many drinking establishments and bawdy houses. Newspapers featured stories of an eruption of Italy's Mount Vesuvius that threatened the city of Naples. Mayor Schmitz, in fact, had urged the citizens to contribute to a relief fund for victims of the volcano. Also in the news that day was the appearance, at the Grand Opera House, of the New York Metropolitan Opera Company. The incomparable tenor Enrico Caruso was featured in a production of Georges Bizet's *Carmen*. After a brilliant performance as Don José, Caruso enjoyed a late dinner and then retired to his suite in the opulent Palace Hotel, only to be rudely shaken out of his sleep as dawn was breaking on Wednesday morning, the eighteenth.

At 5:12 AM the San Andreas fault ruptured beneath the Pacific Ocean about 15 kilometers southwest of the city, ripping both northward and southward. About 145 kilometers north of Point Arena, halfway between Cape Mendocino and San Francisco, the steamer *Argo* suddenly trembled as if it had struck a reef, yet the vessel was in deep water. Farther south, 240 kilometers west of the Golden Gate, the schooner *John A. Campbell* met with a similar experience. Its crew thought it had rammed a derelict, but there was no sign of another ship in the area. Both ships had encountered shock waves in the sea, radiating upward from the rupturing San Andreas fault.

There was a broad zone of destruction along the active part of the fault, as shown by the intensities diagrammed in figure 7-3. In Santa Rosa, 80 kilometers north of San Francisco, every brick building in the city collapsed and more than fifty people died. Blame was placed on poor construction and on alluvial soils, which, being less dense than solid rock, magnified the effect of the earthquake waves. At Point Reyes Station, on Tomales Bay, a railroad train was jolted off the tracks and lay on its side.

Near the southern arm of San Francisco Bay, just outside Palo Alto, the earthquake made a shambles of Stanford University. Opened to students only fifteen years earlier, the university was founded by railroad magnate Leland Stanford as a memorial to his son, Leland Stanford Jr., who had died of typhoid fever. Fourteen buildings were destroyed, but fortunately almost all students and faculty were away for Easter vacation. There were only two fatalities.

While most quake survivors were terrified, the noted psychologist William James was an exception. Then teaching at Stanford, he later wrote:

> My emotion consisted wholly of glee and admiration; glee at the vividness which such an abstract idea or verbal term such as "earthquake" could put on when translated into sensible reality and verified concretely; and admiration at the way in which the frail wooden house could hold itself together in spite of shaking. I felt no trace whatever of fear; it was pure delight and welcome.[3]

About 25 kilometers to the south, twenty-one people died in San Jose, and most of the city's downtown buildings were

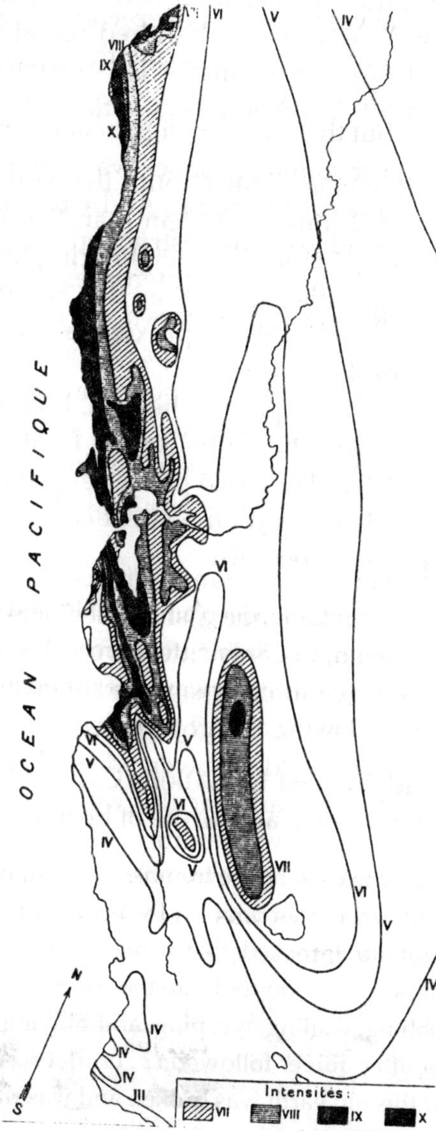

FIGURE 7-3. Zones of equal seismic intensity during the 1906 earthquake, as shown in a French textbook published in 1924. San Francisco Bay can be seen at left center. Values on the Mercalli scale range from IV (felt by many people) to X (buildings destroyed, ground cracked). The zone of greatest destruction, shown in black, extends mainly along the San Andreas fault. (After Montessus de Ballore, *La Géologic Seismologique*, 106.)

wrecked. Nearby, the quake demolished the Agnews State Insane Asylum, and more than a hundred inmates and attendants were killed. Surviving inmates fled into the surrounding countryside, and it was several days before all of them were apprehended.

About 60 kilometers farther south the earthquake badly damaged the Spanish mission of San Juan Bautista, founded over a hundred years before. The neighboring town of Hollister suffered considerable damage, as did Salinas and Monterey. Those cities marked the approximate southern limit of the earthquake's destruction.

In San Francisco the ground heaved, buildings swayed, chimneys toppled, and church bells rang frantically for most of a full minute. A San Francisco police sergeant named Jesse Cook, chatting with a friend on a street corner near the produce market, recalled afterward:

> There was a deep rumbling, deep and terrible, and then I could see it actually coming up Washington Street. The whole street was undulating. It was as if the waves of the ocean were coming towards me, billowing as they came.[4]

A young lady named Exa Atkins Campbell, in a letter to her parents in Louisiana, later wrote of horror:

> The moment I felt the house tremble . . . I leaped out of bed and rushed out to the front door. . . . I was sure the house would fall before I got out. It rocked, like a ship on "rough sea."
>
> Streams of people . . . poured into the streets . . . a mourning, groaning, sobbing, wailing, weeping, and praying crowd.
>
> . . . Quiver after quiver followed . . . until it seemed as if the very heart of this old earth was broken and was throbbing and dying away. . . .
>
> The car tracks were torn up and the iron rails even broken. . . . It is horrible.[5]

The quake collapsed masonry buildings and knocked wood-frame houses askew or smashed them to splinters. Especially south of Market Street, many people died when cheaply built wooden rooming houses and small hotels collapsed upon them as they slept. In the commercial district north of Market, where many buildings were made of brick or stone, the streets were littered with rubble when walls came crashing down. City Hall, a block north of Market Street, suffered enormous damage as columns collapsed and walls crumbled. Stonework shook loose from the building's steel-frame tower, leaving a cylindrical skeleton grotesquely capped by the still-intact dome. In the Mission District, Mission Dolores, dating from 1776, survived almost intact while a newer church next door was damaged so badly that it was later torn down—a telling example of the effect on buildings of different construction.

Telephone and electric lines were down in most parts of the city, and public transportation was severely limited because cable- and horse-car rails had been twisted out of shape by the force of the seismic waves. Damage was most severe where buildings had been constructed upon unconsolidated sediments, as in the area south of Market Street, where stream courses had been filled in, and near the bay, where fill had been dumped into shallow wetlands. Fortunately most of the city's wharves somehow survived the quake, as did the Ferry Building at the foot of Market Street, the terminus of ferry lines that provided transportation across the bay to Oakland.

When the shaking stopped and the noise of crashing buildings subsided, there was a deathly silence punctuated only by the moans of injured people, the muffled cries of those trapped in the rubble, and the awed voices of survivors still too terrified to speak in much more than a whisper. As the dust slowly settled and people began venturing into the streets, many pitched in to help police rescue the trapped and injured. But others began looting, rummaging through the rubble for whatever of value they could find.

The Palace Hotel, on Market Street, was one building that survived intact. Designed to withstand both earthquake and fire, it had a massive foundation, brick walls more than half a meter thick, enormous water tanks in the basement and on the roof, and several kilometers of built-in piping. On the fifth floor, Enrico Caruso was in a state of consternation. It has been said that the excitable singer was afraid the shaking had damaged his vocal chords, that he went to an open window and tried his voice by singing an aria, and that in the street below, people stopped to listen. Thus a legend was born: the great Caruso bravely singing to show that life goes on.

A few blocks away, Fire Chief Sullivan had been asleep in his apartment on the third floor of a fire station when the earthquake struck. A chimney on the adjacent California Hotel crashed through the firehouse roof and carried away part of the apartment's floor, as well as the floors below. Sullivan, rudely awakened, leaped from his bed, fell through the hole, and was mortally injured. Firemen rushed him to a hospital, but he never regained consciousness and died three days later. His experience and leadership were to be sorely missed during those three tragic days.

Immediately after the earthquake, great clouds of dust rose from the ruins into the quiet morning air, along with smoke from scattered fires. The quake had overturned stoves in wrecked wooden buildings, igniting whatever was flammable. Within a quarter of an hour there were as many as fifty fires in the downtown area. When firemen connected their hoses to hydrants, they got only a trickle of water or none at all. The quake had broken water mains serving the heart of the city. Water was pumped from sewers and from whatever storage cisterns remained intact, but that was not enough, and inevitably the fires spread. The firefighters were all but helpless. Only along the waterfront were the fires contained, with water pumped from the bay. Elsewhere, irresistibly, the swelling blazes merged into conflagrations that devoured whole neighborhoods.

At the Presidio, which occupied the northwest corner of San Francisco's peninsula, there were almost two thousand federal soldiers under the command of Brigadier General Frederick Funston. More troops were garrisoned at Fort Mason, at the north end of Van Ness Avenue. Funston quickly realized that the Fire and Police departments would need help fighting fires, maintaining order, and preventing panic. He ordered all available men to report to the chief of police, Jeremiah Dinan, at the Hall of Justice. The first to arrive, from Fort Mason, were sent to take up positions along Market Street. That thoroughfare was crowded with people making their way down to the Ferry Building, hoping to escape to Oakland. When troops arrived from the Presidio, some were ordered to guard the Post Office and the San Francisco Mint. Others, as shown in figure 7-4, were dispatched to help fight fires or to patrol the streets and prevent looting.

The catastrophe that was overtaking San Francisco

FIGURE 7-4. Soldiers patrol a devastated Market Street after the 1906 earthquake. (Courtesy of the Bancroft Library, University of California, Berkeley.)

seemed to galvanize the city's notorious mayor into a position of genuine, even heroic, civil leadership. Immediately after the earthquake Mayor Schmitz made his way to City Hall and, finding it in ruins, hurried to the Hall of Justice, almost a mile away. There he met Police Chief Dinan and acting Fire Chief John Dougherty, who, as a senior member of the department, had taken over for the dying Sullivan. Dinan and Dougherty apprised Schmitz of the scope of the disaster, and the mayor took charge. First he ordered the Police Department to shut down all saloons and other outlets for alcoholic beverages throughout the city. Then he sent telegrams to California's governor, George Pardee, informing him of the calamity, and to the mayor of Oakland, Frank Mott, asking for fire engines, hose, and dynamite.

Schmitz also took the extraordinary step of issuing invitations to San Francisco's leading businessmen to form a committee, which, under his leadership, would govern the city during the emergency. Known as the Committee of Fifty, it included no members of the corrupt board of supervisors, nor did it include political kingpin Abe Ruef.

In addition, Schmitz issued a proclamation that became famous—or infamous, as it has been considered unconstitutional. It read, in part:

> The Federal Troops, the members of the Regular Police Force and all Special Police Officers have been authorized by me to KILL any and all persons found engaged in Looting or in the Commission of Any Other Crime.[6]

Schmitz also sent a telegram to the naval station on Mare Island, in the bay north of San Francisco, urgently requesting marines and fireboats. Two navy fireboats joined tugboats in hosing down the Ferry Building, and the marines worked with firemen striving to contain fires encroaching upon the waterfront.

After Schmitz published his proclamation, a number of looters were indeed shot on sight—along with a few people who were merely assumed to have been looting as they searched for valuables in the ruins of their own homes. These drastic measures were effective during daylight hours but, by the light of burning buildings, criminals rummaged through the ruins at night, largely with impunity. They sought valuables, and also alcohol to drink. Fights broke out as they fought over their loot. Two writers of the time, Charles Banks and Opie Read, graphically described the depravity:

> A crew of hell rats crept out of their holes and in the flame light plunder and revel in bacchanalian orgies. . . . Sitting crouched among the ruins or sprawling on the still warm pavement they may be seen brutally drunk. A demijohn of wine placed on a convenient corner of some ruin is a shrine at which they worship.[7]

The city's hospitals coped with the disaster as best they could. They were all but overwhelmed by patients injured by earthquake or fire. Many hospital buildings had been damaged by the quake, some of them destroyed with great loss of life. Patients were moved elsewhere, many of them to a large exhibition hall called the Mechanics Pavilion, near City Hall. On Thursday one hospital, St. Mary's, even transferred equipment, staff, and patients to a steamboat in the bay.

Bank officials placed money, negotiable paper, and records in fireproof safes or vaults, or they removed the materials from the city. William Crocker, president of the Crocker Bank, hired a boat to take the bank's records to safety in the middle of the bay. Amadeo Giannini, who had founded the small Bank of Italy for the benefit of San Francisco's Italian population, hired two horse-drawn wagons and, personally driving one of them, carried the bank's furniture and funds—all of $80,000—to his home in San Mateo. The building that had housed the bank was destroyed, so on Thursday Giannini took the money to his brother's house on Van Ness Avenue. There, alone among the city's bankers, he reopened for business. The Bank of Italy, later renamed the Bank of America, eventually became one of the great banking houses of the world.

Refugees clogged streets leading to parks and beaches. Many dragged trunks or pushed anything on wheels, from wheelbarrows to baby carriages, loaded with household belongings and valuables. Much of that property was later abandoned as fires threatened the parks and people had to move on. Thousands made their way to Golden Gate Park, the Presidio, or Fort Mason, well outside the fire area, where they set up impromptu camps.

Meanwhile the fires were spreading rapidly. Firemen fought them as best they could, street by street, with what little water was available, but relentlessly the flames advanced. Attempts were made to create firebreaks by dynamiting buildings ahead of the fire—but the firefighters lacked training in the use of explosives. Hesitant to destroy property that was not in imminent danger, they often blew up buildings too close to the fire and succeeded only in creating heaps of readily combustible debris. And sometimes they used too much dynamite, the resulting explosions igniting new fires. Nevertheless the dynamiting continued, sounding like an artillery barrage and causing more harm than good.

In a residential area just north of the Mission District, three or four hours after the earthquake, a woman started a fire in her kitchen stove to cook breakfast. The chimney had been damaged by the quake, and sparks set her house afire. Rapidly spreading to other houses in the neighborhood and blown eastward by the wind, the blaze—dubbed the Ham and Eggs Fire—burned many city blocks. By nightfall the Ham and Eggs Fire had reached what was left of City Hall, where it destroyed the Public Library and many vital city documents.

By late morning on Wednesday the fires south of Market Street had coalesced into a single roaring inferno. Fire Chief Dougherty ordered all available fire engines to Market Street, where they pumped water from the bay and kept that vital thoroughfare open for the steady stream of people heading for the Ferry Building and Oakland, but most buildings on or near the street caught fire anyway. By Wednesday afternoon flames were encroaching upon the Palace Hotel—the largest in the United States at the time and considered among the finest in the world. Its built-in reservoirs and piping system had saved it for several hours, but the reservoirs ran dry, and inevitably the flames claimed another famous landmark.

Three or four blocks west of the Palace, heroic battles were being fought at the Mint and the Post Office. The Mint had its own artesian well, and employees with buckets kept the interior walls wetted down. Soldiers on the roof quenched fires that started from wind-borne embers. The outside walls were blackened by fire, and iron shutters over the windows buckled from the heat, but the massive building survived. At the Post Office, men beat out flames with wet mailbags. To their everlasting credit they lost not a single piece of mail. Starting the next day they would accept letters and notes written on anything—scraps of paper, old envelopes, pieces of cardboard, even wooden shingles—and send them postage-free to relatives and friends of survivors throughout the country.

North of Market Street more fires were raging out of control, leaping from building to building and incinerating block after block of San Francisco's commercial district. In a solid masonry building known as the Montgomery Block, a millionaire named Adolph Sutro had collected a private library of some two hundred thousand volumes, including many rare and irreplaceable books. As the fires advanced, caretakers loaded the entire library into wagons and removed it to the Mechanics Pavilion, over a mile away near City Hall, for safekeeping. The Montgomery Block, as it turned out, was among the few buildings to survive in downtown San Francisco, while the all-wood Mechanics Pavilion, with Sutro's priceless library, burned to the ground in the Ham and Eggs Fire.

A short distance west of the Montgomery Block, dynamiters set off a blast that hurled burning debris into the wooden warrens of Chinatown. Within a few hours the entire district was in ashes, and another ten thousand people joined the streams of homeless refugees making their way to Golden Gate Park, to smaller parks nearby, or to the Presidio.

Updrafts from the rampaging fires created great clouds of smoke that could be seen from ships 150 kilometers at sea. Residents of Oakland and Berkeley, across the bay, saw the clouds tinged red by the flames. As darkness fell that Wednesday evening, people far to the north and south of San Francisco saw the night sky glowing brightly.

The people of San Francisco exhibited a remarkable spirit of purposefulness, indomitability, even a fatalistic cheerfulness, as they began to settle down in refugee camps. In Jefferson Square, two blocks west of Van Ness Avenue, someone was playing a piano. Two young women, glasses of whiskey in hand, are said to have sat on the piano singing "There'll Be a Hot Time in the Old Town Tonight."

When day dawned on Thursday, April 19, however, the outlook for San Francisco was anything but cheerful. Food and drinking water were in short supply. The fires still raged, largely unchecked except along the waterfront. There were more and more casualties and nowhere near enough coffins for the dead. Corpses, of necessity, were left to be cremated by the flames. Wednesday's fires had devastated most of San Francisco's commercial district north of Market Street and an area extending more than a kilometer south from Market and more than 3 kilometers west, from the waterfront to the Mission District.

The fire burned westward, continuing its advance toward Van Ness Avenue. There the firefighters prepared to make a last stand. Mayor Schmitz abandoned the failed plan of dynamiting only buildings that were immediately in front of the fire. He authorized the destruction of all buildings in twenty-five blocks along the east side of Van Ness, extending from the bay south to Golden Gate Avenue, the northern boundary of the area laid waste by the Ham and Eggs Fire. In those blocks were churches, large apartment houses, and many of the finest homes in the city, including the residences of several members of the Committee of Fifty. No matter. They had to go. General Funston ordered field artillery brought in to help the dynamiters. Combined with the width of Van Ness Avenue, the swath of destruction created an effective firebreak.

Meanwhile aid poured into San Francisco. As soon as Governor Pardee received Mayor Schmitz's telegram Wednesday morning he ordered detachments of the National Guard sent to San Francisco, and he wired officials in Los Angeles, asking them to send help. They sent $10,000 that had been collected for victims of Mount Vesuvius, and within hours a relief train carrying doctors, nurses, and medical supplies was on its way from Los Angeles.

On the morning of Friday the twentieth, the conflagration east of Van Ness began to spread northward. With water pumped from the bay, firemen were able to stop the northward advance and keep the fire from jumping Van Ness and threatening the Western Addition. There was nothing to stop the flames from moving eastward, however. One resident, Mary Austin, watched the holocaust from her home in the Western Addition and described it this way:

> We saw the great tide of fire roaring in the hollow toward Russian Hill; burning so steadily for all it burned so fast that it had the effect of immense deliberation; roaring on toward miles of uninhabited dwellings so lately emptied of life that they appeared consciously to await their immolation; beyond the line of roofs, the hill, standing up darkly against the glow of other incalculable fires, the uplift of flames from viewless intricacies of destruction, sparks belching furiously intermittent like the spray of bursting seas.[8]

Some residents of Russian Hill were able to save their houses by beating out the approaching fire with blankets, carpets, and coats soaked with water that had been saved in bathtubs and buckets. But the blaze swept around the hill, devastated the area known as North Beach, and continued on to Telegraph Hill. There, according to legend, Italian immigrants fought the fire with homemade wine from barrels stored in their basements.

By Saturday morning, April 21, the conflagration had burned itself out or been overcome everywhere but north of Telegraph Hill along the bay shore. There, the last assault of the great fire threatened the wharves and piers that were San Francisco's lifeline for rebuilding and recovery. In this last battle weary firemen, sailors, and marines, aided by water pumped from several fireboats, slowly turned back the flames. They were finally extinguished shortly after 7:00 AM. The ordeal was over—and the heart of San Francisco was a charred wasteland.

Some five hundred city blocks had burned. Homes, schools, churches, stores, business offices, factories, warehouses, theaters, restaurants, parks and gardens, libraries, art collections—all were gone. In some places it was impossible to tell where streets had been or where property lines were. Communication and transportation systems were a shambles. City Hall and the County Court House had been destroyed with all their records—among them property deeds, marriage licenses, birth certificates, and business licenses.

The value of buildings destroyed has been estimated at more than $300 million. There is no way of estimating the value of their contents. Insurance companies paid hundreds of millions of dollars in claims. Some went bankrupt as a result. Others defaulted or simply went out of business. Stock markets, too, lost heavily as a result of the disaster, helping to trigger a nationwide money panic in the following months.

No one knows how many people died in the San Francisco catastrophe. Estimates range from three hundred to three thousand. Ironically, although the fires caused most of the destruction, it was the earthquake that caused most of the fatalities. Thousands of people fled the city and never returned. Many quake victims were buried in rubble, their remains later incinerated as the fires spread. Soldiers and National Guardsmen hastily buried unknown numbers of corpses in parks and vacant lots.

Those who survived the earthquake and fire, and had not either fled the city or returned to undamaged homes, remained in the camps that had been established in Golden Gate Park, the Presidio, and elsewhere. There were perhaps one hundred thousand refugees in Golden Gate Park and twenty thousand to thirty thousand in the Presidio. Barracks were built, as well as small houses for families. Many people, having made friends and essentially established new lives, did not leave the camps for months.

In November 1906, as a result of a reform movement, both the mayor and Abe Ruef were indicted for bribery and extortion. Schmitz was convicted, removed from office, and sentenced to jail, but his conviction was overturned on a questionable legal technicality. He ran again for mayor and received a good many votes. Despite his mixed record he was highly regarded because of his firm leadership during the fire—but he failed to win the election. He did, however, later serve two terms on the board of supervisors.

Abe Ruef was found guilty of extortion after a lengthy trial during which two key witnesses died mysteriously and attempts were made to intimidate witnesses, bribe jurors, and assassinate the prosecuting attorney. Ruef was sentenced to fourteen years in San Quentin Prison but, because of political connections, served only four and a half years.

The main significance of the San Francisco earthquake for geologists is that it was the first seismic event to receive intensive scientific scrutiny. It has been analyzed more thoroughly than most other quakes. Before-and-after surveys detected horizontal movement of land on either side of the San Andreas fault and led to an understanding of how the earth's crust is deformed along fault planes.

• • •

San Franciscans began rebuilding their city almost as soon as the fires were out. Businesses reopened within days, sometimes in hastily built temporary quarters. Rubble was removed from the streets and dumped into the bay. Vital services were restored. Most banks were able to open within six weeks. Enormous quantities of lumber were shipped into the city, and houses were rebuilt. The shells of the more substantial buildings downtown were intact, though gutted by fire, and by year's end many of those buildings were restored and open for business.

San Francisco missed a golden opportunity in its reconstruction, however. In 1904 a group of local businessmen had retained a noted architect, Daniel Burnham, to devise a long-range plan for the beautification of the city. Burnham, codesigner of the 1892 World's Columbian Exposition in Chicago, came up with a plan that included wider streets, a new civic center, boulevards around the largest hills to replace the steeply inclined streets, and an extension of Golden Gate Park. His plan was ignored, however, in the rush to rebuild and get back to business. It was quicker and easier to follow the old street grids.

Rebuilding progressed so rapidly, in fact, that by December 1906 city officials had revived a plan, first discussed the year before, to hold a world's fair in San Francisco in 1915. The Panama-Pacific International Exposition did indeed open in 1915, drawing thousands of visitors from all over the United States and around the world, and by that time there was hardly a trace of the calamity that had befallen the city only nine years before.

In 1936 Hollywood celebrated the San Francisco saga with a motion picture that is considered a masterpiece for its time. Titled simply *San Francisco,* it stars Clark Gable, Jeanette MacDonald, and Spencer Tracy. An awesome twenty-minute earthquake and fire sequence, created by state-of-the-art special effects, realistically portrays the horror of the city's ordeal, and a fanciful closing montage shows a modern city rising from the ashes.

A famous modern city has indeed risen from the ashes, and there has been no shortage of books and magazine articles pondering what might happen when the next major earthquake—the next "big one"—strikes San Francisco or some other part of California. With dark humor, people even talk about California's someday "falling into the sea." In 1944 a fantastic tale about an event of such biblical proportions was published in an anthology titled *Continent's End—a Collection of California Writing*. Fittingly called "Departure to the Sea," the story is taken from a satirical novel, *The Flutter of an Eyelid*, by Myron Brinig. It relates that

> California . . . started sliding swiftly, relentlessly, into the Pacific Ocean.
>
> The rugged cliffs that stand over San Francisco Bay crumbled . . . , and buildings of the city collapsed. . . . The waters rose, the shore sank, and in a few minutes, only a few rocks could be seen protruding above the desolation of the sea. . . . Los Angeles tobogganed with almost one continuous movement into the water.[9]

A similarly fictional catastrophe is invoked in a book titled *The Last Days of the Late, Great State of California*, written in 1968 by another American author, Curt Gentry. Starting with an earthquake like that of 1906, only so much stronger that it destroys the entire state, Gentry recapitulates the history of California. The state's cultural, economic, and political evolution up until 1969, the year of the fictional quake, is metaphorically interpreted as a slow-motion version of the ultimate environmental cataclysm.

Another book about earthquakes in California, published in 1972, is *Will California Fall into the Sea?* Despite the whimsical title, author Peter Briggs, in a popular vein, seriously discusses the region's seismicity and its ramifications for the future.

Since 1906 both the state of California and the city of San Francisco have taken a number of measures for protection against future disaster. California has implemented building codes for different types of structures to make them resistant to earthquake damage and fire. In San Francisco, reinforced-concrete reservoirs have been constructed, the cisterns beneath city streets have been repaired and kept full, and saltwater pumping stations have been installed near the bay. In addition, the city has established an Office of Emergency Services.

Not all the lessons of 1906 have been learned, however. In San Francisco and elsewhere, new buildings are often built to only minimal code standards. Construction deadlines and cost concerns often lead to shortcuts in implementing safety factors. Geologists and structural engineers have urged height restrictions for buildings in earthquake-prone areas, but their advice is frequently ignored for the sake of greater immediate return on investment.

Economic pressures and expediency have led to continued building in risky locations. Areas of unconsolidated fill, where earthquake damage was most severe in 1906, were built upon again soon after the disaster. The city expanded into areas where rubble from 1906 had been dumped into the bay. Many of San Francisco's downtown skyscrapers have foundations sunk into filled land, and there is no evidence that they will not fail in a strong earthquake.

Throughout California, new buildings, housing developments, and even whole communities have been built on or near faults. It is not unusual to find schools, churches, banks, supermarkets, oil refineries, bridges, dams, freeways, and water reservoirs located along the trace of the San Andreas fault. Daly City, a suburb of San Francisco, is located directly over the fault.

Across the bay a tunnel of the Bay Area Rapid Transit (BART) system passes through the Hayward fault. In Berkeley, the University of California football stadium straddles the Hayward fault and is being pulled apart at a rate of more than a centimeter a year. In the same area, inexcusably, thirteen schools straddle the fault. Always, it seems, there are economic or political reasons for the issuing of building permits in areas at risk.

Another big earthquake in San Francisco is inevitable. Movement along the San Andreas fault averages 4 centimeters a year. Deep in the earth's crust the stress caused by that motion most likely is released slowly, but the shallow part of the fault near San Francisco has been locked since 1906. Eventually the vast amount of energy stored in the upper part of the fault will be released, probably suddenly.

A warning came on October 17, 1989. During a World Series baseball game in San Francisco's Candlestick Park, a part of the fault that was activated in 1906 broke free about 80 kilometers south of San Francisco, near the city of Santa Cruz. The resulting earthquake had a magnitude of 7.1. It caused many landslides, collapsed freeways and a section of the San Francisco–Oakland Bay Bridge, and—in a tragic echo of 1906—set the Marina District of San Francisco on fire. The Marina District, between Fort Mason and the Presidio, is built on fill, much of it debris from the 1906 quake. The unconsolidated material amplified the seismic waves, many buildings collapsed, and, as in 1906, cooking and heating stoves set the wreckage afire. Called the Loma Prieta earthquake after the name of a hill near its epicenter, the quake killed thirty-seven people, injured almost four thousand, and left twelve thousand homeless.

The northern part of the 1906 rupture, which passes close by San Francisco, remains locked—and highly dangerous. Many geologists think another rupture is overdue. Some think the break may not come for another fifty years. Most are hesitant to make a firm prediction. If an imminent quake were predicted, and the prediction believed, it might well cause panic. A false prediction, on the other hand, could have severe economic repercussions and result in skepticism about future predictions. But when the "big one" does come, it will surely be catastrophic. And it *will* come.

CAUSES OF QUAKES IN THE BAY AREA

The infamous San Andreas fault achieved notoriety because of its association with the earthquake that destroyed much of San Francisco in 1906. But the San Andreas is only one of many quake-producing faults within the California fault belt, which extends more than 2,000 kilometers from an area in the Pacific Ocean off northwestern California to an area off northwestern Mexico. About 100 kilometers wide, the fault belt was created some 30 million years ago as the North American and Pacific tectonic plates collided.

For many millions of years those plates had been separated by another large piece of the earth's crust known as the Farallon plate, named after the Farallon Islands, which lie in the Pacific Ocean about 45 kilometers west of San Francisco. The eastward-moving Farallon plate was slowly being subducted beneath the westward-moving North American plate, the resulting tectonic upheaval giving rise to California's mountain ranges. Meanwhile the Pacific plate was drifting toward the west-northwest.

Eventually almost the entire Farallon plate disappeared beneath North America. Today there are but two tiny remnants—the Juan de Fuca plate, which underlies the Pacific Ocean off the northwestern United States, and the Cocos plate off Central America. Satellite observations indicate that the Pacific plate continues to move west-northwestward at about 4.5 centimeters a year.

As more and more of the Farallon plate was subducted, the North American plate, moving westward—currently at 2 centimeters a year—crossed the boundary between the Farallon and Pacific plates and made contact with the Pacific plate somewhere south of present-day Los Angeles. Because the North American plate was moving toward the west and the Pacific plate toward the west-northwest, they collided at an oblique angle and thus created shearing stresses. Those stresses, in turn, created the

California fault belt, which grew laterally as more and more of the old boundary between the Farallon and Pacific plates slipped beneath the continent.

During the 30 million years that have elapsed since the North American and Pacific plates first came into contact, the cumulative distance over which opposite sides of the California fault belt have moved with regard to each other is thought to be more than 1,200 kilometers. Cumulative slippage along the San Andreas fault, on the other hand, is estimated to be only about 300 kilometers. The difference implies that either the San Andreas must have played only a minor role in the early phases of deformation, or the San Andreas originated later. In either case, it is now the principal fault in the California part of the plate boundary, as shown in figure 7-5, and movement along that fault is the dominant cause of earthquakes in the region. The San Andreas fault extends more than 1,000 kilometers from Cape Mendocino in northern California to the Salton Sea in southern California.

At present, deformation in the California fault belt is controlled by the westward movement of the North American plate at a rate of about 2 centimeters a year and the simultaneous west-northwest drift of the Pacific plate at 4.5 centimeters a year, also shown in figure 7-5. During the last two millennia the average rate of slippage within the California fault belt has been estimated at 3 to 4 centimeters a year.

The San Andreas fault has three main segments. The northern segment extends from Cape Mendocino to San Juan Bautista, near Monterey. A short central segment extends from there to the vicinity of Coalinga, 150 kilometers southeast of Monterey. And the southern segment extends from Coalinga to the Salton Sea. Stress that has accumulated during historical time in the northern and southern segments has been released suddenly from time to time, causing strong earthquakes. In the central segment, how-

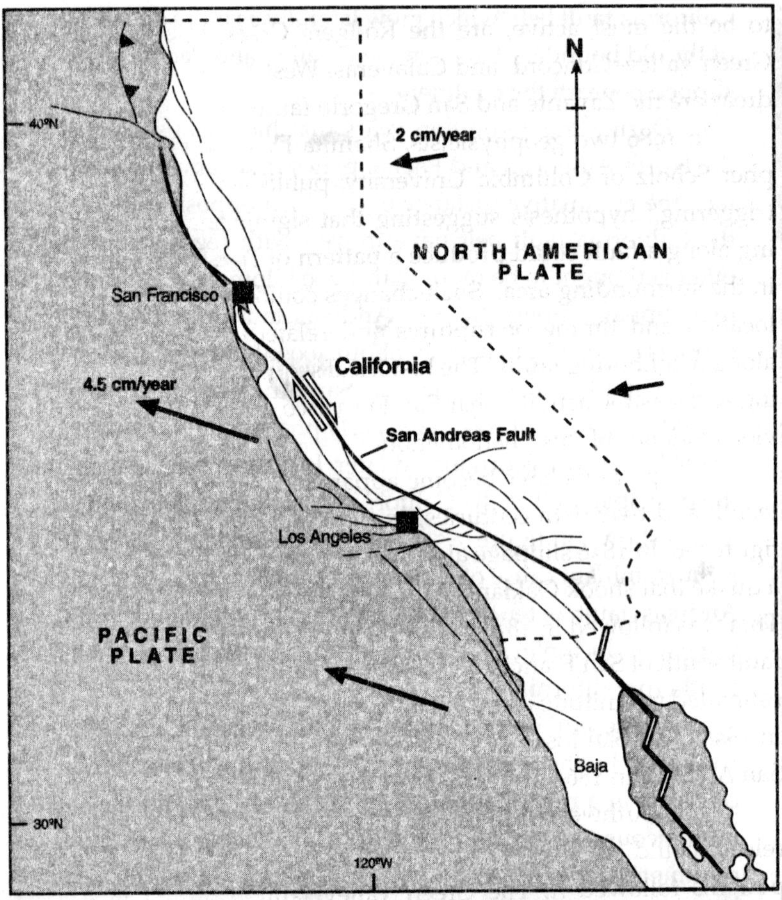

FIGURE 7-5. Plate-tectonic setting of the California fault belt within the state of California. Black arrows indicate present directions and, by their length, relative velocities of plate movement. Open arrows along the San Andreas fault indicate relative directions of crustal movement on either side of the fault.

ever, accumulated stress has been released by a slow creeping movement and minor ruptures, which so far have generated only low-magnitude quakes.

Several major faults branch off from the northern San Andreas, and others run more or less parallel to it as shown in figure 7-6. The largest of the parallel faults, and presumed to be the most active, are the Rodgers Creek–Hayward, Green Valley–Concord, and Calaveras. West of the San Andreas are the Zayante and San Gregorio faults.

In 1986 two geophysicists, Shamita Das and Christopher Scholz of Columbia University, published a "stress-triggering" hypothesis suggesting that significant rupturing along a fault could produce a pattern of stress changes in the surrounding area.[1] Such changes could influence the location and timing of ruptures and related earthquakes along neighboring faults. The historical sequence of rupturing and seismic activity near San Francisco appears to provide evidence of this phenomenon.

Two patterns have become apparent during the nineteenth and twentieth centuries, as shown by the arrows in figure 7-6. In 1836 slippage along the Hayward fault caused a quake that shook Oakland with a magnitude of about 6.8. That was followed in 1838 by rupturing of the San Andreas fault south of San Francisco, causing an earthquake with an estimated magnitude of 7.2. A rupture of the Hayward fault in 1858, near San Jose, was followed by slippage along the San Andreas in 1865, this time near Santa Cruz.

This southwestward migration of the centers of stress release could have been a coincidence, except that similar patterns followed it. The Green Valley fault ruptured in 1892 and caused an earthquake with a magnitude estimated to have been about 6.7. That quake was followed by one in 1898 that originated along the Rodgers Creek fault, southwest of the Green Valley. It had an estimated magnitude of 6.9. Then came the great San Francisco earthquake of April 1906, which originated along the San Andreas fault, still farther southwest, and according to the most recent estimates had a magnitude of about 7.9.

Figure 7-6 also illustrates an interesting pattern of northward migration for more than 100 kilometers along the Calaveras fault. The migration began in 1974 with slippage in the southern part of the fault. Rupturing moved

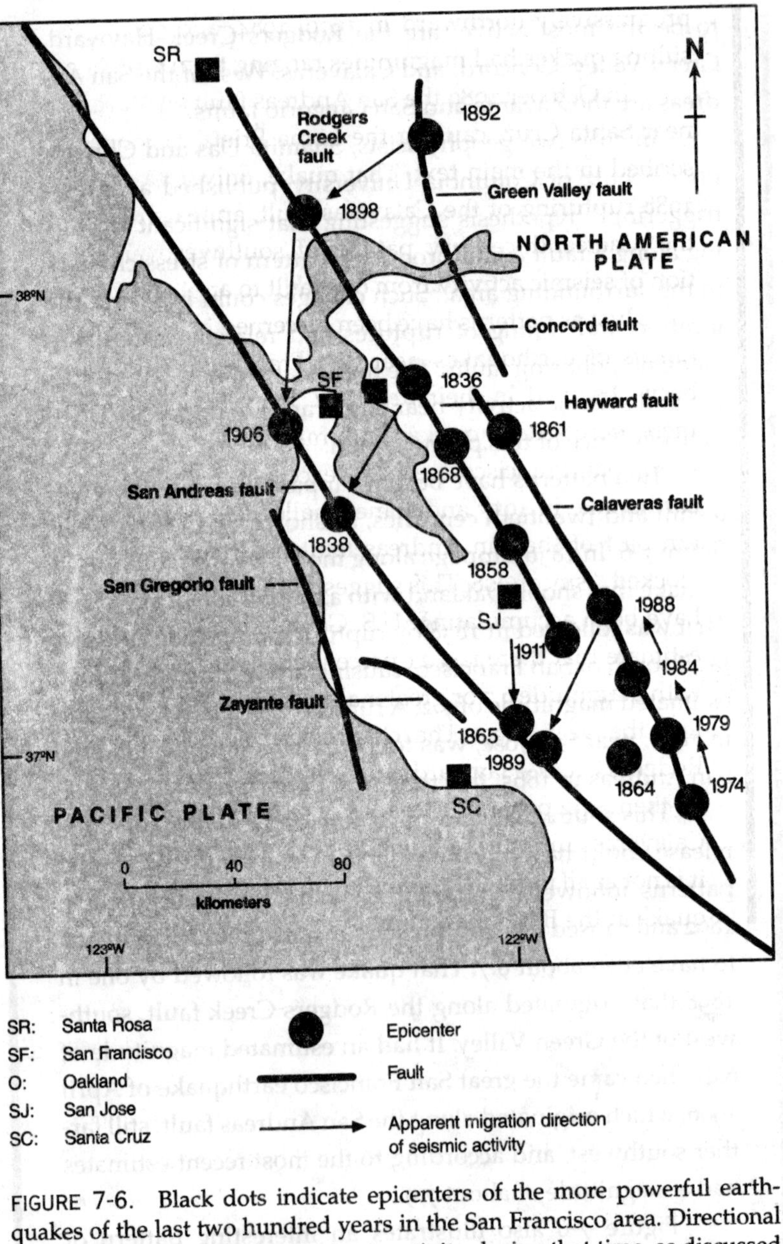

FIGURE 7-6. Black dots indicate epicenters of the more powerful earthquakes of the last two hundred years in the San Francisco area. Directional arrows indicate migration of seismic activity during that time, as discussed in the text.

progressively northward in 1979, 1984, and 1988. The resulting quakes had magnitudes ranging from 5.1 to 6.2.

In October 1989 the San Andreas fault again ruptured near Santa Cruz, causing the Loma Prieta earthquake described in the main text. That quake, only a year after the 1988 rupturing of the Calaveras fault, appears to replicate the nineteenth-century pattern of southwestward migration of seismic activity from one fault to another.

Just as patterns have been discerned in consecutive *locations* of earthquakes near San Francisco, a pattern has been observed in their *frequency*. Between 1836 and 1906 there were sixteen quakes with magnitudes of 6 or greater in the San Francisco area. But except for a magnitude 5.3 earthquake in 1957 and some smaller temblors, the northern part of the San Andreas fault has remained quiet, or "locked," since 1906. This suggests, ominously, that stresses have been accumulating. U.S. Geological Survey scientists estimate that there is a 21 percent chance of an earthquake with magnitude 6.7 or greater along that part of the fault before the year 2030. The chance that slippage along the Rodgers Creek–Hayward fault will produce a strong quake by then is 32 percent. The odds of a strong quake along the Calaveras fault during the same period are 18 percent. Thus it is not at all unlikely that there could be a disastrous earthquake in the Bay Area within the next three decades.

8 • Japan's Great Kanto Earthquake: "Hell Let Loose on Earth"

It was not long before the place turned into a veritable sea of fire,
and one of the most horrible and shocking events
ever recorded in the annals of human tragedy followed;
hell was indeed let loose on earth.

The Bureau of Social Affairs, Home Office, Japan,
The Great Earthquake of 1923

IN JAPAN IT IS CALLED the Kanto Dai-shinsai, the Great Kanto Earthquake Disaster. It happened in September 1923 and was among the most destructive natural calamities ever recorded. The earthquake struck at 11:58 AM on September 1 and devastated an area known as the Kanto plain on Japan's largest island, Honshu. The most extensive area of level land in Japan, the Kanto plain encompasses the capital city of Tokyo as well as Yokohama and many smaller cities and towns in surrounding prefectures. Half of the city of Tokyo was laid waste, and Yokohama—the country's main seaport—was almost totally destroyed. As many as 150,000 people died, most by burning to death in wind-driven fires that followed the earthquake itself.

The shaking, with a magnitude subsequently estimated to have been as high as 8.3, continued unabated for several minutes. The quake was powerful enough to knock seismographs out of commission at the Seismological Institute in Tokyo. It was felt as far as 400 kilometers away, over an area of more then 400,000 square kilometers. A second major quake struck just twenty-four hours after the first, and aftershocks shook the region for almost two years. There was an especially strong aftershock in January 1924, four and a half months after the principal quake.

Tokyo, originally named Edo, grew from a small town that developed around an ancient castle. Edo became the administrative capital of the country in 1603 CE, when the Tokugawa family, which owned the castle, acquired the hereditary title *shogun*. The emperor remained in the old capital city of Kyoto, some 380 kilometers east, until 1868, when the shogunate was overthrown. Edo was then renamed Tokyo, and the emperor, restored to power, made the city his capital. By 1923 the population of Tokyo had reached 2,265,000.

Tokyo has a low sector and a high sector. The "Low City" is Tokyo's downtown, occupying lowlands near Tokyo Bay and along the Sumida River, which winds through the city much as the Thames winds through London. The "High City" is a largely residential area on a range of low hills, underlain by bedrock, west of downtown.

The Tokugawa shoguns drained the lowlands near the mouth of the Sumida, and it was upon filled land in that area that much of the Low City was built. Such unconsolidated ground, saturated with water, tends to liquefy like quicksand during earthquakes. It shakes like jelly, greatly magnifying the effects of seismic waves. Thus the lower sections of Edo, and subsequently of Tokyo, have suffered greatly from earthquakes over the centuries. Fires inevitably followed those events. Whether related to earthquakes or not, fires were so common in Edo that they came to be known by the sobriquet *Edo no hana*, "the flowers of Edo." It was generally accepted in the Low City that no house should be expected to remain standing more than a decade or two.

Yokohama, on Tokyo Bay a short distance south of Tokyo, was originally a tiny fishing village. It became a commercial seaport in 1859 after the opening of Japan to foreign trade by treaty with the United States. By 1923 Yokohama had become a city of half a million people.

Tokyo Bay opens inland from the east side of a larger embayment to the south called Sagami Bay, which in turn opens into the Pacific Ocean. The north and west shores of Sagami Bay form a wide crescent lined with resort cities and fishing villages. During the 1923 earthquake, those cities and villages suffered the greatest damage from the quake itself as contrasted with the fire damage that devastated Tokyo and Yokohama. In some places virtually every house collapsed on September 1.

To compound the chaos, Japan was literally without a government. The country's prime minister had died only a week earlier, and the new prime minister, Gonnohyoe Yamamoto, had not yet made all his cabinet appointments. Thus members of the outgoing government had to deal with the immediate emergency. One of their acts, as quake-ravaged Tokyo and Yokohama burned, was to declare martial law. Yamamoto hastily completed his cabinet appointments the next day. His government remained in office for less than a year, but it guided the nation through the early stages of reconstruction and recovery.

• • •

Japan is visited by calamitous natural events probably more often than any other country in the world. Earthquakes often rock the islands; great, quake-generated sea waves to which the Japanese gave the name *tsunamis*, or "port-waves," not uncommonly crash ashore; and the country has many active volcanoes. Moreover, more typhoons make their landfall in Japan than anywhere else in the western Pacific.

Throughout the country's history, earthquakes have been among the most devastating of those events. Records have been kept faithfully since 481 CE, a time when seismic events were thought to be caused by the wriggling of a gigantic catfish that lived in the sea beneath Japan and supported the islands on its back. There is a powerful quake somewhere in the country every six to seven years, on average. The great number of earthquakes in Japan led to the development there of the first reliable seismograph in 1880. Since the Kanto disaster in 1923 there have been twelve quakes with magnitudes greater than 7.5. One of them, in 1938, had an estimated magnitude of 8.9.

The Japanese islands lie within an immense tectonic zone where the Pacific and Philippine tectonic plates are colliding with the Eurasian plate as shown in figure 8-1. One result of this geological cataclysm has been extensive volcanic activity, which created the island arc we now know as Japan. The northern island of Hokkaido and the northern part of Honshu were formed where the Pacific plate is slipping, or being subducted, beneath Eurasia along the Japan trench. Meanwhile southern Honshu and the islands of Shikoku and Kyushu, in southern Japan, developed where the Philippine plate is being subducted beneath the Eurasian plate along the deep Ryukyu trench.

The Philippine plate is being subducted northwestward at about 4 centimeters a year, and the Pacific plate is being subducted toward the west-northwest at about 10 centimeters a year. Hence the faster-moving Pacific plate is slipping beneath the Philippine plate along the Izu-Bonin trench. Meanwhile Eurasia is moving eastward, over those plates, at about 0.2 centimeter a year. The net rate of subduction, then, is about two and a half times as fast beneath the northern part of the Japanese arc as beneath the southern part. The faster rate of subduction creates more stresses within the earth's crust, leading to more earthquakes in the northern part of the country than in the southern part.

The Kanto earthquake was caused by slippage along the fault that transects Sagami Bay from northwest to southeast, near Oshima Island, as shown in figure 8-2. South of the Boso peninsula that fault curves sharply to the northeast. Motion

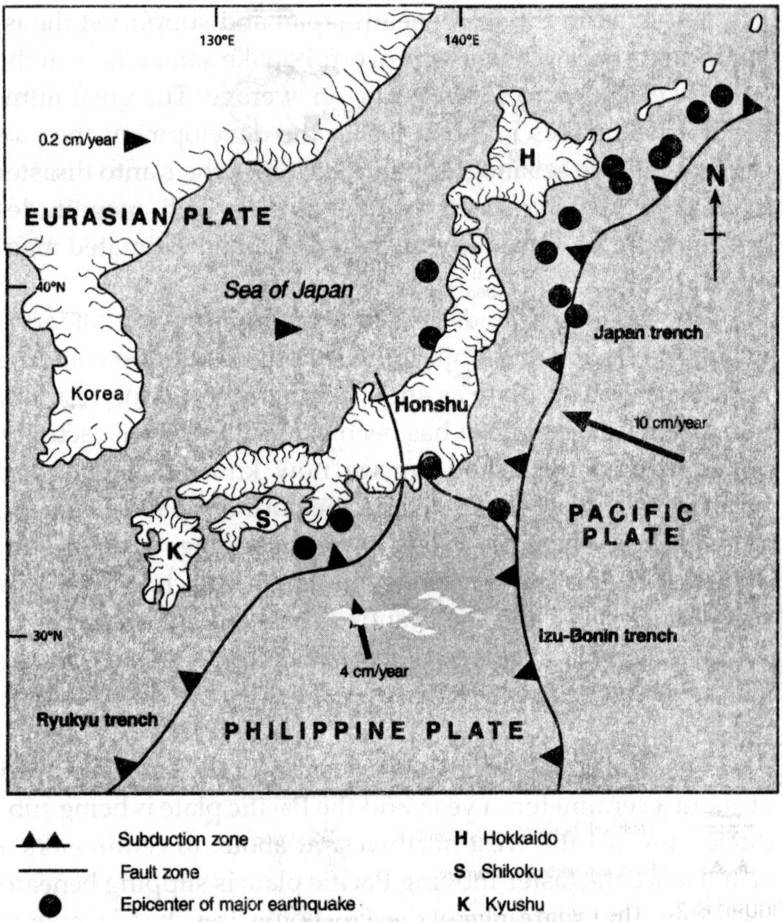

FIGURE 8-1. Plate-tectonic setting of the Japanese archipelago. Arrows indicate present directions and, by their length, relative velocities of plate movement. Also shown are the locations of epicenters of major earthquakes during the last hundred years.

along the Sagami Bay segment was more or less horizontal, with the southwestern block moving northwestward. Along the segment south of the Boso peninsula, however, the motion was partly vertical. In that area the Philippine plate was thrust northwestward, beneath the Boso and Miura peninsulas.

The Philippine plate moved as much as 3.5 meters and

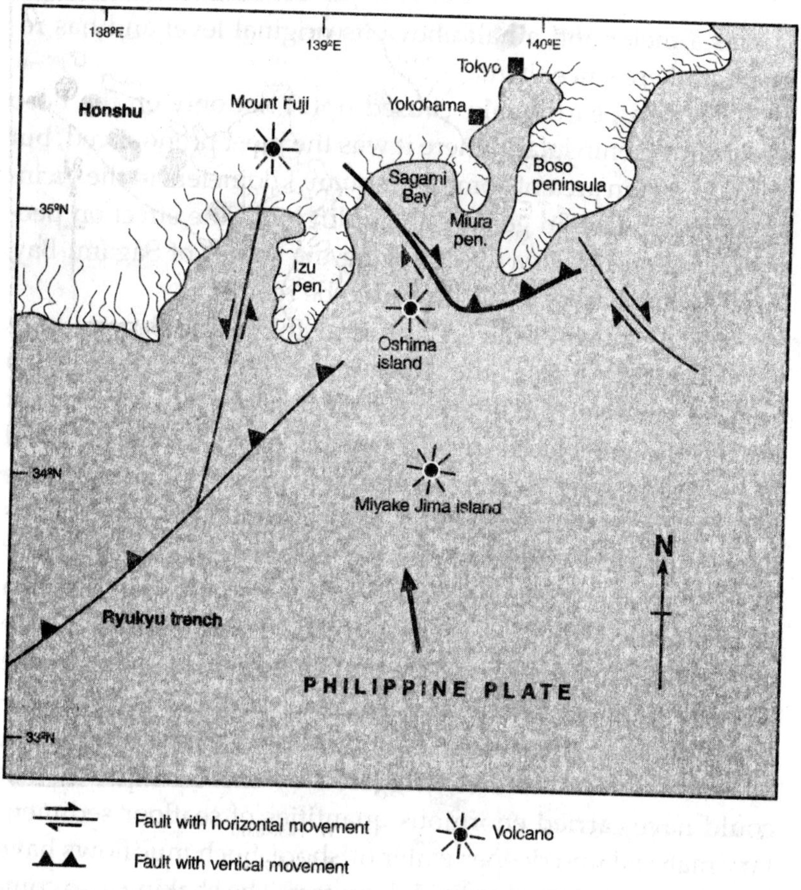

FIGURE 8-2. The Kanto earthquake originated along the northwest-southeast-trending fault that transects Sagami Bay. South of the Boso peninsula, where the fault turns toward the northeast, the Philippine plate is being thrust beneath the peninsula.

uplifted parts of both peninsulas. A man who was swimming in Sagami Bay off the city of Kamakura, a resort at the north end of the Miura peninsula, experienced that uplift firsthand. He felt tremors in the water and rapidly made for shore. As he struggled onto the beach, he felt it rising beneath his feet. The southern part of the Miura peninsula rose about 8 meters that day and remained at that elevation for three days. Then it slowly subsided, about 20 centimeters a day. Four weeks later it was a meter and a half above its original level and has remained there since then.

The 1923 earthquake caused uplift not only on the Boso and Miura peninsulas, where it was the most pronounced, but throughout an area of some 230 square kilometers in the vicinity of Tokyo Bay. In general the uplift had little effect on people living in that area except along the shores of Sagami Bay, where some harbor facilities had to be rebuilt.

While much of the area around Tokyo and Sagami bays was uplifted during the earthquake, soundings taken in Sagami Bay after the quake seemed to show that the floor of the bay in some places, instead of being uplifted, had subsided to an astonishing degree. Compared with known prequake depths, the water was found to be as much as 150 meters deeper near the western shore, 200 meters deeper in the center of the bay, and 230 meters deeper to the south, near Oshima Island, where the bay opens into the Pacific Ocean. Those before-and-after differences cannot be explained solely by the tectonic slippage of crustal rock formations along faults beneath the bay. The differences might be explained, however, by submarine mudflows, triggered by the earthquake, that could have carried enormous quantities of seafloor sedimentary material into deeper water offshore. Such mudflows have been known to travel many kilometers. The shaking also compacted the unconsolidated sediments on the floor of the bay.

Remarkably, the earthquake seriously damaged only four of some two thousand houses on Oshima Island. This relative immunity to the earthquake is attributed to the fact that Oshima is a volcanic island, composed of solid igneous rock, as contrasted with the weaker sedimentary strata beneath the ravaged areas of the Kanto plain.

Seismic vibrations from the September 1 earthquake compacted unconsolidated sediments beneath the Kanto plain, causing the surface to subside in many areas. Near Manazuru, a city on the west side of Sagami Bay, farmers had long obtained their water from wells lined with baked tiles. As the sediments compacted around the wells, their linings were left standing like chimneys, some as high as 3 meters above the surface of the ground.

Near Chigasaki, a city on the north shore of Sagami Bay, the soil settled and revealed seven vertical wooden columns, each more than half a meter in diameter, that had been buried in a rice field. When the shaking ended, the ancient columns stood almost a meter above the field. They were determined to be pilings for a bridge that had been built in 1182.

A few minutes after the principal earthquake, tsunamis inundated the shorelines of Sagami and Tokyo bays. Tsunamis, like all ocean waves breaking on a beach, often are preceded by withdrawal of water from the shoreline. At Miura the sea retreated so rapidly that many fishing boats and small steamers were carried away. A tide gauge at Aburatabo, a nearby village, recorded small oscillations at the instant of the earthquake. Five minutes later the instrument was thrown off scale when sea level suddenly dropped by as much as 4 meters.

Incoming waves that followed the retreating water were highest along the west-central shore of Sagami Bay and at the south end of the Boso peninsula. Near Atami, on the west shore of the bay, the highest wave crested at more than 13 meters, the tsunami gaining height as it rushed into the confines of the city's narrow harbor. When the giant wave receded it carried sixty people to their deaths and washed away 155 houses, many of which had been destroyed only a short time before by the earthquake.

At Ito, some 16 kilometers south of Atami, the tsunami was 9 meters high. It swept 100-ton fishing boats more than 200 meters inland and, upon retreating, carried away some three hundred houses, though the townspeople escaped with no fatalities. In the seaside resort of Kamakura, however, a tsunami 5 meters high washed almost a hundred bathers out to sea.

• • •

In Tokyo the earthquake began with a loud underground rumbling noise and a trembling of the earth, which quickly intensified. Professor Akitsune Imamura, of the Tokyo Seismological Institute at the Imperial University, described the earthquake this way:

> At first, the movement was rather slow and feeble. . . . Soon the vibration became large, and after 3 or 4 seconds . . . I felt the shock to be very strong indeed. Seven or 8 seconds passed and the building was shaken to an extraordinary extent. . . . At the twelfth second . . . came a very big vibration. . . . Now the motion, instead of becoming less and less as usual, went on increasing in intensity very quickly, and after 4 or 5 seconds I felt it to have reached its strongest. . . . During the following 10 seconds the motion, though still violent, became somewhat less severe, . . . the vibrations becoming slower but bigger. For the next few minutes we felt an undulatory movement like that . . . on a boat in windy weather. . . . After 5 minutes from the beginning, I stood up.[1]

Frightened people rushed into the streets from homes, stores, and offices. They stood speechless, terrified, then fled to parks and other open areas as tall buildings swayed and houses crashed to the ground. With the first shock waves Tokyo's telephone and telegraph wires came down, fissures opened in roads, and railway lines within 150 kilometers of the city were disrupted. The city was isolated from the outside world.

The effects of the quake were greatly intensified by the unconsolidated alluvial sediments and filled land beneath the Low City, so that downtown area suffered more damage from the earthquake itself than did the largely residential High City on its bedrock hills. Many downtown masonry structures broke apart. In the Asakusa amusement district a 12-story brick building (Tokyo's tallest), called the Ryounkaku ("Rising-over-the-Clouds Tower"), swayed ominously for a few moments; then the top four stories fell off to one side. Fortunately they landed in a pond instead of crashing into noontime crowds in nearby streets.

Meanwhile about 5 kilometers southwest of Asakusa, near the Imperial Palace, some two hundred dignitaries had gathered for a gala luncheon to celebrate the grand opening of a new 250-room hotel. Called the Imperial, it was designed by an American architect named Frank Lloyd Wright, who had not yet achieved the renown of his later years. The hotel was built upon soft sediment some 18 meters deep. Recognizing the seismic hazard of the site, Wright had incorporated a number of innovative features into his design in an effort to make the building earthquake resistant. Essentially he floated the structure on concrete piles driven into the mud, and he reinforced the walls with steel bars. Among other innovations, he divided the structure into discrete sections that could move independently during a quake, rather than breaking apart.

When the earthquake struck almost at noon the gala luncheon ended abruptly, but the Imperial Hotel survived with little damage. Wright was in the United States at the time, and after the quake a Japanese official sent him the following cablegram:

> HOTEL STANDS UNDAMAGED AS MONUMENT OF YOUR GENIUS HUNDREDS OF HOMELESS PROVIDED [FOR] BY PERFECTLY MAINTAINED SERVICE CONGRATULATIONS[2]

Wright promptly released the cable to news media. Other buildings of modern construction in Tokyo survived as well, but the Imperial—and Frank Lloyd Wright—became famous. In the Western world, legend had it that his hotel was the only building in Tokyo to survive the disaster. Wright's ensuing career placed him in the first rank of architects.*

Despite the violence of the earthquake, that event by itself destroyed relatively few buildings in Tokyo. But immedi-

* The hotel was torn down in 1968 and its facade rebuilt as part of a museum near Nagoya.

ately after the quake began, the city caught fire. Except for a few downtown structures of modern fire-resistant design, Tokyo in 1923 was essentially a gigantic village of wooden buildings built close together in a warren of narrow streets and alleys. Most stores and office buildings were made of wood, and over two million people lived in traditional Japanese houses with light wood frames and interior walls of oiled paper panels. At lunchtime on September 1, open charcoal fires burned in virtually every home. The earthquake toppled cooking stoves, mainly in the downtown area where the tremors were strongest. As frightened people ran from their homes, red-hot coals fell onto straw mats and came to rest against combustible walls. Fires sprang up all over the Low City, spreading rapidly from house to house—a tragic reprise of the "flowers of Edo."

That same day a typhoon was whirling across northern Honshu some distance from Tokyo, creating havoc of its own. Winds related to that storm, blowing from the south over the city, whipped the coalescing flames into a conflagration that eventually destroyed 80 percent of Tokyo's homes.

The fires themselves generated turbulent winds as well. The intense heat produced updrafts, which, to fill the partial vacuum thus created, sucked air through the streets at velocities estimated to have approached 80 kilometers an hour. Converging air currents at street corners developed into firestorms of whirlwinds, which, spiraling upward, carried burning debris that helped spread the conflagration. Some of the fiery whirlwinds developed into tornadoes, which, incinerating everything they touched, sometimes produced so much carbon monoxide that people who had escaped death by fire died from inhaling the poisonous gas. Some, too, no doubt died of suffocation as the fires consumed oxygen, causing billowing, sooty clouds and dense, ground-hugging smoke.

People fled from their ruined and burning homes and raced desperately through debris-choked streets and alleys, driven onward by spreading fires and pressing crowds. Many, carrying clothing and bedding, perished when their belongings caught fire. Those who survived the flames congregated in the few open places—parks, playgrounds, and vacant lots. Many sought refuge on the bridges over Tokyo's rivers and drainage canals. The largest bridges, five of them, spanned the Sumida River. Hundreds of refugees crowded onto them, seeking safety over the water. Though the bridges were made of iron, the floors were of wood. When the flames reached them they caught fire and collapsed into the river. Hundreds of refugees drowned.

The most horrible event in a day of horror occurred at a 6-hectare site on the east bank of the Sumida River that had been occupied by an army clothing depot, where military uniforms had been manufactured. The facility had been moved recently and the buildings torn down, leaving an open area that was to be made into a park. In the interim neighborhood children had been using it as a playground. The southerly wind kept the fires away from that area, and as many as forty thousand people took refuge there.

About 6:00 PM, however, the wind veered to the west, and flames reached the houses surrounding the former clothing depot. Packed into the area, the refugees were trapped when a tornado of fire, smoke, and hurricane-force winds swept down upon them. A government report, published in 1926, described the appalling scene:

> It was not long before the place was turned into a veritable sea of fire, and one of the most horrible and shocking events ever recorded in the annals of human tragedy followed; hell was indeed let loose on earth.[3]

Engulfed in flames and acrid black smoke, unable to escape, forty thousand people burned to death.

The fires continued for three days and turned to ashes some 18 square kilometers of Tokyo, 40 percent of the city's area (see figure 8-3, top). Virtually all of Tokyo's downtown—the Low City—was consumed by the flames, and parts of the

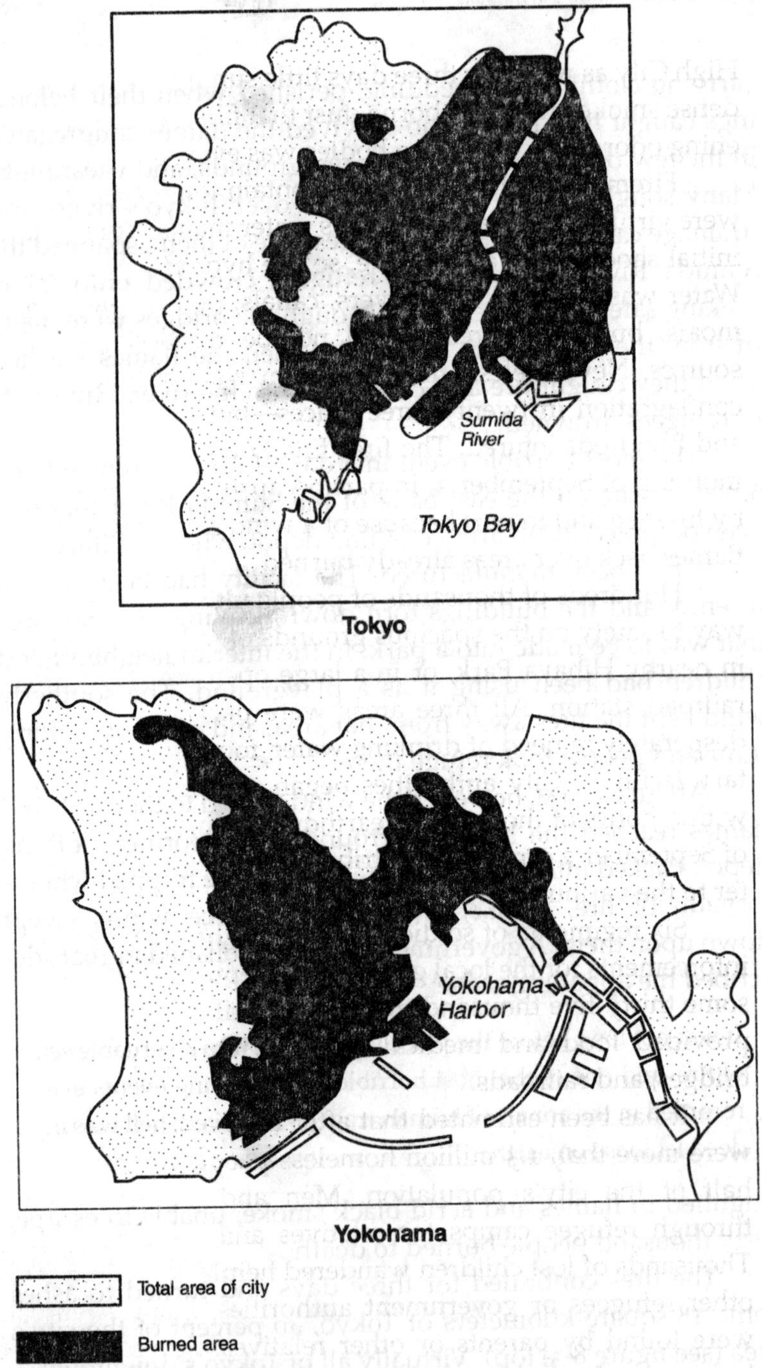

FIGURE 8-3. Areas of Tokyo and Yokohama destroyed by fire.

High City as well. For three days little sunlight penetrated the dense smoke and wind-borne dust that filled the air. The sickening odor of decomposing bodies was everywhere.

Firemen fought valiantly to contain the flames, but they were virtually helpless. The city's water mains broke with the initial shock of the earthquake, so fire hydrants were useless. Water was pumped from rivers, canals, ponds, even ancient moats, but many areas could not be reached from those sources. Nevertheless, heroic firemen were able to stop the conflagration in twenty-three places—but many were killed and hundreds injured. The fires finally died out early on the morning of September 3, in part because of demolition work by firemen and in part because of a wind shift that turned the flames back over areas already burned.

Hundreds of thousands of people ultimately found their way to safety on the spacious grounds of the Imperial Palace, in nearby Hibaya Park, or in a large open area near Tokyo's railroad station. All three areas were packed with refugees desperately in need of drinking water, food, shelter, and sanitary facilities. City authorities began repairing water mains within hours of the primary earthquake, and by the morning of September 2 carts were distributing limited supplies of water to the various refugee camps.

Six regiments of soldiers were brought into Tokyo as reinforcements for the local garrison. By September 8 there were some thirty-five thousand troops in the city. They kept order, provided food and medical supplies, and repaired roads, bridges, and railroads.

It has been estimated that after the Kanto disaster there were more than 1.5 million homeless people in Tokyo—over half of the city's population. Men and women searched through refugee camps for relatives and missing children. Thousands of lost children wandered helplessly. Cared for by other refugees or government authorities, many eventually were found by parents or other relatives. Several hundred, however, whose families had been killed, were placed in foundling homes. As many as 150,000 of the homeless suffered from burns or other injuries, and thousands later died. Surviving doctors in Tokyo, soon aided by medical teams from suburbs and nearby cities, provided what care they could in the refugee camps.

• • •

In Yokohama, as in Tokyo, the first indication of the earthquake on September 1 was a thunderous subterranean rumbling. Then came a sharp vertical shock, and almost all large buildings in the city collapsed into ruins. A massive, crescent-shaped breakwater across the harbor entrance sank into the sea and disappeared. Trees were uprooted, streets cracked, water mains burst, and riverbanks crumbled, tumbling houses into the water. Telephone poles fell, their wires draped like cobwebs over the ruins. Like Tokyo, Yokohama lost communication with the outside world. Continual aftershocks punctuated the terrible scene.

As in Tokyo, fires sprang up throughout the city from lunchtime cooking stoves. And again the flames were fanned by strong winds. They spread rapidly, forming whirlwinds that lifted burning debris and rained it down upon fleeing quake survivors. Unstoppable, the fires consumed almost 8 square kilometers, almost half the area of Yokohama, before burning themselves out (see figure 8-3, bottom).

Driven from ruined homes, desperate people tried to outrun the spreading fires. Those who managed to escape congregated in open places such as Yokohama Park or else swam to ships and barges moored in the rivers or in the harbor. Yokohama Park was mostly submerged beneath as much as a meter of water from broken mains and surfacing groundwater. It was a vast swamp crowded with tens of thousands of refugees standing waist-deep in muddy water.

A passenger on a ship moored in the harbor that September morning recorded his observations of the catastrophe and later published them anonymously in the *Kobe Chronicle,* as follows:

> The first shock lasted possibly a full minute but it seemed like five. The decks . . . were vibrating in a most alarming manner. . . .
>
> About a minute following this lengthy shock, a yellow cloud—very thin at first but growing in size every second—rose from the land; from behind the houses, the docks, the hills beyond. This cloud formed a continuous strip all around the bay, growing in size and deepening in color, travelling at great speed toward the north. This cloud was doubtless caused by the dust from collapsing buildings . . . and soon filled the atmosphere. . . .
>
> Fires ashore assumed huge proportions, fanned by the southerly gale. Sampans and large cargo lighters . . . took fire, broke from their moorings and were carried by the wind and sea across the harbour. There were many of these boat-furnaces travelling rapidly, burning fiercely, making straight for ships at anchor.[4]

All in all, about eighteen thousand buildings in Yokohama collapsed during the earthquake, and more than fifty-five thousand were consumed by fire. It has been estimated that more than 23,400 people died. Many thousands were injured, and most of the survivors were homeless. Their immediate need for food was alleviated by quantities of rice and other provisions brought ashore from ships that survived in the harbor. Warships of the Japanese Navy soon arrived with more food and other supplies.

• • •

Damage from earthquake and fire was widespread in the region of the Kanto plain. In the manufacturing city of Kawasaki, between Tokyo and Yokohama, many factory buildings were demolished with great loss of life. On the Miura peninsula between Tokyo and Sagami bays the port city of Yokosuka, Japan's chief naval base, was largely destroyed. Smaller cities and towns also suffered greatly. In Odawara, on the northwest shore of Sagami Bay, only about 260 of the city's original 5,000 buildings remained standing after the quake. A short distance to the south the village of Nebukawa, in its entirety, was pushed into the sea by a mudflow that coursed down the gorge of the Nebukawa River. Moments earlier a passenger train had pulled into the Nebukawa station. The station, the railroad tracks, the train, and two hundred passengers were swept away.

Many towns and villages in the mountains west of Sagami Bay were reduced to ruins, and large areas of forest were destroyed. Landslides temporarily dammed rivers in many places. When the dams gave way, rampaging streams carried fallen trees and other debris downstream. Bridges were destroyed, farms flooded, and towns devastated.

Seismological stations around the world detected the Kanto earthquake within minutes of the first tremors. Seismologists immediately knew there had been a major event, probably in Japan, but more than that they could not know because there was no communication with that country. The first effort to send news of the disaster to the outside world was made by the Yokohama chief of police using the radio aboard a freighter, the *Korea Maru,* in Yokohama harbor. An English translation reads as follows:

> Today at noon a great earthquake occurred and was immediately followed by a conflagration which has changed the whole city into a sea of fire, causing countless casualties. All facilities of traffic have been destroyed and communications cut off. We have neither water nor food. For God's sake send relief at once.[5]

A radio station in a city about 240 kilometers northeast of Tokyo picked up the message, and an operator there broadcast the following, in English:

> Conflagration subsequent to severe earthquake at Yokohama at noon today. Whole city . . . ablaze with numerous casualties.[6]

That message, received by a radio station in San Francisco at 6:20 AM on September 1, alerted the rest of the world to the Kanto Dai-shinsai, the Great Kanto Earthquake Disaster.

Meanwhile, during the evening of September 1 (local time), the original message from the *Korea Maru* reached the U.S. Asiatic Fleet, which was stationed at Dairen (now Dalian), Manchuria. Admiral Edwin Anderson immediately began loading relief supplies and also summoned other U.S. ships from Asiatic ports as far away as Manila. Less than forty-eight hours later the first American vessels steamed into Yokohama harbor. They stayed for ten days as U.S. Marines went ashore to help clear away debris, construct temporary docks, and erect tents to shelter refugees. Other ships sailed on up Tokyo Bay to relieve the capital city.

It was not long before relief ships from Britain, France, and Italy arrived in Japanese waters, and contributions of money, food, clothing, blankets, and timber for rebuilding flowed in from many countries of the world. Ships from many nations, including Japan, provided free transportation for refugees who wanted to leave the stricken areas.

In the United States President Calvin Coolidge called for contributions by American cities to a Red Cross relief fund. Most gave generously—and San Francisco, to which the Japanese people had contributed a large sum after the earthquake of 1906, raised some $500,000. In response to American aid, Prime Minister Yamamoto is quoted as having said:

> The genuine friendship of the United States government and people demonstrated towards us at the time of our sorrow and distress will, I am firmly convinced, increase the intimacy of the two peoples and eventually further strengthen the links of the world's peace.[7]

An ironic message, given that Japan and America were at war only eighteen years later—and Tokyo, largely a maze of rebuilt wooden houses, was destroyed again in 1945 by firebombing.

• • •

Most victims of the Kanto earthquake devoted their energies to repairing their lives in the days following the disaster, but others looked for someone to blame for their misfortune. It is not unusual for survivors of such an event to seek scapegoats. Rumors swept through the refugee camps. Korean immigrants, it was said, had started the fires and were even poisoning the scarce water supplies. Korea had become a protectorate of Japan in 1905, and Japan annexed the country in 1910. A land-reform law deprived many Korean people of their farms. Dispossessed farmers emigrated to Japan in large numbers to find work as unskilled laborers. Most of them lived in the slums of Tokyo or Yokohama, and virtually all of them were now among the homeless. Koreans traditionally had been looked down upon by native Japanese, and now they became ready targets for rumor mills.

Many Koreans did not speak Japanese, or did so with a noticeable accent. Gangs of vigilantes sought them out, interrogated them, and, if not satisfied with their answers, summarily executed them. A number of Japanese, mistaken for Koreans, are thought to have been killed as well. The police, exhausted and preoccupied with other aspects of the disaster, were unable to control the vigilantes. Estimates of the number of their victims range from several hundred to several thousand.

The atrocities abated only after Prime Minister Yamamoto's government published a warning and the Japanese Army restored order in Tokyo. Ostensibly for protection, thousands of Koreans were sent to a camp in the neighboring prefecture of Chiba. But killings with political overtones continued as the secret police, or Kempeitai, sought out and murdered a number of people they believed to be opposed to the government.

In contrast to the reign of terror conducted by vigilantes and the Kempeitai, the great majority of Tokyo's citizens demonstrated exemplary courage and discipline in response to the catastrophe. There was little panic, looting was rare, and the crowds of refugees in the city's parks remained calm.

There can be little doubt that the Kanto Dai-shinsai was among the most devastating natural catastrophes in history. Possibly 100,000 people were killed outright, more than 100,000 were injured, and well over 40,000 were listed as missing. Assuming that the more seriously injured and most of the missing died, the death toll might well have exceeded 150,000. More people have been killed in other earthquakes. One that struck Edo in 1703 is thought to have killed 200,000, and in 1737 an estimated 300,000 died in India when a quake devastated the area around Calcutta. But no other natural disaster has approached the devastation caused by quake-induced fires in Tokyo and Yokohama. Government buildings, offices, banks, schools, libraries, university buildings, temples, shrines, and factories were destroyed. In fact, the entire Kanto region lost most of its infrastructure. No other natural event in historical time has caused so much damage over so wide an area.

Moreover, Japan lost irreplaceable collections of art, historical documents, books, family heirlooms, and other treasures. One art collection in Tokyo contained thirty-five thousand prints and paintings, among them original works by such noted artists as Utamaro, Sharaku, and Hokusai. The library of the Imperial University contained some seven hundred thousand volumes. All were lost. And almost a million books were destroyed in government libraries.

• • •

In 1978 the Japanese government enacted legislation mandating comprehensive earthquake countermeasures. Evacuation routes have been established in threatened areas, and bridges, harbor facilities, and public buildings have been reinforced. Each year on September 1, called Disaster Preparedness Day in commemoration of the Kanto Dai-shinsai, disaster exercises and training events are conducted throughout Japan. Earthquake drills are held regularly in schools and offices. In Tokyo, emergency supplies including food and blankets are stored at strategic locations in all parts of the city. Streets leading to more than a hundred parks and other open areas are clearly marked.

Since 1923 Japanese scientists have created one of the most sophisticated systems in the world for earthquake prediction. They periodically measure crustal deformation, changes in the water table, and other phenomena that might warn of impending seismic activity. They monitor seismographs around the clock. Early on January 17, 1995, however, all those efforts went for naught when, with no clear warning, an earthquake of magnitude 6.9 struck southeastern Honshu. It devastated the city of Kobe, killed 4,570 people, caused a great many fires, and destroyed many buildings.

Despite efforts by seismologists around the world, the goal of reliable earthquake prediction remains elusive.

THE KAMAKURA EARTHQUAKE OF 1257 AND THE RISE OF THE LOTUS SECT

Kamakura, a city on the northwestern shore of Japan's Miura peninsula, was the capital of Japan in 1257 and the site of a palace owned by the shogun. Though the city was often laid waste by fire and sword in ancient wars, the greatest threats to its citizens have been earthquakes and the resulting destructive sea waves called tsunamis. In 1257 a powerful quake devastated Kamakura and led to famine, plague, and social unrest in the entire region. Graffiti on a wall of the old imperial palace in Kyoto attest to that fearful time:

> At the New Year, ill omens.
> In the land, disasters.
> In the capital, soldiers.
> In the palace, favoritism.
> In the provinces, famine.
> In the shrines, conflagrations.
> In the riverbed, skeletons.[1]

Priests of religious sects, profiting from the general panic, increased their holdings of land and other property and widened their political influence. Government officials were losing control.

People sought consolation in their religions. Yet neither the priests nor the teachings of the Buddhist *nembutsu* establishment, then dominant in the region, provided needed spiritual support. But in Kamakura a political and religious reformer named Nichiren (1222–1282) was teaching the Lotus Sutra, a Buddhist doctrine based on adoration, law, and morality. The social chaos following the 1257 earthquake provided fertile ground for Nichiren's Lotus Sect to take root.

Nichiren regarded all other Buddhist doctrines as heretical and believed they should be suppressed. According to G. B. Sansom, author of *Japan, a Short Cultural History*, his ultimate goal was to found a universal church with its Holy See in Japan.[2]

Although Nichiren's teachings were popular, his attacks on the Buddhist establishment and its powerful leaders led to religious and government persecution. There were attempts on his life. He was imprisoned and even exiled for a time. Yet his faith in his mission remained unshaken, and his followers grew in number.

In 1260 Nichiren, in a treatise titled *Rissho Ankoku-ron* (On the Establishment of Righteousness and the Safety of the Country), predicted a foreign invasion and civil wars. Eight years later emissaries of the Mongol emperor Kublai Khan arrived at the Kyoto court, demanding fealty and threatening invasion. Nichiren's growing influence and the accuracy of his prediction led government authorities to seek his advice. He replied that a Mongol invasion could be averted only if the entire nation adopted his religion. Japanese leaders, however, decided to rely instead on their samurai warriors. Nichiren left Kamakura to spend his remaining years as a hermit in the mountains.

But ultimately Nichiren's predictions came true. The Mongols attacked twice before his death in 1282. They were repulsed only with the help of bad weather and typhoons. The social evils against which Nichiren had preached spread throughout the country. The central authority of Japan collapsed, and civil wars followed. The Japanese people would not know peace for many years. Nichiren's Lotus Sect flowered, however, and today it remains an important part of Japan's religious establishment.

And nature continued to batter Kamakura. Tsunamis generated by offshore earthquakes virtually destroyed the city in 1369 and again in 1494. Kamakura has since been rebuilt, but all that remains of its former glory is a 17-meter-high bronze statue of Buddha in the ruins of the shogun's palace. In the late 1800s an English poet, Mary McNeill Scott, penned an eloquent eulogy:

What do I dream of? Ah! The glories gone;
    Once, all before me, 'twixt the sea and me
Lay a fair city—rose a Shôgun's home.
    Fair Kamakura, ruled by him and me.
Jealous the Sea-God! In one mighty wave
    Swelled his proud heart, the waters rose apace—

Rose and swept inward; at my forehead drave,
Crested the hill tops for a moment's space.
Only one moment. From the insulted land
Swift it receded. Ah! The wreck it bore!
Oh! The fair city built upon the sand.
Oh! The fair city, seen no more—no more.[3]

9 • Peru in 1970: Chaos in the Andes

This is a cosmic terror, an instant danger, the universe caving in and crumbling away. And, meanwhile, the earth lets out a muffled sound of thunder, in a voice no one knew it had. . . . And we are left alone with our dead, with all the dead, not knowing how we happen to be still alive.

Pablo Neruda, *Memoirs*

IT WAS THE WORST natural disaster in the history of the Western Hemisphere. On May 31, 1970, at 3:23 in the afternoon, a massive earthquake struck Peru. With a magnitude of 7.8, it was felt throughout the country—but it was in the department of Ancash, along the coast in central Peru, that the quake was most catastrophic. Entire cities, towns, and villages were destroyed, and some 76,000 people died. Another 140,000 were injured, and as many as 800,000 were left without homes. It has been estimated that 160,000 buildings were ruined. The cataclysm destroyed roads, railroads, bridges, businesses, schools, and government facilities. Water, sewerage, telephone, and electrical systems were put out of operation. All this because of an earthquake that lasted less than a minute.

The department of Ancash, with an area of more than 40,000 square kilometers, comprises lowlands along the Pacific coast and, in the interior, mountainous terrain of the Andes cordillera (see figure 9-1). From the lowlands, which are mostly desert, the land rises eastward to form two northwest-trending mountain ranges, the Cordillera Negra (Black

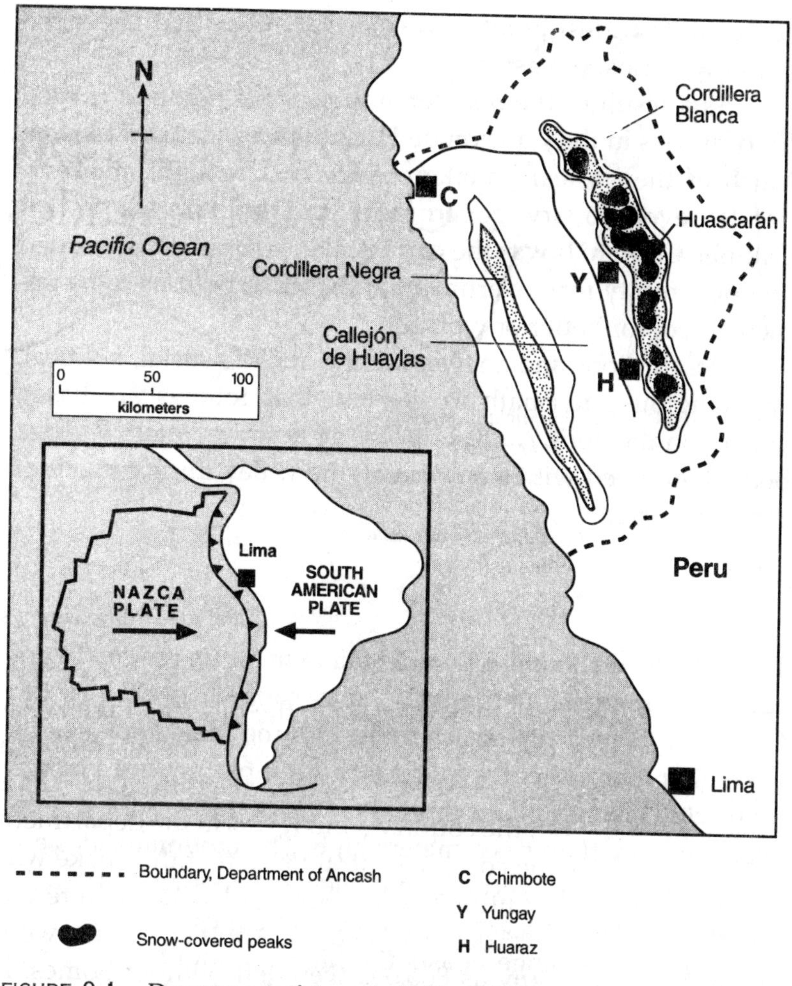

FIGURE 9-1. Department of Ancash, in Peru. The Rio Santa flows northward through the valley known as the Callejón de Huaylas, between the Cordillera Blanca on the east and the Cordillera Negra along the coast. The 1970 earthquake devastated the entire valley.

Mountains) and, farther east, the Cordillera Blanca (White Mountains). Between the Negra and Blanca ranges lies a fertile valley called the Callejón de Huaylas, about 200 kilometers long, through which flows a river named the Rio Santa. The valley is narrow (*callejón* means "corridor"), only 8 kilometers across at its widest point. It was in that valley that the earthquake was most devastating.

As a result of the disaster, a way of life that had existed for centuries in the Callejón de Huaylas was changed forever. Much of the postearthquake change was brought about by Peru's revolutionary government and by reforms in the Catholic Church. It was the earthquake, however, that created an opportunity for government and church policies to be implemented, for better or worse.

Descriptions and analyses of the quake's social, political, and religious aftermath in the text that follows are based largely on the book *No Bells to Toll* by anthropologist Barbara Bode, who lived with survivors in the valley during much of 1971 and 1972.

• • •

The Callejón de Huaylas is widely known for its beauty. To the east, the rugged, perpetually snowcapped peaks of the Cordillera Blanca rise majestically into the blue Andean sky. Far higher than either the Rockies or the Alps, they are a mecca for world-class mountain climbers. At least thirty of the mountains are more than 5,000 meters high. The mountainsides are steep, some nearly vertical, and their glaciers are extremely unstable. Avalanches are common in the Callejón.

The Blanca range boasts the highest mountain in Peru, named Huascarán. Located in the north-central part of the range, it has two peaks, Huascarán Norte, with an elevation of 6,667 meters, and Huascarán Sud, at 6,770 meters. The southern summit (Huascarán Sud) soars more than 4,000 meters above the valley floor. To the west the Cordillera Negra, with a maximum elevation of about 5,000 meters, is lower and not permanently snowcapped, therefore less spectacular, but an imposing range nonetheless.

The Rio Santa flows down the beautiful valley between those mountain ranges, from Conococha Lake in the south, at an elevation of about 4,600 meters, to the town of Huallanca in the north, at 1,400 meters. There it enters a narrow gorge, the Canyon del Pato, and turns west, plunging to the coastal lowlands and emptying into the Pacific Ocean near the city of Chimbote. In the Callejón de Huaylas the river is fed by many tributaries that carry glacial meltwater from the Cordillera Blanca.

Lush farmland, irrigated by water from snowfields in the mountains, extends the length of the Callejón. Even the steep slopes leading up to the mountain ranges support agriculture and provide grazing land for sheep. Valley crops include corn, wheat, barley, and alfalfa, as well as potatoes, which are native to the Andes. The area is near enough to the equator so that palm trees grow in the valley.

Early natives of the Callejón were conquered by the Incas in the late fifteenth century, and only about seventy years later the Incas, in turn, were defeated by Spanish conquistadores. To this day most of the valley's inhabitants speak both Spanish and Quechua, the ancient Inca tongue. Native and Spanish populations have intermarried over the years, and many people in the Callejón today are *mestizo,* of mixed blood. The mestizos traditionally have lived in towns along the Rio Santa and farmed the fertile bottomlands, some owning large estates, or haciendas, while the nearly pure-blooded descendants of the Incas, who resemble their ancestors in appearance, manner, and dress, have been relegated to more marginal lands. These peasants, or *campesinos,* live in villages along the Santa's tributaries and in hamlets high up on the steep mountain flanks. This ethnic stratification has extended, historically, to overt social, economic, and political discrimination in the Callejón.

In the past, the wealthiest town mestizos lived off of surpluses produced on their haciendas by campesino workers, or they operated businesses in the towns. They were owners and managers, dominating the Callejón's economic, political, religious, and social affairs. The campesinos labored on the haciendas, eked out a living farming their own small plots, or *chacras*, on the mountainsides, or worked as servants or manual laborers in the towns. They were expected to defer to mestizos in social or business contacts and to contribute their labor to construction projects in the towns. Nevertheless, the campesinos regularly came down into the towns to sell produce in the open markets, to socialize in cafés, and, on Sunday, to attend Mass in the Catholic Church—where they were expected to sit in the back.

Peruvian General Juan Velasco Alvarado staged a coup d'état in October 1968 and became the country's president. Unlike most military rulers in South America, who traditionally have favored a ruling oligarchy, Velasco Alvarado sought political, economic, and social reforms designed to integrate the mountain campesinos into the broader culture of the nation. His government passed a sweeping agrarian-reform bill calling for basic changes in ideology.

Also during the 1960s the Catholic Church was launching a reform movement inaugurated by Pope John XXIII and the church council known as Vatican II. In Latin America this movement promulgated a new "liberation theology" aimed at improving the lot of oppressed peoples. In 1968 a conference of bishops in Medellín, Colombia, urged radical changes in Latin American society.

Changes resulting from these converging movements had already begun to seep into the Callejón before the earthquake of 1970. Anticipating the government's reform movement, some landowners had begun subdividing their haciendas and selling parcels to the campesinos who worked them. Catholic masses were being said in Spanish and Quechua instead of Latin. Some priests were prohibiting native *costumbres*, festivities traditionally held on Catholic feast days that combined pagan customs dating from the pre-Inca times with processions in which statues of particularly venerated Catholic saints were carried through the streets. The earthquake provided a cruel catalyst for accelerating both political revolution and ecclesiastical change.

The great Andean cordillera owes its structure to forces generated by the collision of the Nazca and South American tectonic plates, as shown in figure 9-1, inset. The Nazca plate, which underlies the Pacific Ocean off the west coast of South America, is moving eastward at about 5 centimeters a year and is sliding beneath the South American plate, which is moving in the opposite direction at 3 centimeters a year. This differential movement, a shortening of the earth's crust by more than 8 centimeters a year, has led to the uplift of the Andes and has created great stresses in the crust. It is the release of those stresses from time to time that causes earthquakes in the region. On average, a strong earthquake shakes Peru once a decade. The city of Lima alone has experienced more than twenty damaging quakes since 1552. The nation's capital, Lima was virtually destroyed in 1746, and damage was especially severe in 1578, 1655, 1687, and 1974.

The American author Thornton Wilder, in his novel *The Bridge of San Luis Rey*, somewhat hyperbolically, but picturesquely, describes the results of stress release beneath the country and offshore:

> In that country those catastrophes which lawyers shockingly call the "acts of God" were more than usually frequent. Tidal waves were continually washing away cities; earthquakes arrived every week and towers fell upon good men and women all the time.[1]

What Wilder failed to mention were avalanches and landslides, which frequently result from earthquakes in Peru. In the Callejón de Huaylas they have been triggered not only by earthquakes but also by chunks of ice and hard-packed snow that break away from the high peaks and plummet down onto steeply sloping, unstable glaciers.

In 1725 an avalanche from Huandoy, the next mountain

north of Huascarán, roared down a narrow gorge and buried the town of Ancash. (The department of Ancash is named for a battle fought nearby in 1839.) The avalanche broke the natural dam of a glacial lake high in the gorge, and an enormous volume of water, carrying with it mud, boulders, and sizable pieces of glacial ice, inundated the town and killed fifteen hundred people. The town was never rebuilt.

A similar phenomenon in 1941 destroyed part of the city of Huaraz, near the southern end of the Callejón. An enormous chunk of ice plunged into a glacial lake high above the city. The resulting wave destroyed the lake's natural dam and carried a mass of rock and mud down a steep canyon into Huaraz, killing some five thousand people.

Another avalanche in 1962 destroyed most of the town of Ranrahirca, about 40 kilometers north of Huaraz, near the city of Yungay. An immense cornice of wind-packed snow at the summit of Huascarán Norte broke loose, dropped hundreds of meters down the mountain's sheer western face onto an unstable glacier, and triggered an avalanche that sent an estimated 3 million tons of ice and snow thundering down a narrow canyon into the town. Scouring the canyon, the avalanche picked up mud, rocks, and other debris and buried all but a small part of Ranrahirca. (The town's name means "hill of many stones," no doubt referring to deposits of earlier avalanches.) Some four thousand people lost their lives. In the June 1962 issue of *National Geographic* magazine, author Bart McDowell prophetically wrote, "No one knows when the mountain will again conjure the fatal formula that sends ice and snow crashing into the valley. Mighty Huascarán . . . keeps counsel only with itself."[2]

Only eight years later the great earthquake of 1970 shook all of Peru. Its epicenter was in the Pacific Ocean some 25 kilometers west of Ancash. Its point of origin, or focus, was 50 kilometers beneath the surface of the ocean. As indicated by the distribution of aftershocks, the fault ripped southward in a wide zone 145 kilometers long. Seismographs in North America recorded at least thirty-seven aftershocks with magnitudes ranging from 4 to 6.3, and there were hundreds of tremors with lower magnitudes.

Fortunately for Peru's coastal cities, and also for Hawaii, the rupture did not extend upward to the seafloor. Thus there was no seafloor movement to trigger the giant sea waves called tsunamis. In May 1960, however, part of the Nazca plate was thrust beneath the South American plate, causing an earthquake with a magnitude of 8.5. Seafloor faulting created tsunamis that sped across the Pacific and caused great damage in the city of Hilo, Hawaii (see sidebar).

Witnesses reported that the 1970 earthquake began without warning. It was felt at first as a gentle swaying motion, which lasted only a few seconds. Then a period of violent shaking lasted about 45 seconds. The area of structural damage was vast, greater than 150,000 square kilometers, and it extended at least 145 kilometers inland. The coastal zone absorbed most of the shaking, and Chimbote was largely destroyed. By far the greatest damage, however, was in the Callejón de Huaylas. Although the Callejón was 130 kilometers east of the epicenter, the unconsolidated sediments in the valley amplified the seismic waves.

That Sunday afternoon, May 31, 1970, the people of the Callejón were busily engaged in ordinary weekend affairs—traveling between towns to visit relatives and friends, listening to radio broadcasts of a world-championship soccer game in Mexico City, buying and selling in town markets, or perhaps enjoying a late lunch. On Huascarán Norte there was a team of mountain climbers from Czechoslovakia. Japanese climbers were high up on a nearby peak.

At 3:23 PM the ground started shaking, mildly at first, then violently. The Japanese mountaineers saw a gigantic mass of ice and rock break loose from the top of Huascarán Norte and fall to the unstable, steeply sloping glacier below, and they photographed the beginning of an avalanche thought to have been as much as 1,000 meters wide. Horrified, they watched the lethal mass annihilate their Czechoslovakian colleagues in their base camp on the slopes of Huascarán far below.

With an initial volume of perhaps 25 million cubic meters, the avalanche hurtled down the steep mountainside at velocities thought to have been as high as 250 kilometers an hour. It picked up great quantities of material from old glacial moraines and stream valleys, including boulders weighing thousands of tons. Friction created by the speeding mass generated enough heat to melt most of the ice and snow, creating a seething torrent, up to 30 meters deep, of mud, rocks, and large chunks of ice. Funneling into a river canyon, the avalanche ricocheted back and forth with changes in the canyon's direction, dropping more than 4,000 meters within a distance of some 16 kilometers (see figure 9-2). Thousands of boulders were tossed from one wall of the canyon to the other. With an unearthly roar, the churning mass sped down into the Callejón, sweeping away peasant hamlets, trees, farm animals, and crops. As many as eighteen hundred people perished before the avalanche had even reached the valley floor.

The juggernaut had such momentum that it crossed the Rio Santa and climbed the foothills of the Cordillera Negra to a height of more than 75 meters above the valley floor, depositing an enormous chunk of glacial ice in the plaza of a village named Matacoto. It dammed the Rio Santa, causing a flood upstream from the dam, then surged down the riverbed, carrying rocks, debris, and hundreds of human bodies all the way to Huallanca at the north end of the Callejón. There, it choked the Canyon del Pato, destroyed a rail line that provided the only exit from that end of the valley, and killed the passengers on a train in the canyon.

As the avalanche roared down from Huascarán, it split into two lobes at a high hill called Shacsha, between Ranrahirca and Yungay. In 1962 the hill had spared Yungay from the avalanche that devastated Ranrahirca. This time Shacsha was overwhelmed, and both towns were buried in seconds,

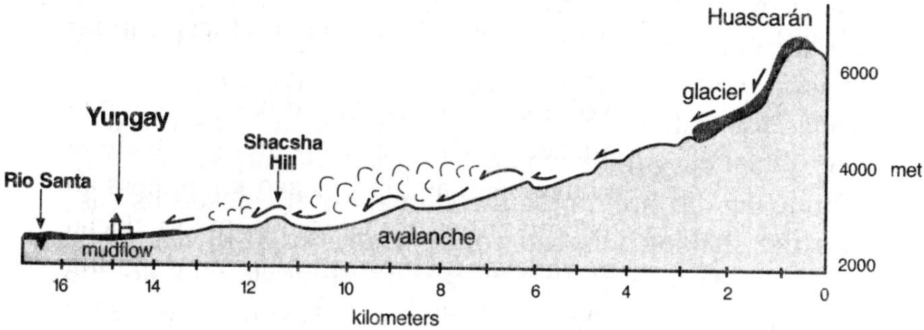

FIGURE 9-2. Schematic cross section along the southwestern slope of Huascarán, showing the avalanche that buried Yungay.

beneath as much as 60 meters of rock- and ice-studded mud. Barely four minutes had elapsed since the first earthquake shocks.

In Ranrahirca, virtually all who had survived the earlier avalanche—some eighteen hundred people—were killed instantly. In Yungay, crowded with campesinos, tourists, and other Sunday visitors, it has been estimated that more than eighteen thousand people lay buried beneath massive layers of mud. Including mountain hamlets in the path of the avalanche, the total number killed probably approached twenty-five thousand. The few stunned survivors saw only the tops of four palm trees above about 20 meters of gray-black ooze that covered the city center. In some low-lying areas the mud was as much as 60 meters deep. An accurate count of survivors and victims was impossible because of the horror and confusion that followed the event.

The capital of one of sixteen provinces of the department of Ancash, Yungay had been noted for the loveliness of its setting in the Callejón. Located in the north-central part of the valley, it had offered a magnificent view of towering, snow-capped Huascarán. The city, in fact, had proudly borne the nickname Hermosura (Beauty). Now it was a wasteland. All that remained of the main part of Yungay was four palm trees in the city center and, somewhat farther east, the top of a prehistoric mound that served as Yungay's cemetery. The mound was surmounted by a colossal concrete statue of Christ, facing Huascarán with arms upraised. Ironically, the Yungaínos had erected the statue as an offering of thanks for being spared in 1962, when the earlier avalanche buried Ranrahirca. The 1970 earthquake did not topple the statue, but it cracked its base. And the shaking released coffins from burial niches in the cemetery. Many broke open to reveal their grisly contents. The earthquake had thus buried the living and exhumed the dead.

Nevertheless, at least three hundred Yungaínos still lived. A group of children, now orphans, had been attending a circus in a soccer field at the edge of the city, barely out of harm's way. And a few people had escaped the avalanche because they happened to be in relatively high locations. One was an area called Aura, an extension of Shacsha hill. Another was the northeast corner of Yungay, called Cochawaín. The third was the cemetery mound, to the top of which ninety-two terrified people had somehow clambered as the avalanche bore down upon them. Isolated there, as on an island, they spent a cold night. Some, having been caught in the torrent of viscous mud but able to struggle free, had had their clothes ripped from their bodies and had donned clothing taken from dislodged corpses. The next day the traumatized survivors made their way to Cochawaín, using a walkway made of coffin lids they laid over the deep mud and tree trunks extended from Cochawaín by survivors there.

A Peruvian geophysicist named Mateo Casaverde happened to be driving through Yungay when the catastrophe struck. He wrote the following account:

> As we drove past the cemetery the car began to shake. . . . I saw several homes as well as a small bridge . . . collapse. . . . After about one-half to three-quarters of a minute when the . . . shaking began to subside . . . I heard a great roar coming from Huascarán. . . . It looked as though a large mass of rock and ice was breaking loose from the north peak. My immediate reac-

> tion was to run for the high ground of Cemetery Hill, situated about 150 to 200 [meters] away. . . .
>
> The crest of the wave had a curl, like a huge breaker coming in from the ocean. I estimated the wave to be at least 80 [meters] high. . . . There was a continuous loud roar and rumble. I reached the upper level of the cemetery near the top just as the debris flow struck the base of the hill and I was probably only 10 seconds ahead of it. . . .
>
> At about the same time, I saw a man just a few meters down the hill who was carrying two small children. . . . The debris flow caught him and he threw the two children towards the hill-top . . . to safety, although the debris flow swept him down the valley, never to be seen again.[3]

As the days passed, the mud dried and subsided around scattered boulders, the four palm trees, and mutilated human corpses. It formed a ghastly gray-white surface covering more than 20 square kilometers. Bordering the Rio Santo, it became known as the *playa*—the "beach." Human remains that could be found were buried in mass graves, or burned. Thousands more remained beneath the mud. Later, grief-stricken survivors placed hundreds of small wooden crosses on the playa, marking places where they thought their loved ones might have been when the avalanche buried them. Eventually the entire area of the mudslide was declared *campo santo*, holy ground.

While Yungay was destroyed by the earthquake-triggered avalanche, other cities and towns in the Callejón fell victim to the quake itself. About 50 kilometers south of Yungay, the city of Huaraz suffered more than most. Possibly as many as twenty thousand people were killed, buried beneath the rubble of fallen buildings. Virtually the entire city center, mostly old adobe-brick buildings, collapsed during the brief moments of the quake. There was so much dust in the air that the few survivors could barely see, and they had difficulty breathing. All that was left of central Huaraz was a vast, deep

FIGURE 9-3. The dome of the cathedral of Huaraz—all that remained of that city after the 1970 catastrophe. (Courtesy of Barbara Bode, author of *No Bells to Toll*.)

field of rubble, punctuated here and there with warped tin roof panels, splintered wooden beams, and, most poignantly, the remains of the city's cathedral, shown in figure 9-3.

An especially poignant tragedy in Huaraz was the death of some four hundred children at the Santa Elena convent school, where they were honoring the birthday of the school's director. With the first mild tremors of the earthquake, the mother superior, in an effort to forestall panic, told everyone to remain quiet—and then she locked the doors. Moments later, when the serious shaking began, no one could escape. The building collapsed on top of them. Among the very few people rescued from the rubble was a poet and novelist named Marcos Yauri Montero, who later wrote:

> A thick mist veiled the air, hiding the sky and the mountains. . . . In front was Santa Elena, converted into a column of rubble,

> from which the bodies of children didn't stop coming. The world was empty. . . . We had died a thousand times. We were all dead.[4]

The tragedy of the Callejón led some of the deeply religious valley people to question the existence of a benevolent God. In her book *No Bells to Toll*, Barbara Bode wrote:

> A few survivors mused ironically on the whereabouts of God that Sunday. Audaciously, Humberto de Jesús wrote: "Tell me, Lord, what were you doing on May 31, 1970, at 3:24 in the afternoon? Perhaps, the answer is that God rests on Sundays and for that reason he didn't realize the earth was trembling. Trembling like a wounded animal that curls up its back, trying not to let death's grin show."

The death of innocent children in the convent school was especially difficult for people to comprehend. Again from Bode:

> In their reflections, people would recall the circus in Yungay, where indeed many children were spared from the avalanche. But then, how might that be reconciled with what happened in Huaraz where as many as 400 children attending festivities in a convent school perished?[5]

Clouds of dust rose into the air not only above the ruins of Huaraz but over the entire 200 kilometers of the Callejón. Within minutes after the earthquake the dust rose to an altitude of more than 5,000 meters in places, obscuring the entire valley. Temperatures dropped almost to freezing. Telephone lines were down. Landslides had buried roads. People in the isolated valley were unable to communicate with the rest of the country. In the ruins of towns and on hillsides where they had taken refuge, frightened people huddled together, building bonfires for warmth. For the first few days, survival was the only matter of importance. Food was scarce, as was clean water because the streams ran muddy. For shelter, homeless survivors made lean-tos from pieces of rubble, or they built primitive huts of cornstalks.

The first news of the disaster reached the outside world from shortwave radio operators in the valley. Officials in Lima were stunned when they received the news, refusing at first to believe the extent of the catastrophe. They sent air-force planes to investigate, but their crews could see nothing on the ground because of the vast clouds of dust. Finally on Tuesday, June 2, the first helicopter was able to penetrate the dust and land near the town of Caraz, a few kilometers north of Yungay.

Four days after the earthquake, the Peruvian air force began dropping packages of food, blankets, and medical supplies in the Callejón. The airport at Caraz had been buried by debris from Huascarán, and it took well over a week to prepare a landing strip at Anta, a small town halfway between Yungay and Huaraz. At last, large quantities of supplies could be flown in, and injured people could be evacuated to hospitals in coastal cities. The disaster overwhelmed the resources of Peru, but eventually help arrived from some seventy nations.

Most of the aid went to cities and towns along the Rio Santa. Many peasant communities in the highlands did not receive aid for months. Some received none at all. Campesinos went down into the valley seeking aid, and some looted the ruins after dark. Others, however, brought food and gave it to survivors in the valley—the only food many valley people had during the days before government aid began to arrive.

Refugee camps sprang up near the ruined towns. Crude lean-tos and cornstalk huts were replaced by shacks made of straw mats, by tents provided by the government, and, eventually, by more substantial prefabricated structures. Among the largest of the camps was one called Pachulpampa, on a hill immediately north of Yungay. It was established by surviving Yungaínos, but campesinos from destroyed peasant villages near and far gravitated to the camp, swelling its population. Pachulpampa soon acquired the name Yungay Norte and eventually assumed much of the role Yungay had played as the provincial capital.

In all the camps, earthquake survivors, traumatized by their losses, lived in squalor. Shacks and tents leaked when it rained. People waited in long lines for handouts of food. They waited in rain, mud, and cold, as the seasons came and went. They waited, and waited, for the government to help them rebuild their towns, and their lives.

Indeed, General Velasco Alvarado's government had a Herculean task. The earthquake had devastated not only the Callejón but coastal areas as well. But instead of immediately launching a program of reconstruction in the valley, the government looked upon the disaster as an opportunity for speeding the process of social reform. The Callejón was a tabula rasa, a blank slate upon which to plan the new Peru. The ravaged valley was an ideal site for starting from scratch, for creating a social experiment designed to right the wrongs of generations.

Launching such an experiment required planning. Studies would have to be carried out, even while the wretched survivors lived in misery. To that end, on June 9, the government established the Commission for the Reconstruction and Rehabilitation of the Affected Zone, known by the Spanish acronym CRYRZA. The mission of CRYRZA was stated, in part, as follows:

> The revolutionary orientation of the Government and the magnitude of the disaster signify a juncture propitious for striving for . . . the transformation of the structures which reigned in the Zone before the cataclysm, accelerating . . . the process of change on which the country is bent.
>
> This objective is in perfect accord with the Revolutionary Government . . . , which has proposed to structure a more just and united society, in which privileges are excluded. . . .
>
> . . . CRYRZA considers that the politics to be followed in fulfilling its specific function most certainly do not consist in a mere physical reconstruction.[6]

The commission was given authority over all aspects of disaster recovery, from the distribution of material aid and medical help to the relocation of survivors and long-range planning for reconstruction and future development. Not surprisingly, CRYRZA's operations soon succumbed to bureaucratic conflict, error, and inefficiency. Months went by, and as 1970 drew to a close little had been done to improve the plight of the refugees.

Among the first governmental edicts after the earthquake was a moratorium on land transactions in the Callejón. And in the ruins of the towns, because it was often difficult to determine where property lines had been, people were forbidden to occupy or build upon their own land. Frustrated at the lack of progress in reconstruction, some refugees attempted to stake out their property, or even rebuild their houses. Soldiers would immediately remove the stakes or dismantle whatever construction had been started.

On the anniversary of the earthquake, May 31, 1971, CRYRZA sent bulldozers to Huaraz to remove the rubble of collapsed buildings, a belated token effort to demonstrate that the bureaucracy was doing something. The bulldozer operators ruthlessly leveled the ruins, in the process destroying buried statues of saints that had been venerated by the natives. People in the Callejón identified with their saints, just as their ancestors had identified with Inca gods. To the pious survivors, the desecration by the bulldozers was another tragedy, a sign that even their saints had been unable to survive the catastrophe that had been visited upon them.

A month after the earthquake the Peruvian government had announced a housing program that would provide temporary, prefabricated building modules for the towns of the Callejón. In Yungay Norte, the hillside refugee camp formerly known as Pachulpampa, such modules had replaced the original huts and tents. Groups of refugees, brought together by kinship, friendship, or common need, inhabited the modules.

By the fall of 1970 Yungay Norte had developed into a

town of considerable size, with stores, municipal offices, a post office, and a bustling marketplace. This business section, constructed entirely of the prefabricated modules, had grown up along a road that had been bulldozed across the avalanche scar to replace the buried valley highway along the Rio Santa. Rows of identical residential modules ascended the hillside above the business section.

Any further construction, however, was delayed by indecision about the future of the town. CRYRZA planners considered Yungay Norte a temporary camp. Because of perceived danger from future landslides, they anticipated relocating the population. The Yungaínos, on the other hand, were determined to rebuild their city where it had been, and they refused to move. In the resulting standoff, there was no permanent reconstruction.

In refugee camps throughout the Callejón, people had been living for a year in crude, temporary housing without electricity, running water, or toilet facilities. They wanted to rebuild their houses, their churches, and their towns. They wanted help in reestablishing their businesses. But CRYRZA, while accomplishing little itself, prohibited any rebuilding. Government officials wanted no construction in the towns until they had perfected their plans for a new society, a redistribution of property, and designs for new, modern cities.

In May 1972, in Huaraz, the government changed the moratorium on land transactions to outright expropriation of privately owned property. CRYRZA was going to redistribute the land equally, some 300 square meters to anyone who could afford to buy the lots. No matter how much land people had owned in the city before the disaster, they now owned nothing and would be allowed to purchase only a parcel of land equal in size to that of all others. Moreover, they were not allowed to design and build their own houses but had to take out long-term loans and buy small, uniformly designed concrete houses from the government. Thus the townspeople lost their property twice—once to the earthquake and again to officials determined to make Huaraz a showcase of the new Peru. And many people, having lost everything, could not afford to buy even the small lots that were being offered.

Meetings were held during May between CRYRZA officials and earthquake survivors to discuss the government's plans. The revolution, the officials said, would not permit a return to the "old reality." But the natives of the Callejón had a strong sense of place. They wanted to live and die where they had always lived, where their ancestors had lived, where, indeed, their dead were buried. They wanted to return to their own pieces of land, whether in the countryside or in the towns.

They questioned the small, uniform concrete houses, which were not *their* houses. Concrete was foreign to the valley. They disliked the long-term loans required for buying the houses, and the interest payments and insurance that would be required. They demanded to know where, two years after the earthquake, CRYRZA's money had gone, what accounted for the interminable delays in rebuilding. "There had to be studies," was the reply.

To the people of the Callejón, CRYRZA had become an object of bitter contempt. The survivors were angry at the way the bureaucracy controlled their lives and frustrated their efforts to rebuild their world. They resented the fact that decisions affecting their future were being made by government officials in Lima, without even consulting them. "This is not *aid*, it's a *struggle*," was the way one woman put it.[7] CRYRZA, in turn, accused the survivors of being antirevolutionary.

Meanwhile the Catholic Church was conducting its own revolution. Like government officials, church reformists saw the Callejón disaster as an opportunity to start with a clean slate. They were eager to achieve progress, and they paid little heed to the spiritual needs of the earthquake survivors. When, after a government-decreed year of mourning, the survivors wanted to resume their costumbres, the festive native customs that for generations had been part of their rites on Catholic feast days, the church prohibited those rites as being rooted in pagan idolatry.

One of those customs, of great importance to campesinos in their mountain villages, was the erecting of crosses on hilltops, where their pre-Inca ancestors had placed icons called *huacas* to protect their homes and crops from landslides, hail, and other misfortunes. Each year, during the pre-Lenten carnival in February, it was customary for the campesinos to carry their crosses down into the valley, parade them through the streets of the towns with great ceremony, take them to the churches, and have them blessed at special masses. Then the crosses would be returned to their hilltops to provide protection for another year. Disregarding the emotional significance of this custom, church reformists considered it merely a senseless pagan tradition, and they forbade it.

There were too many changes in the life of the Callejón. They came too suddenly and too fast for the people to absorb them. On top of the trauma of the earthquake and its aftermath, the revolutionary zeal of CRYRZA and the church reformists was akin to a second calamity. It exacted a high price psychologically.

As Barbara Bode wrote in her preface to *No Bells to Toll:* "The valley swarmed with ideas from external cultural systems." The changes came "too fast for survivors to preserve even an illusion of control." The people "clung tenaciously to their old ways, seeking some sense of continuity, some comfort in the commonplace, in a world suddenly turned surreal."[8] They needed to find some connection between their past, the unbearable present, and an unknown but frightening future. They needed to find meaning in what had happened to them.

The survivors asked why Yungay, Huaraz, and other towns had been destroyed while others had suffered little damage. Why was one part of a town destroyed but not another part? Why were children at a circus spared while those at a convent school were crushed to death? Why was I spared while my wife, husband, child, or friend died? In essence they were seeking a solution to the perennial mystery of whether the universe operates by chance or by design.

Many people blamed the earthquake on atomic-bomb tests being conducted by the French government, despite worldwide protest, on the Pacific atoll of Mururoa, 6,400 kilometers west of Peru. Indeed, in 1973 Peru severed diplomatic relations with France because of the nuclear tests, claiming a relationship between the repeated explosions and the frequency of Andean earthquakes, as well as contamination of the ocean and the atmosphere.

Some people put the blame on the presence of foreigners in the Callejón—tourists, Protestant missionaries from North America, the mountain climbers on Huascarán. Others thought God had punished them for their sins—but which sins? Was it because of the social and religious changes that had begun to seep into the Callejón, or because those changes had not progressed fast enough? Was it because the people had been made to abandon their costumbres, or because they had *resisted* abandoning them?

Or was the disaster perhaps caused by the centuries-long repression of campesinos by townspeople? Those who leaned toward this explanation quoted an ancient Andean myth, predating the Incas, in which a poor wanderer appears in a town and is refused succor. The wanderer turns out to be a god in disguise, and the town is destroyed as punishment. This story is not unlike the parable in Matthew 25: 41–45, often quoted by the Catholic reformists, in which the Lord castigates those who have not helped people in need:

> Depart from me, ye cursed, into everlasting fire. . . . For I was . . . hungered, and ye gave me no meat: I was thirsty, and ye gave me no drink: I was a stranger, and ye took me not in: naked, and ye clothed me not. . . .
>
> Then shall they answer him, saying Lord, when saw we thee . . . hungered, or athirst, or a stranger, or naked . . . and did not minister unto thee?

. . . Verily I say unto you, Inasmuch as ye did it not to one of the least of these, ye did it not to me.

• • •

The disaster resulted in a kind of socioeconomic leveling. A good many of the well-to-do and better-educated mestizos in the towns had been killed, while the largely uneducated campesinos on the mountainsides lost relatively few of their numbers. Moreover, most mestizos lost virtually all their property, while the campesinos lost little. Many campesinos actually gained material possessions as aid poured into the Callejón.

Life in the camps was entirely different from anything the survivors had known before. Everyone, from uneducated peasant to professional mestizo, lived together, coping with economic hardship, physical privation, and social chaos. For the first time, town mestizos had to compete with rural campesinos for basic necessities.

The social leveling created by the earthquake, along with the policies of Peru's revolutionary government, brought about a societal process called *cholification*, representing upward mobility for the masses and downward mobility for the erstwhile privileged classes. Everybody, it was said, was now a *cholo* (literally "half-breed," but as used in this context not meant to be disparaging). Eventually many previously rural cholos took advantage of subsidized government housing and moved into the rebuilt towns. Whereas, for example, old Yungay had been a bastion of the traditional elite in the Callejón, Yungay Norte was a cosmopolitan, cholo town.

Some of the former elite took a philosophical view of cholification and their loss of prestige and of material possessions. "When our things were destroyed," one woman said, "we were not interested anymore in things. Conceived inside the mother, naked, without anything, naked I shall return."[9] But others were less sanguine. They wondered why the campesinos, who never had much to start with and therefore had lost little, should gain from the disaster. As a woman from Yungay put it, "We, the real Yungaínos, have lost everything so we should get more."[10]

As reconstruction finally got under way in the Callejón there was bitterness, too, because rural campesinos, who formerly had been expected to work for town mestizos for little or no pay, now had wage-paying construction jobs and could choose whom to work for and how much to charge for their services. Their labor was no longer available on demand.

Nevertheless, survivors of all classes felt the common bond often shared by those who have experienced a disaster together. Despite their differences, they recognized the need for cooperation in rebuilding their world, changed though it would be. And the presence of unpopular CRYRZA officials and Catholic reformists in the valley tended to unite the natives of the Callejón. The differences between campesino and mestizo were less than their common differences with outsiders. Again a quote from Barbara Bode's *No Bells to Toll*: "Like the interlocking plates of the earth's crust, fates were interlocked. Private lives became related to each other through the event, and to a large extent all lives came to be oriented around it."[11]

The spirit of togetherness was perhaps best expressed in the rebirth of Yungay as a provincial capital. The residents of Yungay Norte, mestizo and former campesino alike, were determined that their city, adjacent to the original Yungay, would retain that name and would continue to play a key role in the affairs of the Callejón. They had resisted government plans to abandon the site altogether, but the officials still wanted to establish the provincial capital elsewhere. Moreover, two other places claimed the name Yungay. One was Aura, the high area near old Yungay that had survived the avalanche. The other was Tingua, a nearby village, which CRYRZA favored as the new capital.

It was in Yungay Norte, however, that most of the old city's survivors had settled. Together with the new postearthquake residents, they worked to establish schools and maintain links with nearby villages, and thus economic viability. And eventually, despite CRYRZA, they reestablished the functions of the provincial capital there. Yungay Norte prevailed, and Yungay, though quite unlike what it had been, was reborn.

Like the Yungaínos, people throughout the Callejón, despite their ordeal, were able to maintain their identity and, to a great extent, their cultural heritage. Even their costumbres eventually survived, despite the efforts of Catholic reformists.

Velasco Alvarado's social revolution, however, did not endure. A high rate of monetary inflation and severe drought during the years following the earthquake interfered with plans for agrarian reform. Many campesinos left the Callejón for coastal cities, where they inevitably gravitated to marginal lives in urban slums. And cholification did not bring the expected social advancement to many of those who moved to valley towns. Class distinctions did not disappear. Social acceptance by surviving members of the higher classes was grudging at best, and former campesinos achieved little political power. After the spurt of new construction, most found only lowly jobs in the towns and, not surprisingly, continued to occupy the lower rungs of society. "The messianic zeal of the Peruvian Revolution had faded into resignation."[12]

The French have an expression for it: *Plus ça change, plus c'est la même chose*—the more things change, the more they remain the same.

IN CHILE—TSUNAMIS, DEVASTATION, AND DARWIN

The west coast of South America is among the world's most seismically active regions. The Nazca tectonic plate, which lies just offshore beneath the Pacific Ocean, is slowly grinding its way eastward under the South American continent. The result, for Chile, which stretches more than 1,500 kilometers from the southern boundary of Peru to Cape Horn, has been innumerable earthquakes. Many have been disastrous in themselves, and many have generated enormous tsunamis that have crashed ashore and destroyed coastal towns and cities.

A strong earthquake struck central Chile on February 20, 1835, while Charles Darwin was visiting that country during the famous voyage of HMS *Beagle*. On March 5 Darwin arrived in the city of Concepción, where the quake had caused great damage. It was "the most awful yet interesting spectacle I ever beheld," he wrote. "Each house, or row of houses, [was] a heap or line of ruins."[1]

The earthquake was followed by a tsunami that devastated Concepción's port city of Talcahuano. Darwin described the tsunami in his book *Voyage of the Beagle*:

> Shortly after the shock, a great wave was seen from the distance of three or four miles [5 or 6 kilometers], approaching in the middle of the bay with a smooth outline; but along the shore it tore up cottages and trees, as it swept onwards with irresistible force. At the head of the bay it broke in a fearful line of white breakers, which rushed up to a height of 23 vertical feet [7 meters] above the highest spring-tides. . . . The first wave was followed by two others, which in their retreat carried away a vast wreck of floating objects.[2]

Darwin wrote, "It is a bitter and humiliating thing to see works, which have cost man so much time and labour, overthrown in one minute." The scientist also wrote about the geological consequences:

> The most remarkable effect of this earthquake was the permanent elevation of the land. . . . There can be no

> doubt that the land round the Bay of Concepcion was upraised two or three feet. . . . At the island of S. Maria (about thirty miles [50 kilometers] distant) the elevation was greater; . . . beds of putrid mussel-shells [were found] *still adhering to the rocks*, ten feet [3 meters] above high-water mark. . . . At Valparaiso . . . similar shells are found at the height of 1300 feet [400 meters]: it is hardly possible to doubt that this great elevation has been effected by successive small uprisings, such as that which accompanied or caused the earthquake of this year.[3]

Thirty-three years later, in August 1868, a powerful earthquake shook northern Chile and killed an estimated twenty-five thousand people. That quake was followed in 1906 by one with a magnitude estimated to have been 8.6, and another in 1939 with a magnitude of 8.3.

In 1960, at the end of May, central Chile was shaken by six major earthquakes within a ten-day period. On the twenty-second the largest, with a magnitude of 8.5, devastated Concepción, which only recently had recovered from the 1939 disaster. More than six thousand people died, and a vast part of the country, about 1,000 kilometers long, was laid waste. The coastline was elevated for 100 kilometers south of Concepción, and farther to the south some 300 kilometers of the coast subsided.

Three tsunamis ravaged the coast soon after the shock of May 22, and as the waves retreated they sucked houses, boats, and people into the sea. The first struck about fifteen minutes after the quake, with a wave 4 to 5 meters high. About an hour later the second tsunami arrived with a wave more than 8 meters high. The third wave had an estimated height of 11 meters. The tsunamis killed more than a thousand people. Caused by movement along faults in the seafloor, they spread westward across the Pacific Ocean. The waves reached Hilo, Hawaii, on May 23, about fourteen hours after the earthquake. They caused much damage and drowned 61 people. The tsunamis then sped on to Japan, where they arrived in the late afternoon, flooding coastal areas and killing 185 people. The May 22 quake released so much energy that water in the Pacific Ocean remained agitated for several days.

Chile, like Peru and Peru's neighbor Ecuador to the north, remains at the mercy of irresistible tectonic forces generated within the earth's restless crust.

10 • The 1972 Managua Earthquake: Catalyst for Revolution

Each abuse of power hastens the destruction of he who exercises it. We will go toward the sun of liberty or toward death. And if we die, our cause will continue to live.

Augusto César Sandino

NICARAGUA, THE LARGEST COUNTRY in Central America, is about the size of the state of Louisiana in the United States and in 1994 had about the same population, roughly 4.3 million. Located between Honduras and Costa Rica, Nicaragua has three physiographic regions: the Caribbean lowlands, the interior highlands, and the Pacific lowlands. Much of Nicaragua was once mantled with tropical forests, but today vast areas have been deforested. The mountainous highlands and the Caribbean lowlands are sparsely populated, but there is rich agricultural land in the Pacific lowlands, and most of Nicaragua's people live there.

Nicaragua has a long history of foreign intervention and political instability. From the arrival of Spanish conquistadores in the sixteenth century until modern times, foreign interests have generally dominated the country politically and economically. An elite minority has benefited financially from this foreign domination, but the great majority of Nicaraguans have remained impoverished. As a result there has been continual unrest, and from time to time populist leaders have emerged to lead nationalist efforts aimed at gaining control of the country's destiny.

One such leader, Augusto César Sandino (1895–1934), is Nicaragua's national hero. Sandino led a guerrilla campaign against a virtual United States occupation of Nicaragua in the 1920s and early 1930s. His forces fought U.S. Marines and the Guardia Nacional, the National Guard of Nicaragua. Pro-U.S. dictator Anastasio Somoza Garcia had Sandino assassinated in 1934, but his name lived on in the Sandinista National Liberation Front (Frente Sandinista de Liberación Nacional, or FSLN). The FSLN was founded in 1961 to protest the violence, repression, and corruption of the Somoza regime. Figure 10-1 graphically illustrates the national feeling of the time.

Support for the FSLN at first came mostly from Nicaragua's *campesinos*, poor farmworkers. The organization had little strength in the cities, hence among people who might be in a position to influence government policies, until 1972. In December of that year an earthquake destroyed much of Managua, the country's capital. Government officials embezzled international relief funds, and National Guard troops openly looted the stricken city. Many citizens who had previously tolerated the Somoza government became foes of the regime and sympathetic to the Sandinistas. As a result, the FSLN rapidly grew in strength and could expand its influence into the capital, finally toppling the Somoza regime in 1979. Thus the Managua earthquake, which lasted barely ten seconds, was a catalyst for revolution.

Nicaragua lies above a zone of tectonic-plate convergence where the Cocos plate, west of Central America, is sliding, or being subducted, northeastward beneath the Caribbean plate at a rate of about 8 centimeters a year. The zone is marked by the Middle America trench, just off the west coast of Nicaragua. The boundary between the Cocos plate and the giant Pacific plate, which underlies most of the Pacific Ocean, is the East Pacific Rise, a broad, submerged ridge that extends southward from central Mexico almost to Antarctica. Molten

FIGURE 10-1. Pro-Sandinista wall painting. (From Sheesley and Bragg, *Sandino*, 21.)

rock, or magma, erupting from rifts in the East Pacific Rise solidified over the eons to create the Cocos plate.

Subduction of the Cocos plate has lifted the westernmost part of the Caribbean plate, creating the Central American isthmus. Arching and fracturing of the earth's crust in that region created the Nicaraguan rift zone, which forms a long, shallow depression in western Nicaragua as illustrated in figure 10-2. Created by subsidence of the crustal block between boundary faults on either side, the depression extends southeastward from the Gulf of Fonseca into northern Costa Rica. It contains two large freshwater lakes, named Nicaragua and

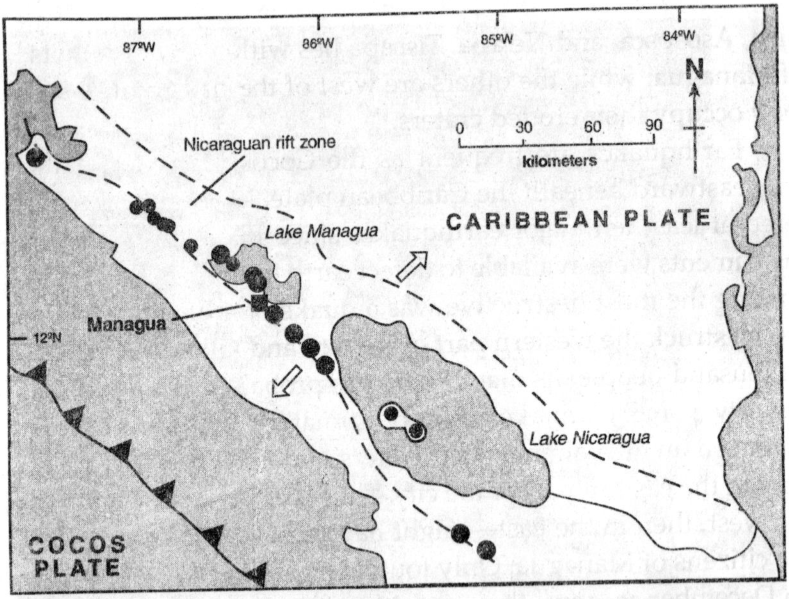

FIGURE 10-2. Plate-tectonic setting of Nicaragua, showing the Nicaraguan rift zone and principal lakes and volcanoes. The Cocos plate is being subducted beneath the Caribbean plate along the line at lower left. White arrows indicate direction of forces responsible for the origin of the rift zone.

Managua, both about 40 meters above sea level. Because sharks swim up the San Juan River from the Caribbean Sea to spawn in the lakes, some geologists believe the lakes may have originated in a Caribbean embayment that was uplifted and isolated from the sea.

As the rift zone subsided, cumulative vertical motion along the faults on either side is believed to have been as much as 1,000 meters. The depression has remained shallow, however, because its subsidence coincided with the rapid deposition of sediments and the products of volcanic eruptions. There are many volcanoes, notably Malaya and Concepción, in and near the rift zone. A chain of active volcanoes trending northwest-southeast is intersected and offset by a north-south-trending chain of four dormant volcanoes—Tiscapa,

Jiloa, Asososca, and Nejapa. Tiscapa lies within the city limits of Managua, while the others are west of the city. Small lakes now occupy their eroded craters.

Earthquakes are frequent as the Cocos plate grinds its way eastward beneath the Caribbean plate. Managua has suffered at least ten major earthquakes since 1844, the first year instruments were available to detect earth tremors in that area. Among the most destructive was a quake on March 31, 1931, which struck the western part of the city and killed more than a thousand people. Its magnitude was probably about 5.6. On January 4, 1968, a quake with an estimated magnitude of 4.6 damaged an area almost 2 kilometers wide and 10 kilometers long in the eastern part of the city. Those earthquakes—first in the west, then in the east—might have served as warnings to the citizens of Managua. Only four years after the 1968 quake, on December 23, 1972, the second most disastrous earthquake in the history of the Western Hemisphere struck the city.*

The main shock, with a magnitude of about 6.2, came at twenty-nine minutes after midnight that morning. Along with a series of strong aftershocks, it affected an area of 270 square kilometers, encompassing the entire city. Most of Managua lay in ruins, three-quarters of the city's buildings having collapsed. Fires following the quake burned out of control because water mains had broken and there was no power for electric pumps. Moreover, parts of the city were flooded by large, quake-generated waves from Lake Managua. Much of Nicaragua's industry, concentrated in Managua, was destroyed. Of the city's estimated population of 450,000, more than 9,000 were killed and more than 22,000 injured. Almost three-quarters were homeless, and half of the survivors who had been employed were jobless. Well over 200,000 people fled the city to find shelter with friends or relatives in rural areas. There, their political beliefs were influenced by campesinos who supported the FSLN. Many of those who fled

* The hemisphere's worst natural disaster was an earthquake that struck northern Peru in May 1970, only a year and a half before, and took at least 76,000 lives.

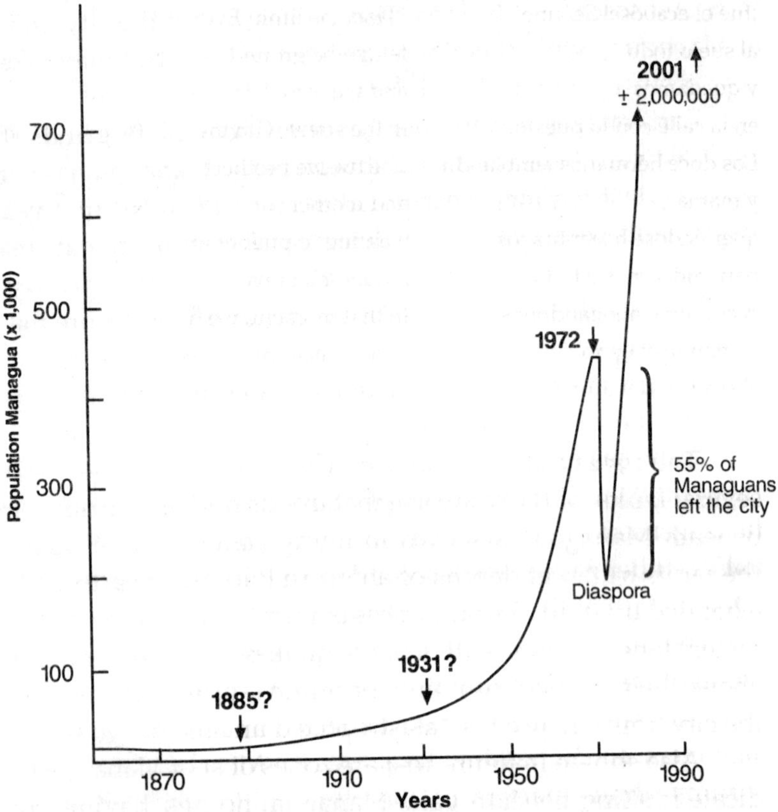

FIGURE 10-3. Changes in Managua's population, showing the abrupt decrease following the 1972 earthquake and subsequent rapid growth. Population declines following the earthquakes of 1885 and 1931 are unknown.

later returned to Managua, bringing revolutionary ideas with them. Figure 10-3 depicts that diaspora, the flow of people back to Managua, and the subsequent rapid growth in the city's population.

In a book titled *Nicaragua in Revolution: The Poets Speak* (*Nicaragua en Revolución: Los Poetas Hablan*) there are several poems about the earthquake. In one of them, "El Hermano Mayor" (The Older Brother), one P. A. Cuadra tells his sister about the disaster:

María, hermana, te cuento	Maria, my sister, I tell you
¡fué el acabóse! Se vino	it was the limit! Everything
al suelo todo	fell to the ground
y quedamos	and we were left
en la calle con lo puesto.	in the street with the clothes on our back.
Los doce hermanos temblando	The twelve brothers trembling
y mamá	and mother
queriéndose hacer brazos	wanting to put her arms
para rodearnos a todos.	around all of us.
A esa hora, ahogándonos	In that moment, we drowned
en polvo, oyendo	in dust, hearing
el estertor del mundo.[1]	the death rattle of the world.

The 1972 earthquake and its aftershocks originated along several faults, part of a swarm that trends northeast-southwest beneath Managua as shown in figure 10-4. Rupturing along the faults began at depths of about 10 kilometers and rapidly extended upward. Surface traces of four faults were 2 to 6 kilometers long. The epicenters of the quakes—the points directly above their focuses, or points of origin—were located within the city limits, hence the catastrophic damage.

Also shown in figure 10-4 are zones of aftershocks that indicate faulting beneath Lake Managua, no doubt accounting for the waves that flooded lakeside areas. The main quake appears to have been caused by the fault that extended beneath the lake. Motion was mostly horizontal, the southeastern block moving northeast relative to the southwestern block. Along the four faults that broke the surface, cumulative horizontal motion ranged from 2 to 38 centimeters.

Aftershocks continued until late January. The two largest, with magnitudes of 5.0 and 5.2, were felt minutes after the first shock on December 23. Like the main quake, they were generated at shallow depths and so caused additional damage to already weakened structures. The extensive destruction and loss of life caused by these earthquakes resulted from a combination of factors: the shallow depths of the earthquakes, the

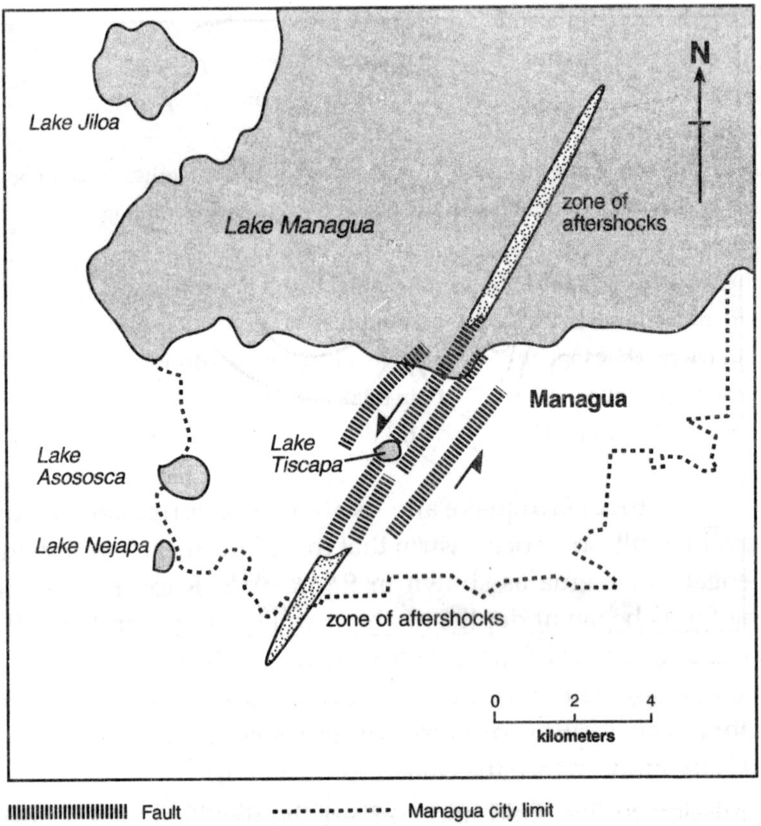

FIGURE 10-4. Faults that were activated in 1972 beneath Managua. Zones of aftershocks indicate that at least one fault extended southwestward and also northeastward beneath Lake Managua.

fact that they occurred directly beneath the city, rupturing of the ground surface, and the generally inferior construction of most of Managua's buildings. It was the damage to poorly constructed buildings that was chiefly responsible for the quake's intensity rating of VII on the Mercalli scale, as illustrated in figure 10-5.

• • •

Nicaragua's history is largely one of adversity. The Spanish conquistadores arrived on the Pacific coast in 1522, their

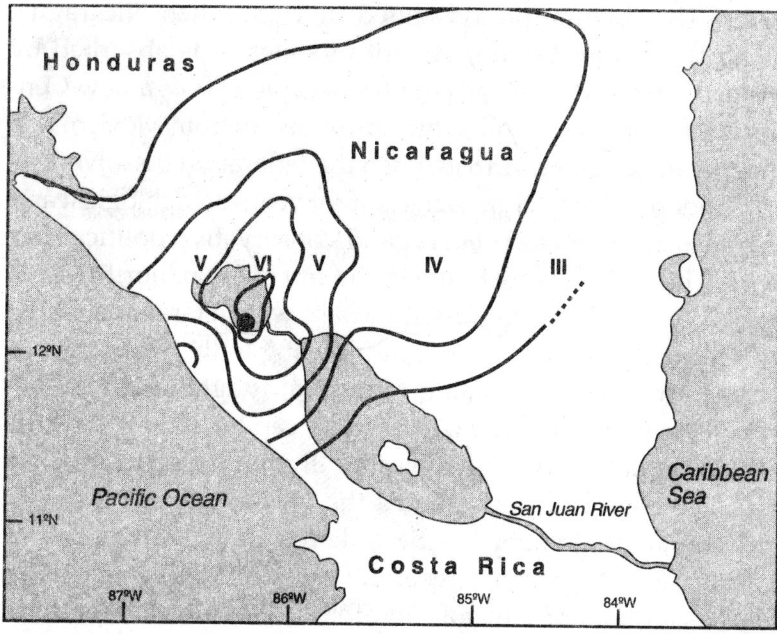

FIGURE 10-5. Zones of equal seismic intensity during the 1972 earthquake, according to the Mercalli scale. The black dot represents Managua. Within the city, the quake's intensity was VII—characterized by "much damage to poorly constructed buildings."

mission to find gold and convert the natives to Christianity. Those first invaders were driven out by natives led by a chieftain known as Diriangén, but two years later Francisco Hernández de Córdoba arrived with a larger band of conquerors and imposed Spanish rule.

The Spanish conquest was devastating to the native population. Many were killed fighting the invaders, many more died from European diseases against which they had no immunity, and still more died in slavery. As a result, Nicaragua's population today is primarily *mestizo*, with mixed native and Spanish blood, and the language and culture are essentially Spanish.

Pirates frequently plundered the Caribbean coast of Nicaragua during the colonial period. They were supported by the British, who eventually occupied key areas along the coast and indeed laid claim to that part of Nicaragua for many years. The colonial period ended in 1822, when Nicaragua, along with other Central American states, was absorbed by Mexico. The next year the country became part of a new Central American federation, which broke away from Mexico. Full independence came in 1838 when the federation dissolved.

Independence, however, brought years of ideological and military strife between liberal and conservative political factions. The liberals were based in the city of León, northwest of Lake Managua. The conservative base was in Granada, at the northern end of Lake Nicaragua. Starting in the 1840s the opposing factions began using Managua, roughly halfway between the two cities, as a compromise capital. Its status as the official capital of Nicaragua was legally confirmed in 1855.

The choice of Managua as the capital was geologically unfortunate, as the city has been damaged by earthquakes at least thirteen times since records were first kept in 1648. The city has an unhappy history in other ways as well. Floodwaters from Lake Managua brought disaster in 1876, an arsenal explosion wrought considerable damage in 1902, and a civil war destroyed much of the city in 1912.

Despite the Managua compromise, struggles between liberals and conservatives continued throughout the nineteenth century. Weakened by the political strife, Nicaragua was a tempting target for foreign intervention, mainly because the world's maritime powers viewed the country as a possible site for a ship canal between the Atlantic and Pacific oceans. Indeed, since colonial times Lake Nicaragua and the San Juan River, which flows from the lake to the Caribbean Sea, had provided a convenient route across the isthmus, with only a short overland trek between the lake and the Pacific Ocean. United States interest in the potential canal route intensified in the mid-1800s because of the California gold rush of 1849 and also because of concerns about British imperial intentions in Central America.

In 1854 the liberals invited an American adventurer named William Walker to aid in their fight with the conservatives. In 1855 Walker helped them take Granada, the conservative stronghold, then accepted command of the Nicaraguan Army and set up a puppet government, which the United States quickly recognized. The next year Walker assumed the presidency of Nicaragua himself. His policies—among them the legalization of slavery and an attempt to establish English as the country's official language—alienated both liberals and conservatives and resulted in civil war. Other Central American countries, alarmed at what appeared to be a United States attempt to take over Nicaragua, sent troops to help in the fight. The United States arranged a truce in 1857, and Walker left the country.

Discredited by the Walker affair, the liberals temporarily lost political influence, and conservatives ruled Nicaragua for more than thirty-five years. In 1893, however, a liberal leader named José Zelaya overthrew the conservative government and assumed dictatorial powers, which he wielded for the next sixteen years. Seeking to protect Nicaragua's national interests, Zelaya refused a request by the United States for the right to assume sovereignty over a proposed canal route. As a result the United States turned to Panama, contriving to have that province declare its independence from Colombia, and in 1903 signed the treaty that led to construction of the Panama Canal.*

Concerned that Zelaya might allow another country to build a competing canal across Nicaragua, the United States sent troops in 1909 to support a rebellion that resulted in Zelaya's downfall. A conservative government was established but was dependent upon the United States to stay in power. Another uprising, in 1912, threatened to topple the conservative regime. Led by a liberal soldier and statesman named Benjamin Zeledón, the rebellion almost succeeded. The United States again sent a contingent of marines to Nicaragua to protect U.S. interests, and the rebels were defeated.

* Volcanism in Nicaragua, brought to the attention of U.S. policy makers in 1902 after the eruption of Mount Pelée on the Caribbean island of Martinique, also played a role in the decision to build a canal in Panama.

Through a series of cooperative presidents, the United States essentially ran Nicaraguan affairs for most of the next two decades. After the 1912 rebellion Benjamin Zeledón was captured and killed by Nicaraguan soldiers, who dragged his body through the hamlet of Niquinohomo, not far from Managua. A teenage boy named Augusto Sandino witnessed the desecration of the liberal hero's body, and he never forgot it.

Born in 1895 of a liaison between the son of a well-to-do planter and a mestizo servant girl, Augusto César Sandino grew up and was educated in the household of his father. He worked with his father until 1920, when, at age twenty-five, he fled Nicaragua after a fight in which he injured a man who had insulted his mother. Sandino found work at a variety of jobs in Honduras, Guatemala, and finally Mexico, where, in Tampico, he was in charge of sales for the local branch of the Standard Oil Company of Indiana. There, in the aftermath of the Mexican Revolution of 1910, he absorbed the political ideals that became his philosophy—pride in his mestizo heritage, sympathy for the campesinos, and resentment of foreign intervention in the countries of Latin America.

Sandino returned to Nicaragua in 1926 and, organizing a fighting force of workers and campesinos, joined a new liberal revolt against the country's conservative government. A leader of the revolt was one Juan Sacasa. When the liberals' general, José Moncada, agreed to a cease-fire in 1927, Sandino refused to sign the agreement. From strongholds in the northern mountains he conducted guerrilla warfare against the conservatives, the U.S. Marines who supported them, and the pro-U.S. National Guard. In 1928 the United States supervised an election in which Moncada was elected president; and four years later, in another U.S.-supervised election, Juan Sacasa assumed the presidency.

Sandino's overriding goal was to rid his homeland of foreign influence. His slogan, *patria libre o morir* (a free homeland or death), like Patrick Henry's "give me liberty or give me death" in an earlier American revolutionary movement, inspired his countrymen. To a charge that his guerrillas were merely bandits, Sandino replied:

> We are no more bandits than Washington was. If the American people had not lost their respect for justice and human rights, they would not so easily forget their past, when a handful of ragged soldiers marched over the snow, leaving bloody footprints behind, in order to gain liberty and independence.[2]

Sandino's campaign attracted increasing support from the Nicaraguan people, and by 1932 it had become apparent that his guerrilla army would not be defeated without a major effort on the part of U.S. Marines, undoubtedly with many casualties. The U.S. Congress refused to back such an effort, and the marines withdrew from Nicaragua in 1933. Sandino, however, continued his campaign against the pro-U.S. conservative government and the National Guard. When the marines left, President Sacasa named as director of the Guard an ambitious Nicaraguan politician, Anastasio Somoza García.

The son of a well-to-do coffee grower, Somoza García had been educated in the United States at the Pierce School of Business Administration in Philadelphia. There he learned to speak English, and he met and subsequently married Salvadora Debayle, daughter of a Nicaraguan aristocrat. Their children, following Spanish custom, were to carry the surname Somoza Debayle.

Somoza García returned to Nicaragua in 1926, became active in politics, and served as minister of war and of foreign relations. Because of his education in the United States and his command of English, he enjoyed cordial relations with U.S. officials in Nicaragua, and he was involved in reorganizing the National Guard. When Somoza was named director of the Guard he lost no time in establishing firm control, purging any officers who he thought might not be loyal to him.

Meanwhile Augusto Sandino had agreed to a peace conference with President Sacasa. The negotiations began in February 1934, but as one of his conditions Sandino insisted on dissolution of the National Guard. On February 21, after dining with Sacasa in the presidential palace, Sandino, his brother Socrates, and two of his generals were murdered by National Guardsmen acting on orders from Somoza García. The Guard followed Sandino's assassination with a bloody slaughter of his sympathizers.

Two years later, in 1936, Somoza staged a coup d'etat, deposed President Sacasa, and had himself named president. Thus began a long, brutal, and corrupt dictatorship, noted for both its duration and its dynastic character. For forty-four years, from 1936 until 1979, the Somoza family controlled Nicaragua's government, the National Guard, and, as time went on, more and more of the nation's economy.

Somoza García broadened the functions of the Guard to include not only national security but control over such public services as communication, transportation, customs, port facilities, airports, health services, and taxation. He condoned, even encouraged, members of the Guard to engage in the various forms of corruption that such control offered, thus dissociating the organization from the Nicaraguan people and ensuring its continued loyalty to the regime. Any opposition was ruthlessly suppressed.

Somoza promoted economic development that benefited the wealthy few but not the great majority of Nicaraguans. He himself became wealthy from investments in agricultural exports and key businesses, and he profited from bribes and from economic concessions to companies both domestic and foreign.

The dictator closely allied himself and his country with the United States, consistently supporting U.S. foreign policy, allowing U.S. military bases to be built in Nicaragua during World War II, and even declaring war on Germany. In addition, in 1954 he provided training areas in Nicaragua for a CIA-sponsored revolution in Guatemala. In return, Somoza received adulation in Washington and funds for equipping his National Guard with modern weapons.

Thus the Somoza government embraced the discordant forces that had been operating in Nicaragua for years—totalitarian rule, government corruption, foreign intervention, and ruthless suppression of dissent. Opposition to the regime became increasingly widespread, and government repression became increasingly more violent. It has been estimated that Somoza García was responsible for the deaths of more than twenty thousand Nicaraguans. Inevitably the opposition, too, became more violent. Finally, on September 20, 1956, at a ball in León in his honor, Somoza García was shot and killed by a young poet named Rigoberto López Pérez, who was himself killed by Somoza's bodyguards.

Anastasio Somoza García had two sons, Luis and Anastasio Somoza Debayle. Both were educated in the United States. Luis studied engineering, and Anastasio graduated from the U.S. Military Academy at West Point. Luis, like his father, went into politics and was president of the Nicaraguan Congress when his father was assassinated. Thus he legally succeeded Somoza García as president of Nicaragua. Anastasio, with his West Point training, had become director of the National Guard. As president, Luis encouraged industrial development and the mechanization of agriculture, bringing in technical advisers from other Latin American countries, but again only the wealthy minority benefited.

In 1961, growing discontent among the poor people of Nicaragua gave birth to the revolutionary movement known as the FSLN, the Sandinista National Liberation Front. Though formally organized in 1961, the Sandinistas had roots in Marxist, anti-Somoza student activities of the 1940s and 1950s. The movement adopted Augusto Sandino's name and was guided by his populist social policies and by his philosophy of resistance to foreign intervention. Moreover, as the FSLN became more militant, it adopted the guerrilla tactics developed by Sandino. His slogan, *Patria libre o morir* (A free homeland or death), became a national rallying cry, and his image—a silhouette of a slouching figure wearing a broad-brimmed sombrero—began to appear on walls and buildings all over Nicaragua.

Strong counterinsurgency campaigns by the National Guard kept the fledgling FSLN from accomplishing very much for several years. The organization grew slowly, but its rural guerrilla forces were no match for the better-equipped Guard, and many Sandinista leaders were killed or imprisoned. Meanwhile, economic conditions in Nicaragua continued to worsen for most of the population. The government became increasingly dependent upon the United States for economic aid and for the military equipment needed to maintain itself in power.

Luis Somoza Debayle's health began to fail in the early 1960s, and he relinquished the presidency in 1963. Friends of the Somoza family held the office until February 1967, when the younger brother, Anastasio, used his power as head of the National Guard to stage a dishonest election and assume the presidency. Luis died of a heart attack two months later.

As director of the National Guard as well as president, Anastasio Somoza Debayle had absolute political and military control over Nicaragua. He established a military dictatorship and, like his father, encouraged corruption in the Guard as a means of ensuring its loyalty. Moreover, he replaced Luis's technical advisers with largely unskilled friends and political allies, leading to more corruption as well as to inefficiencies in government. Anyone who conspired against the regime was subject to imprisonment, torture, and death.

Unemployment soared as agriculture became mechanized and as campesinos were forcibly removed from areas where FSLN guerrillas were active. The displaced people gravitated to the cities, primarily Managua, in a vain effort to find work, and found themselves living in wretched slums. The wealthy elite of Nicaragua continued to grow richer, while the poor became increasingly desperate. Meanwhile the government, because of concerns in the United States about the spread of communism, received millions of dollars in military and economic aid. Most of the money found its way into foreign bank accounts or real-estate investments owned by the Somoza family or their friends.

By the late 1960s the Somoza family owned or had a controlling interest in most of the country's business enterprises. They also owned perhaps a fifth of Nicaragua's farmland and profited from the exporting of agricultural products. Moreover, with controlling interest in a company called Plasmaféresis de Nicaragua, which purchased blood from poor Nicaraguans and exported the plasma, the Somozas even profited from literally selling the nation's blood.

Somoza Debayle's greed, and his government's corruption and violent repression of dissent, led to more and more opposition by populist groups. By 1970 the FSLN had metamorphosed from a small, isolated band of rebels into a well-trained guerrilla army supported by most of Nicaragua's rural population. In the cities there was support for the Sandinistas among some students and among the former campesinos who were now living in urban slums, but most of Managua's middle class tolerated the regime because it brought economic stability.

It was the earthquake of December 23, 1972, that gave the FSLN the broad-based support it needed to become a leading force in Nicaraguan affairs. The earthquake exposed to all the venality of the Somoza regime. Instead of aiding the citizens of Managua or starting to rebuild the city, government officials seized upon the disaster as an opportunity for enriching themselves by channeling millions of dollars of international aid funds into private foreign bank accounts. National Guard soldiers, instead of maintaining order in the stricken city, abandoned their posts. Some went home to aid their families, but many roamed through the ruins, looting whatever of value they could find and selling it on the black market. After two days Somoza Debayle got the Guard reorganized, only to allow its members to plunder and sell relief and reconstruction supplies that had arrived from abroad. The center of Managua remained a rubble-strewn wasteland for years after the earthquake, and thousands of poor people were displaced into shantytowns that sprang up around the city.

The government's blatant corruption and economic mismanagement in the aftermath of the earthquake alienated not only the poor citizens of Nicaragua but also most of those who had accepted the Somoza regime in the past—middle-class businesspeople and many of the wealthy elite as well. In a book titled *Sandinistas Speak*, published in 1982, FSLN leader Daniel Ortega (who would serve as Nicaragua's president from 1984 until 1990), is quoted as saying in an interview:

> Following the 1972 earthquake, the situation of Somoza's regime became more acute and bureaucratic and military corruption more widespread. While this administrative corruption chiefly affected the masses, it also began to affect the . . . bourgeoisie, thus increasing the scope of opposition to the regime.
>
> . . . There was growing internal resistance from all segments of the population. . . .
>
> While Somoza lost more and more political and moral authority, we gained it.[3]

As a result, the resurgent Sandinistas had little trouble recruiting fighting men and women among the displaced campesinos and urban workers in the slums and shantytowns. Thus the 1972 earthquake became a crucial factor in transforming the FSLN from a mostly rural movement into a national crusade supported by urban workers and the middle class.

A turning point came in December 1974, when a group of Sandinistas infiltrated a party in Managua and took hostage a number of Nicaraguan officials, several related to Somoza Debayle. The government was forced to agree to humiliating demands. The FSLN's prestige soared, and Somoza responded by declaring martial law and dispatching the National Guard on missions of reprisal throughout the country. Hundreds of suspected FSLN sympathizers were imprisoned, tortured, and executed.

These egregious human-rights violations were widely publicized, and Somoza Debayle was internationally condemned. Support for the Sandinistas increased even more, and there were widespread calls for revolution. Somoza declared a state of siege in 1975, imposing press censorship and openly threatening his opponents with imprisonment and torture. Repression and violence increased, and in protest there were frequent strikes during the following year.

In 1977 Jimmy Carter was elected president of the United States on a platform that stressed human rights. He promptly curtailed U.S. aid to Nicaragua, inducing Somoza to stop National Guard terrorism and lift the state of siege. This belated relief from total government oppression only paved the way for open criticism of the regime, and *La Prensa*, the main newspaper in Managua, began publicizing the scandalous behavior of Somoza Debayle and his relatives and friends.

In January 1978 *La Prensa* exposed the sale abroad of Nicaraguan blood plasma by Plasmaféresis, the company owned in part by the Somoza family. On January 10 the editor of *La Prensa*, Pedro Chamorro, was assassinated in obvious retribution for the exposé. Chamorro was an internationally renowned journalist who in 1977 had received Columbia University's Cabot Prize for "distinguished journalistic contributions to the advancement of inter-American understanding." Angry crowds demonstrated against the government, and thousands of mourners lined the streets for Chamorro's funeral procession. A two-week general strike idled 80 to 90 percent of Nicaragua's workers, bringing the nation's economy virtually to a halt. The murder of Chamorro focused attention on the excesses of Somoza Debayle's government and spurred great numbers of Nicaraguans to take an active role in opposing the regime and supporting the Sandinistas.

In August 1978 the FSLN captured the National Palace in Managua, along with some two thousand hostages—high-level officials, hundreds of other government employees, and many ordinary citizens who happened to be there on business. After two and a half days of negotiations mediated by Catholic bishops, the FSLN gained a number of concessions including publication of a Sandinista manifesto calling for insurrection, release of Sandinistas from prison, and safe passage out of the country for the assault team. Thousands cheered as the raiders were convoyed to the airport. Whatever legitimacy the Somoza regime had, other than its control of the National Guard, virtually disappeared. Sandinista sympathizers took up arms throughout the country.

The Guard, however, was still a formidable force, fighting, like a cornered animal, for its life. The FSLN spent the next several months recruiting and training new soldiers, preparing for an offensive that would defeat the Guard once and for all and oust the Somoza regime. The offensive was launched in June 1979. Sandinista troops overwhelmed National Guard outposts in all parts of Nicaragua. By the end of June the Guard controlled only the city of Managua, and the FSLN had formed a government in exile.

Meanwhile Somoza and other government officials had been liquidating assets and transferring money to accounts in foreign countries. And on July 17, 1979, the dictator resigned. The United States arranged transportation to Miami, and Somoza and his family stayed there briefly before moving to Paraguay. There, in September 1980, Anastasio Somoza Debayle was murdered.

The day after Somoza's resignation, FSLN troops entered Managua and, before cheering crowds, accepted the surrender of whatever National Guard troops had not already fled the country. Officials of the provisional government, who had taken the oath of office in León on the seventeenth, arrived in the capital on July 20. The Sandinista revolution was over, and the legacy of Augusto César Sandino was vindicated at last.

A number of crucial events stand out in the Sandinistas' long struggle for Nicaraguan freedom: the taking of government hostages in December 1974, public reaction to the assassination of Pedro Chamorro in January 1978, the capture of the National Palace later the same year, and of course the final offensive in 1979. But the Managua earthquake in 1972 was the catalyst, the event that laid bare the consummate corruption of the Somoza regime and rallied popular support for the Sandinista cause.

• • •

As so often happens when a revolutionary regime assumes power in a country, the political pendulum in Nicaragua swung from one extreme to the other after the Sandinistas' victory. Though less repressive than the Somozas had been, the Sandinistas ruled autocratically. Even with financial aid from the Soviet Union, they struggled with a failing economy. In order to stifle protests, they began imprisoning Nicaraguans who held political views different from their own, and for a time they curtailed freedom of the press. The Sandinistas did, however, hold democratic elections—and in 1990 the people of Nicaragua voted them out of power, replacing them with a centrist government headed by Violeta de Chamorro, widow of the slain newspaper editor. A degree of political instability continued in Nicaragua, but because of changes induced by the revolution—for which an earthquake was a catalyst—that nation moved closer to a more just society.

Afterword

IN THIS BOOK we have tried to give earthquakes a human dimension, showing how the aftereffects of seismic activity can resonate in human affairs for years, decades, centuries, or millennia. At the same time we have explained, in terms of plate tectonics, why earthquakes happen.

We have included chapters on seven specific earthquakes of historical significance, and we have described two areas—the Dead Sea region and England—where seismic activity has been reflected in religion and literature. In human terms these events and geological processes have led to consequences ranging from societal disruption to mass destruction, from ancient beliefs to modern movies. From references to earthquakes in the Bible to the 1972 Managua earthquake in Nicaragua, the seismic events treated here, and their cultural, historical, political, and religious aftereffects, attest to the many ways in which geological phenomena and human destiny have been intertwined throughout history.

• Glossary

active fault—a fracture, or fault (q.v.), along which there is recurrent movement of rock formations on one or both sides.

aftershock—an earth tremor that follows a stronger earthquake and that originates at or near the focus (q.v.) of the stronger quake.

alluvial (a-*loo*-ve-al)—pertaining to or composed of alluvium (q.v.).

alluvium (a-*loo*-ve-um)—unconsolidated (q.v.) material such as gravel, sand, and silt deposited by running water, especially during flooding.

amplitude (of waves)—half the height of a wave above the depths of neighboring troughs. Cf. *frequency*.

anticline—an upward fold in rock layers. Cf. *dome, syncline*.

asthenosphere (as-*theen*-o-sphere)—a ductile layer in the upper part of the earth's mantle (q.v.), where magma (q.v.) is thought to be generated. Cf. *lithosphere*.

avalanche—a mass of rocks, soil, ice, or snow, or a mixture of those materials, sliding down a mountainside or hillside. Cf. *landslide*.

basement—see *basement complex*.

basement complex—the rock formations, usually igneous (q.v.) or metamorphic (q.v.), that underlie the particular formations that are the subject of a given investigation.

basin (geological)—a depression in the earth's surface with no outlet; also a bowl-shaped downwarping of rock formations in the earth's crust; also the area drained by a river or smaller stream. Cf. *syncline*.

bedrock—solid rock of the earth's crust, either exposed on the surface or underlying unconsolidated (q.v.) materials.

body waves—seismic waves (q.v.) within the earth's crust.

compaction (geological)—reduction in the volume or thickness of sediments (q.v.).

compression (of the earth's crust)—shortening of the crust in a given area because of the faulting (q.v.) or folding (q.v.) of rock formations. Cf. *extension.*

conglomerate (rock)—a coarse-grained rock composed of rounded sedimentary (q.v.) materials such as pebbles and boulders.

continental crust—rock formations of which the earth's continents are composed. Cf. *oceanic crust.*

continental plate—a tectonic plate composed of continental lithosphere (q.v.). Also see *plate tectonics.*

cordillera—a mountain range or a system of geologically related mountain ranges.

core (of the earth)—the central part of the earth's interior, thought to be divided into a solid inner core and a fluid outer core.

cornice—an overhanging formation of snow or ice on a mountain.

creep (of a fault)—slow deformation of rock formations on either side of a fault (q.v.), with no abrupt rupturing of the fault.

crust (of the earth)—the solid outermost part, or shell, of the earth.

dome (geological)—a roughly circular or elliptical uplift (q.v.) of rock formations in the earth's crust. Cf. *anticline.*

downwarp—see *basin, syncline.*

ductile—see *plastic.*

earthquake—movement caused by the rupturing, or faulting (q.v.), of rock in the earth's crust.

earthquake focus—the point within the earth where a rock formation first ruptures to cause an earthquake. Cf. *epicenter.*

earthquake waves—elastic (q.v.) waves produced by an earthquake.

elastic—capable of returning to an original form after deformation. Cf. *plastic.*

epicenter—the point on the earth's surface directly above the focus (q.v.) of an earthquake.

escarpment—a cliff or steep slope in the topography (q.v.) of the earth.

evaporite—a sedimentary (q.v.) rock composed of materials deposited by the evaporation of seawater.

extension (geological)—the fracturing and pulling apart of a segment of the earth's crust. Cf. *compression.*

fault (in rock)—a fracture, one side of which has been displaced relative to the other in a direction parallel to the fracture. See *faulting, thrust fault.*

fault block—a segment of the earth's crust bounded by faults.

faulting—the rupturing, or fracturing, of rock in the earth's crust. See *fault, thrust fault.*

fault scarp—a steep slope or cliff formed by vertical or nearly vertical movement along a fault (q.v.).

fault zone—a zone, perhaps many kilometers wide, that contains many faults.

filled land—artificially created land composed of rocks, soil, or other materials such as debris from earthquakes and construction sites.

fissure (in rock or in the ground)—a fracture along which the two sides have separated.

focus—see *earthquake focus.*

folding (in rock)—the bending of layers of rock in the earth's crust. See *anticline, syncline.*

foreshock—an earth tremor that precedes a larger earthquake and that originates at or near the focus (q.v.) of the main quake.

formation (geological)—a body of rock, all of which exhibits uniform or similar characteristics.

fracture (in rock)—any break, such as a fissure (q.v.) or fault (q.v.), caused by mechanical stress.

frequency (of waves)—the number of wave crests or troughs that pass a given point per unit of time.

geodetic (geo-*det*-ic)—related to the size and shape of the earth.

geology—the study of the planet earth and its history, including its life-forms, the materials of which it is made, the processes that act on those materials, and the results of those processes.

geophysics—the study of the earth by using quantitative physical methods.

glacier—a large mass of ice formed by the compaction and recrystallization of snow, including both small mountain glaciers and continental ice sheets.

gravimetric (grav-i-*met*-ric)—related to the earth's gravitational field.

groundwater—water in the zone of saturation within the earth's crust.

gypsum (*jip*-sum)—a mineral composed of calcium sulfate, often found in evaporite (q.v.) deposits.

hypersaline (*hy*-per-*sa*-line)—containing a higher concentration of salt than normal seawater.

hypocenter—see *earthquake focus*.

igneous (*ig*-nee-us)—pertaining to rock formed by the solidification of molten material, or magma (q.v.), generated within the earth. Cf. *metamorphic, sedimentary*.

intensity (of earthquakes)—a numerical measurement that relates to the surface effects of an earthquake in a given locality. See *Mercalli scale*.

intrusive rock—rock formed from magma (q.v.) that has been forced, or intruded, into a preexisting rock formation.

island arc—a chain of volcanic islands such as those that form above a zone of subduction (q.v.), where one tectonic plate (q.v.) is descending beneath another; the earth's curvature gives many such chains an arcuate shape like that of the Japanese archipelago or the Aleutian Islands of Alaska.

landslide—downslope movement of large amounts of soil and rock material.

limestone—a sedimentary (q.v.) rock composed mostly of calcium carbonate deposited in an ancient sea.

liquefaction (lick-wa-*fak*-shun) (of sediments)—the process by which the particles of unconsolidated (q.v.), water-saturated sedimentary (q.v.) materials become separated by water, the whole then acting as a liquid.

lithosphere (*lith*-o-sphere)—a layer of the earth comprising the crust (q.v.) and the uppermost, solid part of the mantle (q.v.); the lithosphere resists plastic flow and lies directly above the asthenosphere (q.v.).

locked fault—a fault (q.v.) in which accumulated stress has been insufficient to overcome friction and cause movement of rock formations on either side of the fault.

loess (luss)—a thick, unstratified (q.v.), presumably windblown deposit of silt.

Love waves—seismic push-pull waves (q.v.) that move along the surface of the ground, named for A. H. Love, a British mathematician.

magma (*mag*-ma)—molten rock generated within the earth. Cf. *igneous*.

magnitude (of earthquakes)—a measure of the energy released by an earthquake. See *Richter scale*.

mantle (of the earth)—the part of the earth between the crust and the core, comprising most of the earth's volume.

marl—unconsolidated (q.v.) sedimentary (q.v.) material usually comprising clay, calcium or magnesium carbonate, and shell fragments.

meltwater—water derived from the melting of snow or ice, especially water flowing in, under, or from a melting glacier (q.v.).

Mercalli (Mer-*cal*-ee) scale—a numerical scale of earthquake intensity (q.v.), devised in 1902 by Giuseppe Mercalli, an Italian geologist, to classify the surface effects of an earthquake.

metamorphic (met-a-*mor*-fic)—pertaining to rock derived from the alteration of preexisting rock by physical or chemical conditions within the earth's crust. See *igneous, sedimentary*.

mid-ocean ridge—see *oceanic ridge*.

mudflow—a flowing mass of mostly fine-grained earth material mixed with water.

oceanic crust—rock formations that underlie the earth's oceans. Cf. *continental crust*.

oceanic ridge—in midocean, a high, broad swelling of the seafloor, with a central rift valley (q.v.), the site of seafloor spreading (q.v.).

oceanic rift—a rift (q.v.) in the ocean floor.

plastic—capable of being deformed without rupturing. Cf. *elastic*.

plate—see *plate tectonics*.

platelet (*plate*-let)—a small tectonic plate. See *plate tectonics*.

plate tectonics—the theory that segments of the earth's lithosphere (q.v.), called tectonic plates, move about, giving rise to earthquakes and volcanic activity.

primary waves—see *push-pull waves*.

push-pull waves—seismic waves (q.v.) propagated by alternating compression (push) and expansion (pull); also called P waves or primary waves because they reach seismographs before the slower shear waves (q.v.), or secondary waves. See *seismograph*.

P waves—see *push-pull waves*.

radiocarbon—carbon 14, a radioactive isotope used in determining the age of materials in which it occurs.

Rayleigh waves—earthquake waves that move along the earth's

surface with an elliptical motion, named for Baron Rayleigh (John William Strutt), a British physicist.

rhomboid (*rom*-boid)—a four-sided plane figure, or parallelogram, in which the angles are oblique, opposite sides are of equal length, and adjacent sides are unequal.

Richter scale—a scale of earthquake magnitude (q.v.) devised in 1935 by C. F. Richter, an American seismologist.

rift (in the earth's crust)—a regional trough, bounded by fault zones (q.v.), where the lithosphere (q.v.) has ruptured by being pulled apart.

rift valley—the valley formed by a rift, specifically the deep central cleft along the crest of an oceanic ridge (q.v.).

rock salt—an evaporite (q.v.) consisting of coarsely crystalline sodium chloride, or native salt, deposited by the evaporation of seawater.

salt dome—a massive columnar body of rock salt (q.v.) that has been forced upward through a zone of weakness in overlying rock formations.

sand blow—an eruption of liquefied sand forced upward through an earthquake fissure by the weight of overlying material. See *liquefaction.*

scarp—see *escarpment.*

seafloor spreading—movement of the seafloor away from either side of an oceanic rift (q.v.) as magma (q.v.), welling up through the rift, continually creates new oceanic crust (q.v.); seafloor spreading results when two tectonic plates move away from each other. See *plate tectonics.*

secondary waves—see *shear waves.*

sedimentary—pertaining to rock formations or unconsolidated (q.v.) materials composed of sediments (q.v.) originally deposited by water or wind. Cf. *igneous, metamorphic.*

sediments—solid fragmental materials that have been transported and deposited by wind, water, or ice, or materials chemically precipitated from aqueous solutions.

seismic (*size*-mic)—pertaining to earthquakes and earth vibrations.

seismic waves—see *earthquake waves.*

seismograph—an instrument for detecting and recording vibrations in the earth.

seismology—the study of earthquakes and of the earth's internal structure.

shear waves—earthquake waves propagated by a shearing motion, with oscillation perpendicular to the direction of propagation; also called S waves, or secondary waves, because they reach seismographs after the faster push-pull waves (q.v.), or primary waves. See *seismograph.*

shield—a large region where basement (q.v.) rock is exposed on the earth's surface.

snowfield—a large area that is more or less permanently covered with snow.

specific gravity—the ratio of the weight of a given volume of a substance to the weight of an equal volume of water.

spreading—see *seafloor spreading.*

strain—deformation of a solid material as a result of stress.

strata—layers of rock, usually sedimentary (q.v.) in origin.

stress—the force per unit area acting on a solid material.

subduction—the descent of one tectonic plate beneath another. See *plate tectonics.*

submarine (adjective)—beneath the surface of a body of water.

subsidence (sub-*side*-ence)—sinking or downwarping of an area on the earth's surface or of part of the earth's crust.

subterranean—beneath the surface of the earth.

S waves—see *shear waves.*

syncline—a downward fold in rock layers. Cf. *anticline, basin.*

tectonic (tek-*tahn*-ic)—pertaining to structural and deformational features within the outer part of the earth. See *plate tectonics.*

tectonic plate—see *plate tectonics.*

temblor—an earthquake (q.v.).

thrust fault—a fracture, or fault (q.v.), caused by the thrusting of one part of the earth's crust over another.

tidal wave—a term sometimes mistakenly applied to a tsunami (q.v.) or to a sudden rise of sea level caused by onshore winds.

topography—the configuration of the earth's surface.

tremor (seismic)—a shaking of the earth, a minor earthquake.

tsunami (tsu-*nom*-ee)—a sea wave produced by a sudden disturbance of the ocean floor, as by an earthquake, or by volcanism (q.v.).

typhoon—a tropical cyclone in the western Pacific Ocean ôr the Indian Ocean, equivalent to a hurricane in the Atlantic Ocean.

unconsolidated—loose, not solidified or cemented together.

unstratfied—not occurring in layers, or strata (q.v.).

uplift (geological)—as a noun, a part of the earth's crust that has been raised above nearby crustal rock; as a verb, to raise a portion of the crust.

volcanism—processes related to the formation of a volcano (q.v.).

volcano—a vent in the earth's surface through which magma (q.v.), associated gases, and fragmental material can erupt; technically includes fissures (q.v.) as well as volcanic mountains, but in this book, for simplicity, we limit the term to volcanic mountains.

water table—the top of the zone of saturation by groundwater (q.v.) within the earth's crust.

• Notes and References

PREFACE

Notes

1. C. P. Snow, *The Two Cultures* (Cambridge: Cambridge University Press, 1959).
2. Trevanian, *The Summer of Katya* (New York: Crown Publishers, 1983), 99.

1.• EARTHQUAKES: ORIGINS AND CONSEQUENCES

Notes

1. Dutton, *Earthquakes*, 12, 14.
2. Aristotle, *Meteorologica*, 209.
3. Franklin, "Conjectures," 1–2.
4. Hough, *Earthshaking Science*, 131.

Cited References

Aristotle. *Meteorologica*, trans. H.D.P. Lee. The Loeb Classical Library. Cambridge, Mass.: Harvard University Press, 1952.

Dutton, Clarence Edward. *Earthquakes: In the Light of the New Seismology*. New York: G. P. Putnam's Sons, 1904.

Franklin, Benjamin. "Conjectures concerning the formation of the Earth, etc., in a letter from Dr. B. Franklin, to the Abbé Soulavie." *Transactions of the American Philosophical Society* 3, no. 1 (1793): 1–5.

Hough, Susan Elizabeth. *Earthshaking Science: What We Know (and Don't Know) about Earthquakes*. Princeton, N.J.: Princeton University Press, 2002.

Montessus de Ballore, Comte de. *La Science Séismologique*. Paris: Armand Colin, 1907.

Other Sources

Bolt, Bruce A. *Earthquakes and Geological Discovery*. New York: Scientific American Library, 1993.

Michell, John. *Conjectures concerning the Cause, and Observations upon the Phaenomena of Earthquakes*. London, 1760.

SIDEBAR: INDUCED EARTHQUAKES

Note

1. David M. Evans, "Man-Made Earthquakes in Denver," *Geotimes* 10, no. 9 (May–June 1966): 11–18.

SIDEBAR: MARK TWAIN'S EARTHQUAKE ALMANAC

Note

1. Bernard Taper, ed., *Mark Twain's San Francisco* (New York: McGraw-Hill, 1963), 124–128.

2.• IN THE HOLY LAND: EARTHQUAKES AND THE HAND OF GOD

Notes

1. Twain, *Innocents Abroad*, 342–357.
2. Strabo, *Geography*, 293–295.
3. Twain, *Innocents Abroad*, 342–344.
4. Ben-Menahem, "Four Thousand Years," 20,205.
5. Emerson, "Geological Myths," 334.
6. Strabo, *Geography*, 297.
7. Neev and Emery, *Destruction of Sodom*, 128.
8. Ben-Menahem, "Four Thousand Years," 20,205.
9. Bruins and Van der Plicht, "Exodus Enigma," 213–214.
10. Josephus, *Whole Genuine Works*, 36–37.
11. Ben-Menahem, "Four Thousand Years," 20,205.
12. Josephus, *Whole Genuine Works*, 304.

13. Ibid., 304–305.
14. Ben-Menahem, "Four Thousand Years," 20,205.

Cited References

Ben-Menahem, Ari. "Four Thousand Years of Seismicity along the Dead Sea Rift." *Journal of Geophysical Research* 96, no. B12 (November 10, 1991): 20,195–216.

Bruins, H. J., and J. Van der Plicht. "The Exodus Enigma." *Nature* 382 (July 18, 1996): 213–214.

Doré, Gustave. *La Sainte Bible*. Toves, France: Alfred Mame et fils, 1864.

Emerson, B. K. "Geological Myths." *Science* 4, no. 89 (September 11, 1896): 328–344.

Josephus, Flavius. *The Whole Genuine Works of Flavius Josephus*, according to Havercamp's edition, by William Whiston. London: William Baynes and Son, 1821.

Kashai, E. L., and P. F. Croker. "Structural Geometry and Evolution of the Dead Sea-Jordan Rift System as Deduced from New Subsurface Data." *Tectonophysics* 141, (1987): 33-60.

Neev, David, and K. O. Emery. *The Destruction of Sodom, Gomorrah, and Jericho*. New York: Oxford University Press, 1995.

Shmuel, Marco, and Agnon Amotz. "Prehistoric Earthquake Deformations Near Masada, Dead Sea Garden." *Geology* 23, no. 8 (August 1995): 695–698.

Strabo. *The Geography of Strabo*, vol. 7, trans. Horace Leonard Jones. The Loeb Classical Library. London: William Heinemann, 1930.

Twain, Mark. *The Innocents Abroad*. New York: Harper & Brothers, 1869.

Other Sources

Finkelstein, Israel, and Neil Asher Silberman. *The Bible Unearthed*. New York: The Free Press, 2001.

Keller, Werner. *The Bible as History*. New York: William Morrow & Co., 1981.

Ruby, Robert. *Jericho*. New York: Henry Holt & Co., 1995.

3.• THE DECLINE OF ANCIENT SPARTA: A TALE OF HOPLITES, HELOTS, AND A QUAKING EARTH

Notes

1. Flaceliere, *Greek Oracles*, 64.
2. Michell, *Sparta*, 4–5.
3. Edmonds, *Elegy*, 67.
4. Plutarch, *Lives*, 71, in "Lycurgus."
5. Durant, *Life of Greece*, 81.
6. Ibid., 87.
7. Edmonds, *Elegy*, 1–73.
8. Durant, *Life of Greece*, 242.
9. Plutarch, *Lives*, 589, in "Cimon."
10. Diodorus, *Diodorus*, 289.
11. Ibid.

Cited References

Diodorus Siculus. *Diodorus of Sicily*, vol. 4, trans. C. H. Oldfather. Loeb Classical Library. Cambridge, Mass.: Harvard University Press, 1946.

Durant, Will. *The Story of Civilization: Part II, The Life of Greece*. New York: Simon and Schuster, 1939.

Edmonds, J. M., trans. *Elegy and Iambus, being the remains of all the Greek elegiac poets from Callinus to Crates excepting the Choliambic writers, with the Anacreontea, in two volumes*, vol. 1. The Loeb Classical Library. New York: G. P. Putnam's Sons, 1931.

Flaceliere, Robert. *Greek Oracles*, trans. Douglas Garman. London: Elek Books, 1965.

Michell, Humphrey. *Sparta*. Cambridge: Cambridge University Press, 1952.

Plutarch. *The Lives of the Noble Grecians and Romans*, trans. John Dryden, rev. (1864) by Arthur Hugh Clough. New York: Modern Library.

Other Sources

Burn, A. R., and Mary Burn. *The Living Past of Greece*. London: Herbert Press, 1980.

Higgins, Michael Dennis, and Reynold Higgins. *A Geological Companion to Greece and the Aegean*. Ithaca, N.Y.: Cornell University Press, 1996.

Hooker, J. T. *The Ancient Spartans*. London: J. M. Dent and Sons, 1980.

Huxley, G. L. *Early Sparta*. Cambridge, Mass.: Harvard University Press, 1962.

Piper, Linda J. *Spartan Twilight*. New Rochelle, New York: A. D. Caratzos, 1986.

Talbert, R.J.A. *Plutarch on Sparta*. New York: Penguin Books, 1988.

Todd, Stephen. *Athens and Sparta*. London: Bristol Classical Press, 1996.

SIDEBAR: EURIPIDES, HOMER, AND ARISTOTLE

Notes

1. Renault, *Bull*, 297–306.
2. Homer, *Iliad*, 221–225.
3. These and the following quotations are from Aristotle, *Meteorologica*, 199–219.

Cited References

Aristotle. *Meteorologica*, trans. H.D.P. Lee. The Loeb Classical Library. Cambridge, Mass.: Harvard University Press, 1952.

Homer. *The Iliad* (Book 13), trans. Alston Hurd Chase and William G. Perry Jr. Boston: Little, Brown and Co., 1950.

Renault, Mary. *The Bull from the Sea*. New York: Pantheon Books, 1962.

Other Sources

Euripides. *Hippolytus*, trans. Rex Warner. In *Three Great Plays of Euripides*. New York: New American Library, 1958.

4.• EARTHQUAKES IN ENGLAND: ECHOES IN RELIGION AND LITERATURE

Notes

1. Carrick, *Wycliffe*, 138
2. Musson, *British Earthquakes*, 39.

3. Melville, "Seismicity of England," 370.
4. Ibid., 372.
5. Snare, "Satire," 22.
6. Ibid., 23.
7. Ibid.
8. Heninger, *Sidney and Spenser,* 649.
9. Snare, "Satire," 20.
10. Spenser, *Faerie Queene,* 120–121.
11. Ibid., 122.
12. Ibid., 134–135.
13. Ibid., 138–139.
14. Shakespeare, *Complete Works,* 479.
15. Ibid., 634.
16. Ibid., 1198–1199.
17. Lyell, *Principles of Geology,* 513–514.
18. Heath, "Earthquake at Port Royal," 333.
19. Parker, "Disaster Response in London," 223.
20. Wesley, *Collection of Hymns,* 158–159.
21. Wesley, "Journal," 165.
22. Ibid., 168.
23. Hales, "Causes of Earthquakes," 671–672.
24. Ibid., 676–677.
25. Ibid., 669–670.
26. Niddrie, *When the Earth Shook,* 31.
27. Wesley, "Serious Thoughts" 3–5.
28. Ibid., 12–13.
29. Ibid., 14–15.
30. Darwin, *Journal of Researches,* 305.
31. Gribbin, *Shaking Earth,* 18.

Cited References

Carrick, J. C. *Wycliffe and the Lollards.* Edinburgh: T. & T. Clark, 1908.

Darwin, Charles. *Journal of Researches into the Natural History and Geology of the countries visited during the Voyage of H.M.S. Beagle Round the World, under the Command of Capt. Fitz Roy, R.N.* New York: D. Appleton Co., 1898.

Gribbin, John. *This Shaking Earth.* New York: G. P. Putnam's Sons, 1978.

Hales, Stephen. "Some Considerations on the Causes of Earthquakes." In *Philosophical Transactions, Giving Some Account of the Present Undertakings, Studies, and Labours, of the Ingenious, in Many Considerable Parts of the World,* 46:669–681. London: Royal Society, 1752.

Heath, Emmanuel. "A full account of the late dreadful Earthquake at Port Royal in Jamaica." In *A True and Particular Relation of the Dreadful Earthquake Which happen'd at Lima, the Capital of Peru, and the neighboring Port of Callao, on the 28th of October,* 1746, appendix, 327–341 London: T. Osborne, 1748.

Heninger, S. K., Jr. *Sidney and Spenser: The Poet as Maker.* University Park: Pennsylvania State University Press, 1989.

Lyell, Charles. *Principles of Geology.* London: John Murray, 1832.

Melville, Charles. "The historical Seismicity of England." *Disasters* 5, no. 4 (1981): 369–376.

Musson, R.M.W. *A Catalogue of British Earthquakes.* Technical Report WL/94/04. Edinburgh: British Geological Survey, January 1994.

Neilson, G., R.M.W. Musson, and P. W. Burton, "The 'London' Earthquake of 1580, April 6." *Engineering Geology* 20 (1984): 113–141.

Niddrie, David. *When the Earth Shook.* London: The Scientific Book Club, 1961.

Parker, Dennis J. "Disaster Response in London: A Case of Learning Constrained by History and Experience." In *Crucibles of Hazard: Mega-cities and Disasters in Transition,* ed. James K. Mitchell, 186–247. New York: United Nations University Press, 1999.

Shakespeare, William. *The Complete Works,* ed. G. B. Harrison. New York: Harcourt, Brace and Co., 1952.

Snare, Gerald. "Satire, Logic, and Rhetoric in Harvey's Earthquake Letter to Spenser." *Tulane Studies in English* 18 (1970): 17–33.

Spenser, Edmund. *The Faerie Queene,* ed. Thomas P. Roche Jr. Harmondsworth, England: Penguin Books, 1978.

Wesley, John. *A Collection of Hymns for the of the People called Methodists,* ed. Franz Hildebrandt, Oliver A. Beckerlegge, and

James Dale. In *The Works of John Wesley*, vol. 7. Nashville, Tenn.: Abingdon Press, 1984–.

———. "Rev. J. Wesley's Journal." In *The Works of The Rev. John Wesley, A.M., Sometime Fellow of Lincoln College, Oxford*, vol. 2, 11th ed. London: John Mason, 1856.

———. "Serious Thoughts Occasioned by the late Earthquake at LISBON." In *The Works of the Rev. John Wesley, M. A., Late Fellow of Lincoln-College, Oxford*, 10:3–25. Bristol: William Pine, 1772.

5.• THE GREAT LISBON EARTHQUAKE AND THE AXIOM "WHATEVER IS, IS RIGHT"

Notes

1. Lyell, *Principles of Geology*, 505.
2. Bakewell, *Introduction to Geology*, 251.
3. Singleton, *Great Events*, 4, 1609–1616.
4. Voltaire, *Candide*, 34
5. Batista et al., "Constraints."
6. Kendrick, *Lisbon Earthquake*, 75.
7. Ibid., 137–138.
8. Voltaire, *Candide*, 36.
9. Pope, *Essay on Man*, 12, 15.
10. Voltaire, *Poéme sur le désastre*, 6.
11. Ibid., 7, 8–18.
12. Voltaire, *Candide*, 34–37.

Cited References

Bakewell, Robert. *An Introduction to Geology*, ed. Benjamin Silliman. New Haven, Conn.: Hezekiah Howe, 1833.

Batista, M. A., P.M.A. Miranda, J. M. Miranda, and L. Mendes Victor. "Constraints on the Source of the 1755 Lisbon Tsunami Inferred from Numerical Modeling of Historical Data." *Journal of Geodynamics* 25, no. 2 (1998): 159–174.

Boscowitz, Arnold. *Earthquakes*. London: Routledge and Sons, 1890.

Kendrick, T. D. *The Lisbon Earthquake*. Philadelphia: J. B. Lippincott, 1955.

Lyell, Charles. *Principles of Geology*, 2d ed. London: John Murray, 1832.

Pope, Alexander. *An Essay on Man*, ed. Frank Brady. The Library of Liberal Arts. New York: Bobbs-Merrill, 1965.

Singleton, Esther. *The World's Great Events*, 5 vols. New York: P. F. Collier & Son, 1904.

Voltaire (Jean François Marie Arouet). *Candide, or Optimism*, trans. John Butt. New York: Penguin Books, 1947.

———. *Poème sur le désastre de Lisbonne*. In *The Works of Voltaire*, 42 vols., revised and modernized, with critique and biography by the Right Honorable John Morley, notes by Tobias Smollett, new translation by William F. Fleming, and introduction by Oliver N. G. Leigh, 16:5. New York: The St. Hubert Guild, 1901.

Other Sources

Michell, John. *Conjectures concerning the Cause, and Observations upon the Phaenomena of Earthquakes*. London, 1760.

SIDEBAR: THE WONDERFUL "ONE-HOSS-SHAY"

Note

1. Oliver Wendell Holmes, "The Deacon's Masterpiece, or The Wonderful 'One-Hoss-Shay'—a Logical Story," in *American Poetry and Prose*, ed. Norman Foerster (New York: Houghton Mifflin Co., 1947), 802–817.

6.• NEW MADRID, MISSOURI, IN 1811: THE ONCE AND FUTURE DISASTER

Notes

1. Fuller, *New Madrid Earthquake*, 10–11.
2. Johnston and Schweig, "Enigma."
3. Audubon, *Journals*, 234–235.
4. Johnston and Schweig, "Enigma," 345–348.
5. Fuller, *New Madrid Earthquake*, 76.
6. Ibid., 70.
7. Lyell, *Principles of Geology*, 452–453.
8. Penick, *New Madrid Earthquakes*, 96.
9. Ibid., 94–95.

10. Fuller, *New Madrid Earthquake*, 89–90.
11. Ibid., 90.
12. Penick, *New Madrid Earthquakes*, 1.
13. Ibid., 116–117.
14. Ibid., 117.
15. Ibid, 101–103.
16. Warren, *Brother to Dragons*, 90–91.
17. Penick, *New Madrid Earthquakes*, 122–123.
18. Stewart and Knox, *Earthquake America Forgot*, 74.
19. Ibid., 264.

Cited References

Audubon, Maria R., ed. *Audubon and His Journals*. New York: Charles Scribner's Sons, 1897.

Fuller, Myron L. *The New Madrid Earthquake*. Cape Girardeau, Mo.: Ramfre Press, 1912. (First published by the U.S. Government Printing Office, bulletin 394, 1912.)

Johnston, Arch C., and Eugene S. Schweig. "The Enigma of the New Madrid Earthquakes of 1811–1812." *Annual Review of the Earth and Planetary Sciences* 24 (1996): 339–384.

Lyell, Charles. *Principles of Geology*, 11th ed. New York: D. Appleton & Co., 1872.

Montessus de Ballore, Comte de. *La Science Séismologique*. Paris: Armand Colin, 1907.

Penick, James Lal, Jr. *The New Madrid Earthquakes*. Columbia: University of Missouri Press, 1981.

Russ, D. P. "Style and Significance of Surface Deformation in the Vicinity of New Madrid, Missouri." In *Investigations of the New Madrid, Missouri, Earthquake Region*, ed. F. A. McKeown and L. C. Pakiser, U.S. Geological Survey Professional Paper 1236 (1982): 95–144.

Stewart, David, and Ray Knox. *The Earthquake America Forgot*. Marble Hill, Mo.: Gutenberg-Richter Publications, 1995.

Warren, Robert Penn. *Brother to Dragons*. New York: Random House, 1979.

Other Sources

Edmunds, R. David. *Tecumseh and the Quest for Indian Leadership.* Boston: Little, Brown and Co., 1984.

Hamilton, Robert M., and Arch C. Johnston. *Tecumseh's Prophecy: Preparing for the Next New Madrid Earthquake.* U.S. Geological Survey Circular 1066. Washington, D.C.: U.S. Government Printing Office, 1990.

Sieh, Kerry, and Simon Le Vay. *The Earth in Turmoil: Earthquakes, Volcanoes, and Their Impact on Humankind.* New York: H. Freeman and Co., 1998.

Sugden, John. *Tecumseh: A Life.* New York: Henry Holt and Co., 1998.

Tucker, Glenn. *Tecumseh: Vision of Glory.* New York: Russell and Russell, 1973.

SIDEBAR: A DISASTROUS REPRISE?

Note

1. Philip L. Fradkin, *Magnitude 8* (Berkeley: University of California Press, 1999), 226–231.

7.• EARTHQUAKE, FIRE, AND POLITICS IN SAN FRANCISCO

Notes

1. Thomas and Witts, *San Francisco Earthquake,* 24.
2. Twain, *Roughing It,* 139–140.
3. Abbott, *Natural Disasters,* 90.
4. Thomas and Witts, *San Francisco Earthquake,* 69.
5. Canby, "Earthquake," 95.
6. Bronson, *Earth Shook,* 45.
7. Banks and Read, *San Francisco Disaster,* 103.
8. Jordan, *California Earthquake,* 355.
9. Brinig, "Departure to the Sea," 238–239.

Cited References

Abbott, Patrick L. *Natural Disasters,* 2d ed. New York: McGraw-Hill, 1999.

Banks, Charles E., and Opie Read. *The History of the San Francisco Disaster and Mount Vesuvius Horror.* [Chicago?]: C. E. Thomas, 1906.

Bolt, Bruce A., "The Focus of the 1906 California Earthquake." *Bulletin of the Seismological Society of America* 50, no. 1 (February 1968): 457–471.

Brinig, Myron. "Departure to the Sea." pp. 236–241. In *Continent's End—a Collection of California Writing*, ed. Joseph Henry Jackson. New York: Whittlesey House, McGraw-Hill, 1944.

Bronson, William. *The Earth Shook, the Sky Burned.* Garden City, N.Y.: Doubleday, 1959.

Canby, Thomas Y. "Earthquake—Prelude to The Big One?" *National Geographic* 177, no. 5 (May 1990): 76–105.

Jordan, David S., ed. *The California Earthquake of* 1906. San Francisco: A. M. Robertson, 1907.

Montessus de Ballore, Comte de. *La Géologie Seismologique.* Paris: Armand Colin, 1924.

Morris, Charles. *The Great Earthquake of* 1906. N.p., 1908.

Thomas, Gordon, and Max Morgan Witts. *The San Francisco Earthquake.* New York: Stein and Day, 1971.

Twain, Mark. *Roughing It.* New York: Harper & Brothers, 1871.

Other Sources

Briggs, Peter. *Will California Fall into the Sea?* New York: McKay Co., 1972.

Gentry, Curt. *The Last Days of the Late, Great State of California.* New York: Putnam and Sons, 1968.

Heppenheimer, T. A. *The Coming Quake.* New York: Times Books, 1988.

Kennedy, John Castillo. *The Great Earthquake and Fire: San Francisco,* 1906. New York: William Morrow, 1963.

Meyer, Larry L. *California Quake.* Nashville: Sherbourne Press, 1977.

Sieh, Kerry E., and Simon LeVay. *The Earth in Turmoil: Earthquakes, Volcanoes, and Their Impact on Humankind.* New York: W. H. Freeman & Co., 1998.

SIDEBAR: CAUSES OF QUAKES IN THE BAY AREA

Note

1. Shamita Das and Christopher H. Scholz, "Earthquake Source Mechanics," *Geophysical Monograph* 37. (Washington, D.C.: American Geophysical Union, 1986.)

8.• JAPAN'S GREAT KANTO EARTHQUAKE: "HELL LET LOOSE ON EARTH"

Notes

1. Leet, *Causes of Catastrophe,* 2–3.
2. Bush, *Two Minutes to Noon,* 143.
3. *Great Earthquake,* 56
4. Bush, *Two Minutes to Noon,* 64, 90.
5. Ibid., 127.
6. Ibid.
7. Ibid., 161.

Cited References

Bush, Noel F. *Two Minutes to Noon*. London: A. Barker, 1963.

The Great Earthquake of 1923 *in Japan*. Bureau of Social Affairs Home Office, Japan, 1926.

Leet, L. Don. *Causes of Catastrophe: Earthquakes, Volcanism, Tidal Waves, and Hurricanes*. New York: McGraw-Hill, 1948.

Other Sources

Davison, Charles. *The Japanese Earthquake of* 1923. London: Thomas Murby & Co., 1931.

Kodansha Encyclopedia of Japan. Tokyo: Kodansha, 1983.

Seidensticker, Edward. *Low City, High City*. New York: Alfred A. Knopf, 1983.

———. *Tokyo Rising*. New York: Alfred A. Knopf, 1990.

SIDEBAR: THE KAMAKURA EARTHQUAKE OF 1257 AND THE RISE OF THE LOTUS SECT

Notes

1. *Mongol Conquests,* 50.

2. Sansom, *Japan*, 335.
3. Milne, *Seismology*, 193.

Cited References

Milne, John. *Seismology.* London: Kegan, Trench, Trubner and Co., 1898.

The Mongol Conquests: Time Frame AD 1200–1300 (by the editors of Time-Life Books). Alexandria, Va.: Time-Life Books, 1989.

Sansom, G. B. *Japan, a Short Cultural History*. New York: Appleton-Century-Crofts, 1943.

9.• PERU IN 1970: CHAOS IN THE ANDES

Notes

1. Wilder, *Bridge of San Luis Rey*, 16–17.
2. McDowell, "Avalanche!" 878.
3. Bolt, *Earthquakes*, 122–123.
4. Bode, *No Bells*, 120.
5. Ibid., 113, 118.
6. Ibid., 176.
7. Ibid., 216.
8. Ibid., xli.
9. Ibid., 216.
10. Oliver-Smith, *Martyred City*, 148.
11. Bode, *No Bells*, 111.
12. Ibid., 477

Cited References

Bode, Barbara. *No Bells to Toll: Destruction and Creation in the Andes.* New York: Charles Scribner's Sons, 1989. (Reprinted in 2001 as an Authors Guild Backinprint.com edition.)

Bolt, Bruce A. *Earthquakes and Geological Discovery*. New York: Scientific American Library, a division of HPHLP, 1993.

McDowell, Bart. "Avalanche!" *National Geographic* 121, no. 6 (June 1962): 855–880.

Oliver-Smith, Anthony. *The Martyred City*. Albuquerque: University of New Mexico Press, 1986.

Wilder, Thornton. *The Bridge of San Luis Rey*. New York: Grosset & Dunlap, 1927.

Related Reading

Bode, Barbara. "Disaster, Social Structure, and Myth in the Peruvian Andes: The Genesis of an Explanation." *Annals of the New York Academy of Sciences* 293 (July 1977): 246–274.

Erikson, Kai. *Everything in Its Path*. New York: Simon and Schuster, 1976.

Plafker, G., and G. E. Erikson. "Nevados Huascarán Avalanches, Peru." In *Rockslides and Avalanches*, ed. B. Voight, chap. 8. Amsterdam: Elsevier Scientific, 1978.

Stein, William, *Hualcan: Life in the Highlands of Peru*. Ithaca, N.Y.: Cornell University Press, 1961.

SIDEBAR: IN CHILE—TSUNAMIS, DEVASTATION, AND DARWIN

Notes

1. Darwin, *Journal of Researches*, 303–304.
2. Ibid., 305.
3. Ibid., 308, 310.

Cited Reference

Darwin, Charles. *Journal of Researches into the Natural History and Geology of the countries visited during the Voyage of H.M.S. Beagle Round the World, under the Command of Capt. Fitz Roy, R.N.* New York: D. Appleton and Co., 1898.

Related Reading

Moorehead, Alan. "The Earthquake." In *Darwin and the Beagle*, chap. 9, New York: Harper & Row, 1969.

10.• THE 1972 MANAGUA EARTHQUAKE: CATALYST FOR REVOLUTION

Notes

1. Aldaraca et al., *Nicaragua*, 216–217.
2. Sheesley and Bragg, *Sandino*, 51.
3. Borge et al., *Sandinistas*, 56.

Cited References

Aldaraca, Bridget, Edward Baker, Iliana Rodríguez, and Marc Zimmerman, ed. and trans. *Nicaragua in Revolution: The Poets Speak (Nicaragua en Revolución: Los Poetas Hablan)*, vol. 5, *Studies in Marxism*. Minneapolis: Marxist Educational Press, 1980.

Borge, Thomás, Carlos Fonseca, Daniel Ortega, Humberto Ortega, and Jaime Wheelock. *Sandinistas Speak*. New York: Pathfinder Press, 1982.

Sheesley, Joel C., and Wayne G. Bragg. *Sandino in the Streets*. Bloomington and Indianapolis: Indiana University Press, 1991.

Other Sources

Amador, Carlos Fonseca. "Nicaragua: Zero Hour." In *Nicaragua: Unfinished Revolution*, ed. Peter Rosset and John Vandermeer, 168–189. New York: Grove Press, 1986.

Booth, John A. *The End and the Beginning: The Nicaraguan Revolution*, 2d ed. Boulder, Colo.: Westview Press, 1985.

Brown, R. D., P. L. Ward, and G. Plafker. *Geologic and Seismologic Aspects of the Managua, Nicaragua, Earthquakes of December 23, 1972*. Geological Survey Professional Paper 838. Washington, D.C.: U.S. Government Printing Office, 1973.

Chamorro, Violeta Barrios, with Sonia Cruz de Baltonado and Guido Fernández. *Dreams of the Heart: The Autobiography of President Violeta Barrios de Chamorro of Nicaragua*. New York: Simon & Shuster, 1996.

Merrill, Tim L., ed. *Nicaragua, a Country Study*. Washington, D.C.: Federal Research Division, Library of Congress, 1994.

Walker, Thomas W. *Nicaragua: The Land of Sandino*. Boulder, Colo.: Westview Press, 1986.

Related Reading

La Femina, Peter C., T. H. Dixon, and W. Strauch. "Bookshelf Faulting in Nicaragua." *Geology* 30, no. 8 (August 2002): 751–754.

• Index

Note: "f" after page number indicates a figure or caption; "n" after page number indicates a footnote; "t" after page number indicates a table.